Mystic Endowment

Harvard University
Center for the Study of World Religions

Religions of the World

Editor: Lawrence E. Sullivan

Cambridge, Massachusetts

Mystic Endowment

Religious Ethnography
of the
Warao Indians

Johannes Wilbert

Distributed by Harvard University Press
for the
Harvard University Center for the Study of World Religions

Library of Congress Cataloging-in-Publication Data

Wilbert, Johannes.
    Mystic endowment : religious ethnography of the Warao Indians /
Johannes Wilbert.
        p.   cm.   —   (Religions of the world)
    Includes bibliographical references and index.
    ISBN 0-945454-04-X : $34.95. — ISBN 0-945454-05-8 (pbk.) : $24.95
    1. Warao Indians—Religion and mythology.   2. Warao Indians—
Philosophy.   3. Human ecology—Venezuela—Orinoco Delta.   I. Title.
II. Series: Religions of the world (Cambridge, Mass.)
F2319.2.W3W514 1993
299'.882—dc20   93-10164
                                                                            CIP

Foreword

Johannes Wilbert develops a theme throughout his extraordinary essays, each one of which illumines another facet of Warao ecology of mind. The theme is bold and deceptively simple: the environmental, material, and social processes that construct everyday Warao life are endowed with a religious significance and even a mystical value. To this direct assertion Wilbert immediately adds a complicating amendment: the Warao mystical endowment does not stand apart from material life. It is not a metaphysics (or superstructure or disembodied ideology)—lying somewhere beyond the physical world. Rather, the Warao ability to experience life religiously is embedded in their material existence.

This book journeys through Warao material existence in ways that provide a reader unusual satisfaction. The travel and the satisfaction occur on several levels. On the first level, the tour of Warao mountains, forests, and rivers becomes, on the second level, a survey of Warao cosmology. Wilbert proves an expert guide to an elaborate world of ideas and symbolic actions. A sense of satisfaction derives from his thorough interweaving of these first two levels to a degree that is rare in an ethnography. By the end, the reader has both a feel for the open-ended process of Warao creativity and a richly detailed sense of the material, social, and intellectual contexts of imaginative creativity.

The book covers so much ground because Wilbert is a ceaseless learner. These essays were produced over the course of the past twenty years, a large part of the lifetime of Wilbert's research on the Warao. On a third level of travel, then, the book retraces Wilbert's intellectual pilgrimage. Although Wilbert does not frame these essays in a biographical narrative, each one is a blaze along the trail of his mature life's work. Throughout his professional life, the Warao have stimulated Wilbert to redraw the contours of his discipline and to resite the landmarks of his own intellectual map.

A reader can admire Wilbert's knowledge, which is both broad and detailed. The combination of Wilbert's curiosity, intellectual agility, and discipline is genuinely satisfying. He puts on display the vocation of the ethnographer. His cultivation of knowledge in many subfields of science and his respect for the significance of the tiniest details are coupled with his constant attention to the larger perspective of general principals of Warao thought and overarching themes of Warao culture. The resultant pleasure is the sort one derives from watching a successful juggler, who keeps all objects in motion, and yet, somehow at the same time, in place. He strikes a dynamic balance between a focus on elementary parts and moving whole. One finds this shifting focus at work, for instance, in the essay entitled "The Calabash of Ruffled Feathers" (pp. 133–43). While attending to the details of the haft, pebbles, and gourd-head of the shaman's rattle, on the one hand, Wilbert delineates, on the other hand, the shamanic view of the world and the medical physiology of ecstasy. Similarly, in "The Fiddle and the Dancing Jaguar" (pp. 247–73), the detailed construction of musical instruments and their accompanying dance-movements allow Wilbert to examine the Warao estimation of sweeping changes that have taken place in their long-term cultural history, whether in the realm of staple foods or race relations.

In order to understand Warao religious life, then, Wilbert had to examine material culture and natural history at the same level of telling detail that the Warao understand them. His task is not made easier by the fact that the Warao adapt quickly to change: the change evident in the introduction of new cultigens, new and deadly diseases, new meteorological lore, and so on.

Wilbert credits the Warao with keen powers of observation and a shrewd capacity to enfold metaphors drawn from the material environment into complex patterns of reasoning. One of the marks of Warao culture is the creation of these rich but entangling metaphoric snares— the creation of systems that are both ecological and cognitive. "The Warao have an ecosystemic approach to every physical and biological part of the earth. A tree does not exist in isolation. Like everything else in the environment, it functions as one part of a system of associated parts. Together they form a characteristic unit in which each part is interdependent." (p. 72, fn. 12).

Mystical properties of matter are best disclosed in practical processes, those actions that efficaciously conform human life to matters at hand. Wilbert has taken these matters seriously, learning the natural history of plants, the life cycle of forests and rivers, and the peculiarities of the life forms of animals, fish, or insects that inhabit the Warao ecology. Taking his cue from the Warao, Wilbert obliged himself to study a bewildering array of ethnosciences and a great deal about their nearest counterparts in Western science: pharmacology, botany, meteorology, entomology, astronomy, open-ocean navigation, ethnomedicine, musicology, and architecture. Agriculture, boat making, food preparation, house construction, and musical performance disclose powers peculiar to their material elements—specific woods, crops, insects, tides, birds, and seasonal shifts in the microenvironment. Human labors reveal significant powers, which appear in the image of specific matters. Labor is, in this view, also an act of the religious imagination, a labor distinctive of human beings. In order to understand how Warao society functions on its base of material resources, Wilbert found that he had to understand well Warao religious life.

Brief mention of Wilbert's treatment of canoe building (pp. 25–86) serves as illustration. The construction of a canoe is a grand ceremonial labor for the master builder and the supporting community. The Warao fashion ocean-going canoes from trees that embody Dauarani, the Mother of the Forest. Carved in the image of her birth canal, the canoes are, in every sense, vessels of life for Warao culture. Of course, they are the material conduits of the life they signify because of their place in forestry, long-distance trade, and historical migration. But Wilbert takes us much further. He demonstrates that these material conduits of life also signify the mystical knowledge acquired and transmitted in canoe construction. Like all life-giving vessels, the canoes keep vital fluids in their place—the waters of ocean flood and amniosis; the liquefaction of mystical death that occurs when the master builder is swallowed by the canoe; and the dizzying flow of enigmatic life experiences exemplified by the intoxicated, mystical love-making between boat maker and Forest Mother, whose womb is both birth canal and coffin (p. 73).

Through canoe construction and its experiences of ecstatic death, the community taps its mystic endowment. In the canoe-vagina, community members travel not only from one place to another but from one quality of being to another throughout their entire life cycle. They acquire the experiences that make them fully cultured human beings, who are vital, reflective, and creative because they are centered on the experience of mystical death demanded of those who traffic with the forest, the river, and the sea. Taking his cue from the Winikina Warao, Wilbert presents the canoe as a complex cipher of what it means to become a human being in transit through the world, with the capacity to learn about the world and its history by passing from life to death and back to life again. After reading Wilbert's essay, one better understands why these people of the Orinoco Delta call themselves "Warao," meaning "Boat People."

Warao culture sustains itself because it has become intimate with powers inherent in diverse matters. The Warao have become familiar with the structures of matter and have responded to them appropriately. This intimacy, analysis, and response to matter are evident in the material artifacts of Warao culture: not only the canoe, but also the fiddle, the drum and rattle, medicines, cultigens, the house, and so on.

Wilbert helps us contemplate these practical artifacts. For the Warao, the practical and the contemplative are inseparable, for contemplation is a part of the process of harnessing material life for practical purposes. The powerful structures of material life are made known through human speculation and imagination. Thoughtful life and the exact sciences arise in the encounter with and the contemplation of the specific matters that comprise the viable world. Indeed, mystical experience is a sign of the effective power intrinsic to material life.

In the course of teaching about Warao culture, Wilbert's patient scrutiny of the relationship of surface to depth, his vivid writing, and his stimulating insights serve up new ways of thinking about culture. Wilbert explores the human imagination—his own as well as that of his Warao instructors. How does the imagination proceed when it encounters diverse matters? Humans create models based on the perceived structures of matter and use them as complicated artifacts to communicate information about the world and the processes of knowledge that affect and reshape it in fruitful, meaningful ways.

Wilbert's attention to the value of multiple disciplines in understanding religion makes *Mystic Endowment* a valuable contribution to the "Religions of the World" book series, published by the Harvard University Center for the Study of World Religions. The Center fosters excellence in the historical and comparative study of religion. The book series encourages multiple disciplinary approaches to the full range of religious expressions: in art, medicine, law, literature, music, liturgy, economy, anthropology, and the cosmological sciences.

Kathryn Dodgson Taylor deserves special acknowledgment for her excellent work in preparing the manuscript and managing the production and publication of this volume.

Lawrence E. Sullivan, Director
Harvard University Center
for the Study of World Religions

Preface

This book contains ten research articles on Warao religious ethnography which were written by the author over a period of almost twenty years (1972–1991). Some of the publications in which these articles originally appeared are either out of print or difficult to locate, and two articles appear here for the first time.

For purposes of publishing them as chapters in a book, the articles have been edited for uniformity of punctuation; improvement of diction; and correction of factual errors, statistical data, and outdated chronological information. Although repetitive explanatory phrasing was largely eliminated, a number of redundant passages remained to facilitate contextual understanding.

Johannes Wilbert
23 June 1992

Acknowledgments

Grateful acknowledgment is made for permissions to reprint the following:

Chapter One: Regents of the University of California, for Wilbert, J. "Geography and Telluric Lore of the Orinoco Delta." *Journal of Latin American Lore* 5(1):129–50 (1979).

Chapter Two: Regents of the University of California, for Wilbert, J. "To Become a Maker of Canoes: An Essay in Warao Enculturation." In J. Wilbert, ed., *Enculturation in Latin America*. Latin American Studies 37:22, 303–58. Los Angeles: UCLA Latin American Center Publications (1976).

Chapter Three: Dumbarton Oaks, Trustees for Harvard University, Washington, D.C., for Wilbert, J. "Eschatology in a Participatory Universe: Destinies of the Soul among the Warao Indians of Venezuela." In Elizabeth P. Benson, ed., *Death and the Afterlife in Pre-Columbian America*, pp. 163–89 Washington, D.C.: Dumbarton Oaks Research Library and Collections (1975).

Chapter Four: Peter T. Furst, for Wilbert, J. "Tobacco and Shamanistic Ecstasy among the Warao Indians of Venezuela." In Peter T. Furst, ed., *Flesh of the Gods: The Ritual Use of Hallucinogens*, pp. 55–83. New York: Praeger (1972).

Chapter Five: The Society for Art Publications, Toronto, Ontario, Canada, for Wilbert, J. "The Calabash of the Ruffled Feathers." In *Stones, Bones and Skin: Ritual and Shamanistic Art*. Toronto: *Artscanada*, December 1973/January 1974:90–93.

Chapter Six: University of Utah Press, for Wilbert, J., "The House of the Swallow-tailed Kite: Warao Myth and the Art of Thinking in Images." In Gary Urton, ed., *Animal Myths and Metaphors in South America*, pp. 145–82 (1985).

Chapter Seven: Regents of the University of California, for Wilbert, J. "Warao Cosmology and Yekuana Roundhouse Symbolism." *Journal of Latin American Lore* 7(1):37–72 (1981).

Chapter Eight: Regents of the University of California, for Wilbert, J. "The Warao Lords of Rain." In Giorgio Buccellati and Charles Speroni, eds., *The Shape of the Past. Studies in Honor of Franklin D. Murphy*, pp. 127–45. Los Angeles: UCLA Institute of Archaeology and Office of the Chancellor (1981).

Contents

Maps, Tables, and Figures

MAPS

TABLES

FIGURES

Mystic Endowment

Chapter One

Geography and Telluric Lore
of the Orinoco Delta

THE LAND

The Orinoco Delta proper (lat. 8°25′–10° N, long. 60°40′–62°30′ W)
has been recognized as the home of the Warao Indians since early Indo-
Hispanic times. On their forays up the Orinoco, European voyagers
crossed the borderlands of the delta throughout the age of discovery,
and from the 1590s on the Warao are mentioned in the literature
pertaining to this northern region of South America.[1]

The Orinoco Delta, a fan of alluvial deposits covering approximately
18,000 square kilometers, is bounded on the south by the Rio Grande
and on the west by the Manamo River. The Manamo branches off from
the Orinoco at Barrancas, the apex of the triangle. Barrancas is about
200 kilometers along the Rio Grande from the Atlantic Ocean and
approximately the same distance along the Manamo from the Caribbean
Sea. The waters of the Orinoco are carried through the delta by the
Rio Grande, its principal channel, and through nine so-called *caños*

[1] Several scholars have assisted me in researching aspects of the natural sciences pertinent to this essay. I am particularly indebted to the following scientists of the Museum of
Natural History of Los Angeles County: Dr. Peter Keller, Curator of Mineralogy; Mr. William B. Lee, Curator of Ethnology; and Dr. John Wright, Curator of Herpetology. Special
thanks are due also to Dr. Tj. H. van Andel, Professor of Geology, Stanford University, who
provided much of the geomorphological information concerning the Gulf of Paria, Trinidad,
and the Orinoco Delta. Dr. G. Reichel-Dolmatoff was kind enough to read the manuscript, a
courtesy I gratefully acknowledge. Several of his suggestions have been taken into consideration in the final draft of this chapter. Dr. Inga Steinvorth Goetz generously provided the aircraft that enabled me to reconnoiter the Warao world and to locate the world mountains on
Trinidad and on the outskirts of the Orinoco Delta. The research for this chapter was made
possible in part by a grant from the Ahmanson Foundation which I gratefully acknowledge.

known as Manamo, Pedernales, Tucupita, Cocuina, Macareo, Araguao, Araguaito, Sacupana, and Merejina. Connecting these distributaries, innumerable smaller *caños* form a labyrinthine network of navigable waterways throughout the entire delta. The region is splintered by these crisscrossing streams into a multitude of islands of varying size (map 1.1).

Topographically, the Orinoco Delta may be divided into three transversal zones (map 1.2). The prelittoral zone of the upper delta is completely fluvial. Its Orinoco-connected distributaries, which carry suspended sediments, are known as brown-water rivers. They are bordered by sand levees 3 to 4 meters high and, beyond the levees, by

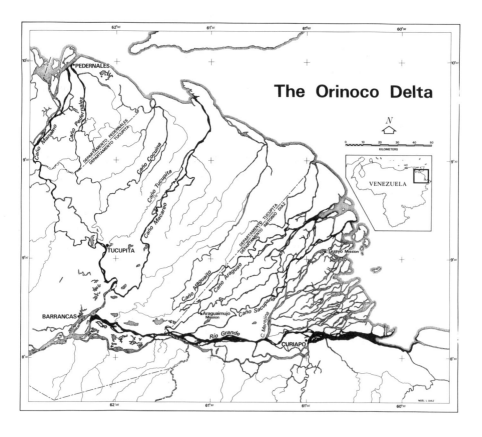

MAP 1.1
The Orinoco Delta

strips of sandy loam about 100 to 200 meters wide. Farther away from the rivers the loam becomes silty, grading into clays, peaty clays, and, in the backswamps, into peat. Although only the lowest parts of these backswamps are permanently inundated, seasonal flooding covers the entire area, except for the crests of levees. Stretches of clays that dry irreversibly during the dry season and run along the outer margin of

MAP 1.2
Geomorphology of the Orinoco Delta

the levees make the latter look 10 to 20 kilometers wide. Point bars are frequently seen in the area, and oxbow lakes and silted-up channels appear throughout the levee system. The prelittoral zone is now largely deforested, but originally the levees were covered by rain forest and the backswamps by 15-meter-high bucare (*Erythrina glauca*), swamp forest interspersed with stands of moriche palms (*Mauritia flexuosa*, manaca *Euterpe* sp.), and heavy undergrowth.

The littoral zone, a coastal strip 10 to 30 kilometers wide permanently flooded by tidal waters and excessive rains, is drained by a network of swamp streams, many of them unconnected with upland rivers which carry rich humic acids. These black-water streams, which contain no minerogenous matter, flow over the peaty and clayey swamp floor without the restraint of levees. The strong longshore drift, however, deflects the estuaries of all delta rivers in a northwesterly direction, a phenomenon that has created along the convex coastline long, low, subparallel or diverging sand ridges separated by mud flats and covered with shrubby dune and beach vegetation. The littoral zone, topped by a 30- to 50-centimeters-thick layer of soft humic clay, is covered by mixed swamp and mangrove forests. Mangroves stabilize the coastline and islands that are exposed to maximal tidal influence. Farther inland, the 20-meters-high mixed swamp forest either covers entire islands, as in the southeastern region, or features belts of trees (like *Symphonia globulifera*) with plank roots and superficial rooting. Clusters of moriche, manaca, and temiche palms grow in the interiors of interfluvial islands.

The intermediate zone, wedged between the prelittoral and littoral zones, is a tidal area. Although not permanently inundated by the sea, it is subject to seasonal flooding, especially along its southern and western fringes. Natural levees border the middle courses of such *caños* as the Macareo, the Araguao, and the Sacupana, but as levee building here is minimal, the levees are discontinuous. Wide regions of the intermediate zone are covered by low-lying, featureless, and frequently peaty or clayey marshes and backswamps. Probably because of seasonal fluctuations in the water level, reduced sedimentation, and a decreased supply of nutrients, interfluvial plains are marked by a series of bucare forest (typical of the prelittoral zone), palm swamp, and herbaceous swamp. Palm swamps support an open, bushlike vegetation, and their peaty and permanently waterlogged soft soil provides ideal conditions for palm groves of moriche, temiche, and manaca. Herbaceous swamps, with more or less permanently inundated soils of humic clay and very soft peat, create a mosaic pattern of low vegetation, including ferns, sedges, and shrubs as well as floating grasses, moriche palms, and stunted trees (Müller 1956; 1959, 4–6; van Andel 1956, 1967; van Andel and Sachs 1964, 44–45; Vila et al. 1960, 355–56; Voorde 1962).

The average mean temperature in the Orinoco Delta is 26 degrees Celsius; the humidity ranges from 60 to 80 percent. The periods of heaviest rainfall are from May to October (especially in June) and of least rainfall from November to April (especially the first three months of the year). But rainy days, sometimes with heavy showers, may come at any time during the year. The annual precipitation varies from 150 to 300 centimeters. Northwesterly trade winds of moderate velocity, which sweep across the delta incessantly, mitigate the hot climate of this tropical land.

The tidal zone of the intermediate and littoral delta is the major distribution area of the modern Warao Indians; it is inhabited by roughly 75 percent of the total population of about 20,000. The upper delta, where most of the residual Warao live, has been unsafe for the Warao since the pre-Columbian arrival in the peripheral delta regions of Neo-Indian societies. Devastating neighbors—aggressive Arawak and cannibalistic Carib as well as colonial slave traders and prospectors of various kinds—have all been shunned by the Warao.

COASTAL ADAPTATION

The traditional geography of the Warao homeland, however, includes all three delta zones. In addition, it encompasses the region between the Rio Grande and the mountain ranges of the Sierra de Imataca and the Altiplanicie de Nuria to the south, and the island of Trinidad and the ocean to the north. The traditional history of the Warao goes further back than their discovery in the sixteenth century, for they speak of times when the Serpent's Mouth was dry and the island of Trinidad was connected with the mainland. This geographical condition apparently prevailed until 6,000 years ago, when the water level of the Caribbean Sea was lower than it is today and when the Orinoco discharged its waters only through the southern delta into the Atlantic Ocean (van Andel pers. comm.; cf. van Andel and Postma 1954, 142).

Although the memory of an event so remote in time seems unlikely to have been retained by a people lacking a written record, it does suggest that the Warao certainly do have an oral historical tradition.

In general, the Warao are a water- rather than a land-oriented people; until recently (i.e., the 1930s) they engaged in sea traffic between the mainland and Trinidad. There can be no doubt that the plank canoes of the Warao were able to negotiate interinsular distances, and toponymic and trait-distributional evidence suggests that Waraoan-speaking mariners covered even longer distances coastwise and across the open sea (Wilbert 1957, 11–14).

Rather than regarding the Warao as a deculturated people representing an "extreme case of culture loss," as Steward and Faron (1959, 62, 441–42) have suggested, I recognize them as fully developed Meso-Indians with a nonagricultural and nonceramic culture based on specialized microenvironmental exploitation of the resources of the deltaic zones. Perfectly at home on the water, and true to their tribal name (meaning "boat people"), their ancestors may have been among the shell gouge- or *gubia*-using inventors of dugout canoes along the northern seaboard of South America. Ever since the *gubia* made its appearance some 3,500 years ago, these Meso-Indian mariners must have traveled throughout the southern Caribbean and beyond. Other early voyagers in the area probably included hunters and gatherers who had preceded the Meso-Indians and certainly such relative newcomers to the West Indies as the pre-Columbian Saladoid people and the historic Arawak and Carib who had acquired the art of navigation from the canoe people 3,000 and 2,000 years ago, respectively, before running their mentors out of the Caribbean (Cruxent and Rouse 1974).

I suggest that the ancestors of the present-day Warao were among those Meso-Indian navigators, and that, before the Caribbean became unsafe for them, the Warao launched their vessels not only from the estuaries of the Orinoco Delta but also from ports outside their present habitat on coastal islands, the bogland of the Gulf of Paria, and the swampy littoral of Guiana. It was mainly to escape the expansionist Neo-Indian intruders that the Warao retreated from those peripheral regions into the labyrinthine refuge of the delta, where they weathered the Arawak and Carib conquest of the West Indies and outlived the genocide of the Indo-Hispanic era. Throughout the centuries of their seclusion, however, they have kept the seafaring tradition of the canoe people alive, while at the same time settling down to acquaint themselves with the full potential of their aquatic econiche.

In their long-term occupancy of the Orinoco Delta, the Warao, facing stringent environmental conditions in converting a marginal refuge area into a viable homeland, undertook an intensive investigation of the physical and biological characteristics of their world. I believe that the Warao, far from treating the delta as a homogeneous wasteland, carefully inventoried the different microenvironments of their world, placed themselves squarely in its center, and made their cultural-ecological wisdom a lasting part of their tribal lore. Besides keeping the Warao psychologically sane in their involuntary confinement, this achievement also enabled them to exploit fully the precarious environment of the delta in a nondestructive way, as they have done for centuries and possibly even millennia.

MYTHIC GEOGRAPHY

In my fieldwork among the Warao I concentrated on the Hoanarao subtribes (the black-water people—Mariusa, Winikina, Arawabisi) of the central delta. When discussing cosmic space these Indians like to refer to themselves as "we here in the center." This anthropocentric worldview is expressive of the sacred-rock cult which holds that all terrestrial and celestial coordinates converge in Hoanarao territory. The cult seems to be specific to this tribal subgroup, and its distribution area covers the very heartland of the delta (Heinen and Ruddle 1974, 118; see chapter 3 below). (See maps 1.3 and 1.4.)

The Hoanarao picture the earth as a disk resting on a world sea and scarred by riverbeds. This view is less a mental picture than the way these Indians actually see the physical reality of the earth. Because their land lacks hills or other elevated vantage points, the Warao are restricted to viewing the earth at sea level. To them it thus seems to be a dark, narrow band that cuts across their field of vision, separating the water below from the sky above (fig. 1.1). Accordingly the earth disk must be quite thin, for if a hole is dug or an uprooted tree leaves a crater the water quickly seeps in and fills the cavity. The waterlogged earth is able to float only because its center is firmly supported by a serpentine earth monster whose four horned heads point in the cardinal directions. The convex deltaic coastline and, especially, the horizon

visible across the sea empirically verify that the earth is circular and
that it is surrounded by water. The Warao term *hobahi* (earth) actually
means "surrounded by water"; the rim of the disk is referred to as
hobahi akari, "where the earth breaks off."

For the Hoanarao, who adhere to the sacred-rock cult, the earth's
cardinal points of north and south are marked by two petrified world
trees which have assumed the form of mountains and serve as abodes

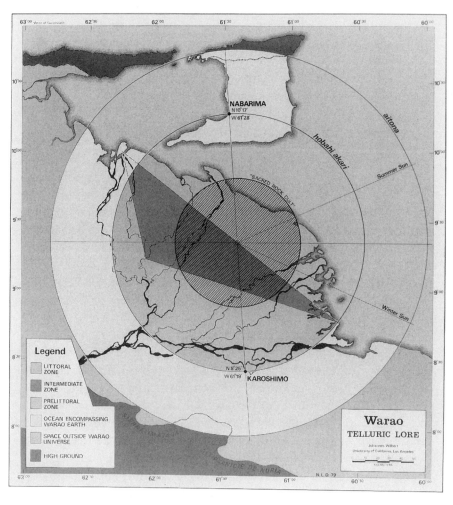

MAP 1.3
Warao telluric lore

of two directional earth-gods. Having come to realize that many strategic markers of Warao cosmology are modeled after physical prototypes, I have searched the delta and adjacent regions for mountains that might fit the mythical description of these two particular ones. The reliance on cartographic hints and the use of low-flying aircraft and of motorboats made the task of finding the mountains at the earth's edge relatively easy.

The abode of the northern earth-god, known as Nabarima or "Father of the Waves," is located on the west coast of central Trinidad near

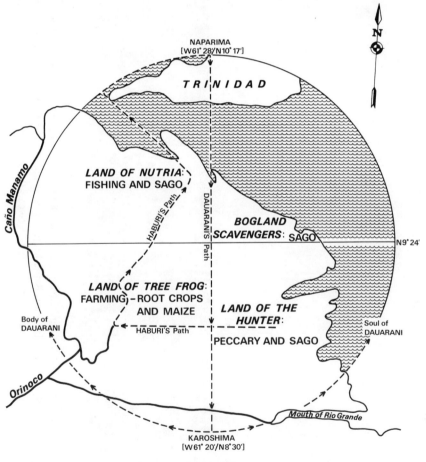

MAP 1.4
Hobahi, land of the Warao

F‌ɪɢ. 1.1

Warao view of the earth, from the *caño* Merejina looking south across the Rio Grande toward the Sierra de Imataca. This elevation is the highest one visible to the Warao anywhere in the delta. The dark line is the contour of the forest on the plain between the Rio Grande and the Sierra. (Photo Johannes Wilbert)

the town of San Fernando (lat. 10°17′ N, long. 61°28′ W). The mountain, though only 192 meters high, stands nearly alone and thus is remarkably conspicuous at the westernmost end of the central range of Trinidad. Approached from the south, Naparima Hill[2] (its Warao name used by Trinidadians), which seems to be standing at the end of the broad peneplain of southern Trinidad, is visible from miles away. An Upper Cretaceous formation, Naparima Hill consists of argillite rock colored yellow and blue-green. The entire north side of the hill is presently being quarried for road metal.

The mountain of the southern earth-god, known as Karoshimo or "Red-Neck," is located in the piedmont area south of the Rio Grande. Although the mountain is referred to on Venezuelan maps as Cerro Manoa (lat. 8°25′ N, long. 61°19′ W), the Criollos[3] whom I questioned use its Warao name, Cerro Caroshimo. Like its northern counterpart, Karoshimo is rather isolated on the surrounding plain and is not very high (150 m). Karoshimo, with its highly ferruginous Paleozoic quartzites enriched with hematite, boasts the first commercial iron mine (opened in 1883) in Venezuela.

It is remarkable that the northern and southern earth-gods are aligned along a north-south axis with a deviation of only 9 minutes or 12 kilometers; transiting marker stars must have provided these geographical bearings. The diameter of the terrestrial disk measures 212 kilometers, meaning that the total surface of the Warao earth is 35,300 square kilometers. The disk's radius of 106 kilometers fixes the center of the earth, of the distribution area of the Hoanarao, and of the sacred-rock cult, so that we must take these Indians literally when they refer to themselves as the inhabitants of the center of the earth. Furthermore, by using the radius of 106 kilometers one can plot the terrestrial disk and observe how perfectly the entire delta is included in the Warao earth: from the mouth of the Rio Grande to the southeast, the line touches the southernmost *caño* (Caroshimo) of the delta system;

[2] In Waraoan the phoneme [p] is limited to word-medial position and its pronunciation varies from [p] to [b] according to regional dialectical usage. As the toponym "Naparima" is spelled this way on the map of Trinidad, I retain the *p* when referring to the mountain itself. When the name of the earth-god is meant I render it as "Nabarima" according to Hoanarao pronunciation.

[3] Criollo: a Venezuelan whose ancestors have interbred for several generations among whites, Indians, and blacks.

flowing from west to east, it intersects the very apex of the delta, leaving only a small portion of the northwest corner outside its ambit. It would be difficult to find a more satisfactory center for the Warao world. The outer circle traces the *aitona*, the edge of the Warao universe, between the Guayana shield and the northern mountain ridge of Trinidad. To the Hoanarao it is only natural that the earth's center should so precisely identify their own territory while at the same time marking the hub of the world axis, which rises up from that point to the center of the celestial dome. In the absence of eastern and western earth-god mountains, the path of the equinoctial sun marks the imaginary east-west divider of the earth and partitions it into four quadrants.

To the Warao, man is a relative newcomer on the earth, having put in his appearance long after most plants and animals had established themselves. The history of life on earth is recorded in a myth of origin, in scores of etiological tales, and in specialized sets of lore handed down from generation to generation by different groups of people. Much of this lore is common knowledge, but a substantial part of it is retained in the minds of specialists like shamans, herbalists, craftsmen, and others.

The myth of origin has been celebrated by Lévi-Strauss (1966, 184) as the most brilliant example of the American oral tradition. It is known, with certain variations, throughout the delta as the Haburi myth; I have compared some fifteen different versions of it from all parts of the area. Among the Hoanarao the myth is cast in a cultural-geographical framework lacking in versions that prevail elsewhere. The Hoanarao versions collected among the Winikina, when viewed from the special perspective of this discussion, illuminate the ecological premise set forth in the introductory section.

The Haburi myth first introduces a protohuman inhabitant of the southeastern quadrant of the earth, commonly referred to as the "Roaster" because he hunted and roasted peccary. Although his hunting grounds were not lacking in moriche groves, the Roaster had no moriche sago to eat because there were no women to prepare it for him. One day, desperately craving sago, he climbed a tall manaca palm (*winamoru*) and, using it as a vehicle, flew to the northwestern corner of the earth. There he encountered the giant river otters (*Pteronura brasiliensis, hoetobu, etobu*), who were fishermen.[4] They lived close to the *morichals*, where two of their women discovered that the hunter of peccary was secretly eating their moriche sago. After his capture by the otter-women, the Roaster agreed to marry them—they were two sisters—and to take them to his part of the earth.

Soon after the younger sister had given birth to Haburi, a baby boy, the hunter was killed by a feline ogre, who then pursued the fleeing women and the infant to the house of Wauta, an old frog-woman who lived in the southwestern quadrant of the earth. Wauta, a tree frog (*Phrynohyas venulosa*), was a farmer who raised manioc and maize. Unbeknownst to the two sisters, she transformed Haburi into a young man who, ignoring his origin, committed incest with his own mother. Unaware of the transformation, the woman did not recognize her son in the guise of the youth.

Learning about his incestuous act from his otter relatives, Haburi and the betrayed woman and her sister schemed their escape. To implement their plan, Haburi invented the dugout canoe and the paddle, and the three of them fled to the northern earth-god mountain Nabarima. At first following the refugees toward the north, the frog-woman was eventually left behind in the central part of the earth, where she was transformed into a "honey-eating" frog (*dokoriaba*). The refugees entered the northern mountain and stayed there permanently. The canoe and the paddle, however, transformed themselves into tree serpents, the canoe becoming a (female) red *cachicamo* (*Colophyllum lucidum* Benth., *bisi*) and the paddle turning into a (male) white *cachicamo* (*Colophyllum* sp., *babe*).

The canoe-serpent, together with her companion, returned to the center of the earth where she was transformed into Dauarani, the Mother of the Forest, and became humanity's first priest-shaman. Disliking the wet swamp in the earth's central region, Dauarani left her companion behind and went to Karoshimo, whence she traveled to the edge of the world (*aitona*) and settled at the points of sunrise (her soul) and sunset (her body) of the winter solstice. It was after Dauarani's arrival at the center of the earth that man first appeared, in the form of the Warao. They occupied the only free space still available, the land portions and the ocean of the northeastern corner of the earth, which even today accommodates the majority of the Hoanarao.

---

[4] A smaller species of otter (*Lutra enduris, dau ubutu*) frequents the lesser *caños* of the delta, but here I am talking about the giant river otter (*Pteronura brasiliensis*).

MYTHIC ECOLOGY

Myths convey different messages to different people, according to acquired levels of understanding. To the Warao child the Haburi saga is a story crackling with adventure, detailing ogre chases, feats, and triumphs. To the average adult, on the contrary, the episodic itinerary of the myth explains a terrestrial arrangement of resources and corresponding means of exploitation. To the sages of the tribe the myth conveys deep religious truths, establishing as it does a link between humanity and the gods. Before outlining the ethnogeographical dimensions of the Haburi myth, I first discuss the ethnoecological aspects.

The southeastern quadrant of the earth with its chenier system of elevated ground is an ideal locale for the peccary, which provides the Roaster with his favorite food. White-lipped (*Tayassu pecari*) and collared peccaries (*Tayassu tajacu*) are found in many parts of the delta, but when the Orinoco's annual floods inundate the prelittoral zone they force peccary herds to migrate to the coastal ridges. There, small bands of collared peccaries (as few as six) or larger herds of white-lipped peccaries (as many as 200) find dry land where they can rest and where they find food.

In contrast with the seasonal abundance of land animals, the scarcity of fish in the southern section of the southeastern quadrant is marked. Present-day Criollos and Indians who frequent this area turn of necessity to agriculture and ranching. Thus, Haburi's father, the Roaster, had chosen an ideal spot for his life as a hunter. A Warao tradition holds that the first human couple emerged from the island of Burohoida, at the mouth of the Sacupana River. If applied to Haburi and his family, this tradition places them in the middle of peccary country, whence the women and the infant boy fled to the land of Wauta, the frog-woman, whose domain was the earth's southwestern quadrant. As noted earlier, the largest part of this area is fluvial; it features Orinoco-related levees, backswamp, and marsh deposits. It was here that Haburi, the son of a hunter and a fisherwoman, learned how to till the soil; Wauta had a field of manioc and a field of maize right behind her house.

Wauta's house in the southwestern quadrant is located in that part of the delta where early Neo-Indians like the Saladoid and the Barrancoid practiced agriculture at least 3,000 years ago. Warao oral lore frequently recalls clashes between their ancestors and the "Red-

Faces" (probably Carib), until the Warao finally yielded the high ground to the intruders and retreated permanently into the lower delta. Now that these once feared Indians have disappeared, Hoanarao of Mariusa origin have entered the Macareo area to engage in agricultural pursuits themselves. Mostly mission-educated Indians, they live side by side with Criollo agriculturalists.

The northwestern corner of the earth lacks natural levees, even along major *caños* like the Manamo and the lower Macareo. Nevertheless, many a Warao song lauds the region's abundance of *morichals* and sago, of moriche wine, and, above all, of fish in the rivers and lagoons. The number of species of edible fish is large, and they rate high in productivity and quality (Barral 1964, 272–73). It is hardly surprising, then, that the giant fish otter finds this part of the earth very compatible. Groups of twenty individuals of this playful nutria frequent the rivers and at times even venture across the sea to visit islands on the continental shelf. The otter feeds mainly on fish, crabs, and frogs, but waterfowl and small mammals also contribute to its diet; in fact, the otter, like the nutria, is practically omnivorous (Harris 1968, 50–91).

The northeastern corner of the earth was the last area to be populated by human beings, the Hoanarao. This quadrant, consisting mainly of water, is, except for Trinidad, wholly situated within the littoral zone of the delta. Hoanarao territory, bypassed by the major rivers of the delta, is drained mainly by nonfunctional *caños*. Here the first Warao lived as swamp foragers who collected and gathered their foodstuffs instead of hunting for major game animals, fishing for large species, or growing crops. The Hoanarao lived that way until the 1940s, and indeed some of them, even today, follow the same pattern. It should be noted, however, that the Mariusa of the Hoanarao, as swamp foragers, specialized in the hunting of manatee (*Trichechus manatus*), especially during the dry season. At that time this species, which is abundant in the region, seeks the deeper waters of the estuaries of the northeastern rivers in the littoral zone (Mondolfi 1974, 15).

Thus, according to the Haburi myth, the four quadrants of the earth were inhabited in primordial times by beings who selectively exploited their respective environments. Among them were hunters, fishermen, farmers, and gatherers, and it is safe to conclude that the Warao have been cognizant of these techniques of food procurement since prehistoric times. A cultural classification on the basis of any one food-quest activity is therefore bound to be inadequate and misleading. The swamp foragers, the Hoanarao, most closely resemble fishermen, as both engage in fishing and both exploit *morichals* for sago as their staple food. The fishermen, however, exploit an abundance of riverine species, whereas the foragers hand-catch mainly two herring-sized species of fish in swamp lagoons and backland *caños*. The foragers also differ from the fishermen in their reliance on marine hunting, for which the Hoanarao, especially the Mariusa, are famous.

The Mariusa, known in the sixteenth century as Tivitivi, were then considered a distinct population inhabiting the delta. In their central position, isolated from all other Warao subtribes, the Mariusa may have preserved a Paleo-Indian life-style based on systematic foraging and on hunting of large species of marine fauna like the manatee, a life-style antedating that of Meso-Indians in the Caribbean area. While certainly distinct, the two culture styles, of the marine hunters and swamp foragers on the one hand and of the riverine fishermen on the other, nevertheless resemble each other closely. Also, as illustrated by the Warao, they reveal specific microecological adaptations which here, as in the Antilles, have continued side by side for extended periods of time and may have been practiced by the same or by closely related peoples.

The cultural habitat of the hunter of peccaries is quite alien to the Hoanarao foragers. He does not know how to prepare moriche sago, the Warao staple food. Like Haburi's kinfolk, the otters, the Warao eat birds and rodents, but they have a traditional aversion to hunting large mammals that have "blood like people." Indeed, the Warao refer to such animals as "people of the forest." Many mammals, like the giant river otter, for instance, are metamorphosed ancestral Warao, and white-lipped peccaries are transformed Warao children; the thought of eating them repels most of the traditional Hoanarao. That some of the southern Warao do partake of peccary meat is symptomatic partly of ecological adaptation and partly of acculturation. Arawak and Carib in this region along the Rio Grande are avid peccary hunters, and, through centuries of coexistence, the Warao of the hunter's quadrant probably learned to take advantage of so rich a source of protein, especially because fish are relatively scarce along the southern Rio Grande.

To the earliest Warao, the culture of the agricultural frog was even more alien than the hunter's culture. Wauta, the frog-woman of the

Warao, owing to her agricultural life-style, her shamanistic power (which can magically turn infants into adolescents), and other mythological characteristics, merges with Tarunmio, the frog-woman of the neighboring Cariña-Carib of western Venezuela, and with the frog-woman Kano(bo)-aru of the Carib of Surinam (Civrieux 1974, 420–22; Roth 1915, 133–35). In fact, the Guyana frog-woman's name, Kono(bo)-aru (spelled Kanobo-aru in the Warao language), is fully intelligible to the Warao, to whom it means "Cassava of the God." The Carib frog-woman plays a role in the famous twin-hero cycle of South America, and in several versions of the Haburi myth twins also appear, although all other characteristics of the twin-hero cycle are missing.[5] The mixing of hero stories may also have resulted from the Warao-Carib acculturation that occurred when mission Warao lived on Cariña territory in the eighteenth century and when refugee Warao in Guyana lived in close proximity to Carib.[6] The Hoanarao, whose Haburi tradition forms the basis of my discussion, were isolated throughout this period and did not experience similar uprooting interventions.

SHAMANISTIC ETHNOGRAPHY

Warao mythical geography, as transmitted from one generation to another in oral lore, is a lesson in human ecology and resource management. I cannot describe here in detail a particular genre of Warao folk literature, known as *namonina a re*, transformation stories, except to point out that it delineates the etiology of a large number of plants and animals and the physical features of Warao land. *Namonina* descriptions of life-forms are often quite detailed. They explain, for instance, where a particular tree originated, why it grows in one spot rather than another, why it looks the way it does, what special properties it has as food or as raw material, and who are the tree's companions— birds, animals, insects, snails, and so on. In other words, *namonina* lore

---

[5] Among the missing characteristics are birth of the twins by cesarean section, their revenge on their mother's murderers, and their testing by their father.

[6] Roth's (1915, 130–33; Wilbert 1970, 357–61) version of the Haburi myth shows the extent of the merging of the Haburi tale with the Carib twin cycle. The fact that the southeastern Warao (descendants of the refugee Warao) place Wauta in the east rather than in the west may have originated in the historical exile of several hundred Warao who fled from the western delta to Guyana in order to escape the colonization program of a certain governor.

expresses the Warao conception and interpretation of the physical, botanical, and zoological environments and their interrelationships in the Warao universe.

As indicated earlier, Warao craftsmen, such as canoe makers and basket weavers, or professionals, such as shamans, rainmakers, herbalists, and musicians, all dominate, at varying levels of competency, that part of Warao ethnoscience which relates to the objects, activities, and events of the social and material world in which they function. To do so efficiently means to be a *uasi* (expert) authorized to appropriate for himself or herself the prerequisite resources of his or her profession. The use of these resources is contingent upon the individual's understanding of the salient aspects of his/her profession, craft, or art and upon his/her own expertise. In a way, all true Warao *uasi* are religious practitioners who mediate the powers of their natural and supernatural environments.

Some individuals attempt to acquire encyclopedic knowledge about the conceptions and classifications of their world. By preparing themselves for several careers they usually achieve a position in an elite of shamans and *uasi* who study and contemplate the ulterior meanings of Warao lore. In their thinking the Haburi myth is not an adventure story for children, nor is it an ethnoecological blueprint of residence, subsistence, and territoriality patterns. Instead, to the initiated sage the myth of Haburi is the genesis of priest-shamanism. In this connection it is noteworthy that one of the early actors in the myth is the species of manaca palm the Warao call *winamoru*. Though scarce in the littoral zone, it thrives on the higher ground of the intermediate delta. Since the manaca palm is the priest-shaman of the trees, there is nothing strange about its ability to fly.

Before embarking on his mission, Haburi's father, the personification of the manaca-shaman, had acquired the paraphernalia belonging to the highest rank of priest-shamanism: the sacred stones and the sacred rattle. The *winamoru* palm, it is believed, carries a rock crystal in the form of a 5-centimeter-long hexagonal pyramid in its root pedestal and a rounded quartzite pebble in the stem section immediately below the crown. The pebble is located close to the fronds that function as the rattle's "resonance chamber," perpetually swaying and rustling in the trade winds some 20 meters above the ground. Presumably poisonous to other birds, the fruit of the palm attracts only *cotorra* parrots of the Psittacidae family, whose tail feathers, when plucked from live specimens, adorn the shaman's rattle. The leaf stipule of the *winamoru* provides the only acceptable wrapping for the shamanic cigar, which produces the food of the gods in the form of tobacco smoke and induces the trance in which the shaman flies to communicate with the spirit world.

To the initiated listener, therefore, the role of the *winamoru* palm in the Haburi myth presents the tree-shaman as an ideal guardian of the sacred rocks kept in Hoanarao temples. Nothing is more difficult for a Hoanarao shaman in the northeastern quadrant of the earth than to acquire the sacred rocks, the rattle, and the cigar, the sine qua non of his profession. To do so he has to seek the company of the *winamoru* palm. There is, of course, no stone in the alluvial delta which would not have been carried there by man. Rock crystal is found in the vicinity of Karoshimo and in Naparima country on Trinidad (Joseph 1970, 7). In other words (and as prefigured in the two crystals in the palm stem), the earth of the Warao is placed in a symbolic force field that emanates from metamorphic rock crystals at its north and south poles. Most Hoanarao priest-shamans can only hope to obtain a mountain crystal, believed to be the "son" of the respective god. The sacred rocks now in Hoanarao temples have all come down to their present owners through a long chain of predecessors, the first of whom are said to have undertaken the perilous journey to either mountain in order to acquire a crystal in symbolic exchange for human lives.

Similarly, the rounded quartzite pebbles must be acquired either from metamorphic rocks on offshore islands or in the piedmont region of the Sierra de Imataca, in the south. A powerful rattle contains from 120 to 200 pebbles carefully assembled over a long period of time. It is very difficult for a novice shaman to obtain these prized possessions, for he has to spend years in long voyages across the sea or journeys through enemy territory. Even to pluck a sufficient number of tail feathers from live *cotorra* birds, caught from behind a blind on top of the *winamoru* palm, is a dangerous and time-consuming task, not to speak of the difficulty of acquiring sufficient quantities of tobacco. Tobacco, not grown by the Warao, also has to be procured abroad. One informant told me that shamans gravitate toward the *winamoru* tree-shaman because he is the first to appear in the initiatory trance of the novice shaman; he is an accomplished shaman who holds out both the promise and the hope of obtaining a shaman's paraphernalia and of achieving the highest rank of the office through possession of a sacred rock. The Haburi myth points to the south and to the north because rock crystals and quartzite pebbles are found in both regions.

To acquire a calabash rattle like the one the tree-shaman possesses is also fraught with difficulties and dangers for a novice shaman in the northeastern quadrant of the earth, mainly because the calabash tree (*Cresentia cujete*) does not grow in the littoral zone but, like the manaca palm, flourishes only on higher ground. Again, the Hoanarao aspirant who wanted to acquire a calabash large enough to hold the sacred quartz pebbles had to travel into "foreign" lands.

Even after assembling all these symbols of his office, the tree-shaman of the myth, in order to function as a shaman, had to approach the otters, for they possessed all the commodities needed for the celebration of the cult festival. They had the moriche sago offered to the gods for use in ritual bathing. The directional gods of the earth and the universe lack fresh water because they live either at the outer edge of the sea that surrounds the earth or at the extreme poles of the earth.[7] The otters also had fish which, together with sago, is the ritual food for the cult festival. Furthermore, the gregarious river otters lived in bands large enough to produce the amounts of moriche sago necessary for the annual festival. Finally, they had children on whom the directional gods prey and for whose protection the cult festival is celebrated in the first place.

The Wauta episode of the Haburi myth is enormously complex from an ethnoecological point of view, but for the religious practitioner it points not so much to manioc and maize production as to the supply of tobacco. Communication with the gods is impossible without tobacco. Originally, to obtain *Nicotiana rustica* of high nicotine content, Warao shamans had to authorize dangerous expeditions into Wauta country on the western fringe of the delta or to Trinidad. Approaching the house of the Wauta frog-woman, the women heard her chant and swing the rattle. She was feeding the stones in her rattle with tobacco smoke and was smoking to communicate with the spirit world. Once defeated by Haburi, the frog-woman became *dokoriaba*, "sweet

---

[7] Naparima Hill on Trinidad is actually located in an area of acute shortage of potable water.

mouth," owner of vast quantities of honey. In a diluted form honey is consumed as a ritual drink by the common participants in the cult festival, and in its natural state it is offered to the gods and eaten by the shamans.

Haburi, son of the tree-shaman and the river otters and foster son of the frog-woman, has all the required shamanic accoutrements. He violates the protohuman social order of the tree-shaman by committing incest, but he establishes the new social order of Dauarani by inventing the dugout canoe (which, metaphorically, represents the vulva and the womb of the goddess). The new order includes not only the priest-shaman and the supreme spirits at the north and south poles of the earth, but also the cardinal and intercardinal gods who reside on mountains beyond the world sea surrounding the earth.

The foregoing bare outline of the Haburi myth and some of its ethnogeographical associations may help to substantiate my premise that the Warao, through intensive study of their world, have created a cosmic order within an apparently chaotic marginal econiche considered by outsiders as hostile to and incompatible with human nature. The water surrounding the terrestrial disk is inhabited by a huge tail-biting serpent, the "Snake of Being." When provoked by human transgressions of the world order, she rises from the sea, swallows any boats she may encounter, or sends earthquakes and hurricanes. She can actually be seen rising out of the coastal waters in the form of far-stretched sandbanks of Amazonian and Orinoco alluvium that occasionally build up high enough to become visible above the water level. Otherwise, as long as humanity abides by the rules of Warao life, the *uroboros* serpent remains submerged in the sea and breathes calmly in tempo with the rhythm of the tides.

From an ethnoecological point of view, the Warao universe is inherently capable of being transported to and established in another milieu. Its dynamics stem from an existing contract of compelling mutuality between man and the supernaturals who, like partners, rely on each other to provide goods that are lacking to either side. To establish such a contract the Warao had to inventory their environment carefully and exchange regional resources. As a navigational people they are mobile and accustomed to traveling, to trading, and to recording transactions mentally over long spans of time until a particular arrangement is realized. For example, the novice shaman spends years in acquiring the paraphernalia of his office through interzonal exchange with fellow Warao or on overland and overseas journeys to deal with foreigners.

This example characterizes the spirit of the canoe peoples of the Caribbean; the Warao may be the only surviving indigenous coastal society to have preserved this spirit to the present day. It is the spirit of an intellectually active and physically mobile society accustomed to living on an earth securely anchored within the round of the world snake that encircles it and sustained by the knowledge that as long as humans live according to established cultural norms they can live safely at the center of their universe. A north-south dynamics is built into this worldview, inasmuch as the terrestrial disk is suspended between the earth-god mountains of Nabarima and Karoshimo, because the east represents the unapproachable world of the God of Origin (in the Atlantic Ocean) and the west, the ominous region of the underworld. On their journeys across the sea the Warao could always remain in the center of the universe as the circle of the horizon traveled with them, and, if need be, they could establish a new home wherever two mountains could serve as the poles of their earth and the abode of the two earth-gods.

Considering the overseas travel of the Warao in connection with their present land, one may wonder if the application of an insular worldview of the Orinoco Delta does not, in fact, represent an extreme case of environmental adaptation forced upon Warao cosmology by the historic population displacements alluded to earlier. True, the extreme familiarity of the Warao with their present habitat is certainly indicative of a longitudinal study that may have taken thousands of years. I am also impressed, however, by the mobility of the Warao universe; its movable center could have been taken along in the minds of the navigators, who would enjoy the security of always being physically and psychologically in the middle of the world and of residing close to the tidal heartbeat of the Snake of Being.

Chapter Two

Carpenters of Canoes

INTRODUCTION[1]

The name Warao designates specifically a single person and generically the entire tribe. The word is derived from *wa* (canoe) and *arao* (owner). The Warao are owners of canoes. In this society, therefore, to become an expert canoe maker is tantamount to becoming a man, and the worst one can say about a man is that he is *wayana,* "without canoe." This designation places him on the bottom rung of the socioeconomic ladder, on a level with paupers. It identifies him as an incompetent commoner among the living and may assign him a place among the undistinguished souls of the dead.

The fame of the Warao as expert canoe builders was established in early colonial times, when Sir Walter Raleigh referred to them as "Carpenters of *Canoas.*" According to Raleigh the Warao "make the most and fairest houses, and sell them into *Guiana* for gold, and into *Trinedado* for *Tobacco...*" (1970 [1596], 52). Subsequent documentation also attests to the proficiency of Warao shipwrights. In colonial times they were still "the most famous boat-builders" who furnished "nearly the whole colony of Demarara with canoes" (Robert Schomburgk in Raleigh 1970 [1596], 49; Penard and Penard 1907–8, 1:124). Eventually Warao dugouts were in use throughout the European

[1] I gratefully acknowledge the comments on a draft of this chapter made by my colleagues Dr. Robert Edgerton, Dr. Walter R. Goldschmidt, Dr. Thomas La Belle, and Dr. Thomas Weisner. Dr. Clinton R. Edwards gave me advice on technical terminology of canoe making. Ms. Charlotte Treuenfells edited part of the manuscript. Most of the ethnographic data were collected among the Winikina-Warao. How far they can be generalized as representative of all Warao subtribes remains to be uncovered through future research. The fieldwork for this chapter was supported in part by a grant from the Ahmanson Foundation.

colonies in Guiana, where English, Dutch, French, and Spanish colonists preferred to purchase canoes made by Warao craftsmen to those of any other artisans, Indian or European (Hilhouse 1834, 328; Schomburgk 1847–48, 1:144). There was scarcely a traveler in the seventeenth, eighteenth, or nineteenth century who failed to admire Warao canoe makers as "wonderful specimens of untaught natural skill" (Bernau 1847, 343) and to deem their products "most excellently adapted to the wants of the Indians, though shaped and hollowed with crude implements and without any assistance from the rules of art" (Brett 1868, 166). In the twentieth century there is abundant evidence that the Warao have continued to live up to their reputation for making the best dugouts, whether for domestic use on the mainland or for export to Margarita Island (Méndez-Arocha 1963, 196) and elsewhere.

In view of the antiquity of canoe making and its importance to the Warao, further examination of this success story should reveal data not only on skill-training and technology but also on certain social and ideational dimensions of Warao enculturation. Each generation has one imperative: in each generation, to raise as many canoe makers as needed to fulfill the requirements of an environment in which canoes are essential for survival. Furthermore, examination of the enculturation processes of skill-training, socialization, and moral education as related to the art of canoe making should demonstrate that they are designed to permit a man to realize his capacity and "to so utilize the technology, to so implement the ideas—value, religion, philosophy—and to so act within the socioeconomic organization that the traditional adjustment of the culture to the outer world is not upset" (Henry and Whithorn Boggs 1952, 261).

At least four major reasons support the choice of canoe making as a vehicle for probing the process of enculturation among the Warao. First, canoe making is a cultural category of demonstrable antiquity, its roots probably reaching back into prehistory. Solid historical documentation covering almost four hundred years positively establishes the dugout as an ancient artifact of Warao technology. Second, canoe making is a dominant category of Warao culture, which concerns all members of the society, especially the males, young and old, and permits a longitudinal study of enculturation from infancy through adulthood. Third, canoe making, pervading all systems of Warao culture, sheds light on the interrelationship of technological features with aspects of both social and value systems. Finally, because canoe making pertains to the universal category of transportation, it lends itself to comparative studies (cf. Williams 1972, 206–7).

THE MODEL

A theoretical model underlies the descriptive and analytical sections of this chapter (fig. 2.1). It shows the relationship of several factors that have an important bearing on the phenomenon of enculturation in a homogeneous tribal society. The model may also apply to the study of education in heterogeneous societies, but that is not the basic intent of its design.

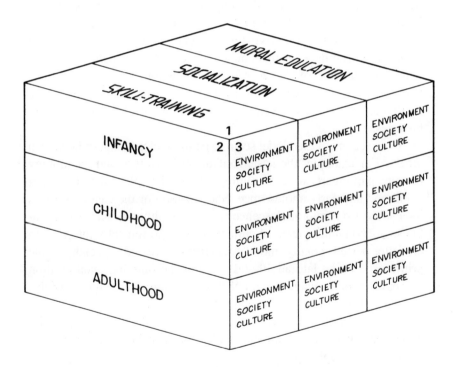

FIG. 2.1.
A model for the study of enculturation. (1) Goals of enculturation (process dimension); (2) Life-cycle stages (time dimension); (3) Ambience of enculturation (space dimension).

According to the dimensions of the model, enculturation is studied as processes of skill-training, socialization, and moral education effected during infancy, childhood, and adulthood, in a given environment, society, and culture. The interrelationships in this process may be diagramed in the form of a cube in isometric projection.

The focus on canoe making puts the whole life cycle of a male Warao into the model's frame of reference, even though infancy and childhood seem to be periods of less intensity in the total learning process than do adolescence and adulthood. At least the data presently available yield less information about the early life stages than about the later ones. Nevertheless, I believe that the data are deceptive and that early years of child training may well be as relevant to the enculturation process as the later periods of manhood. Even the existing data suggest that cultural conditioning of the child toward canoe making is strongly promulgated by various agents at all stages, but additional research through projective tests is needed to substantiate that suggestion. The data for this chapter were collected mainly from the Winikina subtribe of the Warao, among whom I have been intermittently engaged in fieldwork since 1954. I used standard ethnographic methods, including interviews, participant observation, and life histories.

Some sectors of the model seem to be more closely interrelated than others. For example, the system of material culture and technology pertains particularly to skill-training which takes place mainly during childhood and early adolescence. Socialization of the canoe maker is intensified from mid-adolescence to early adulthood, with aspects of the socioeconomic system of culture coming prominently into play in the latter period. Finally, moral education is stressed especially in the prime of life and late adulthood, linking the ongoing enculturation processes with the value system of Warao culture. These relationships, of course, reflect tendencies rather than sharp distinctions, for in real life skill-training, socialization, and moral education are parallel processes functioning in all stages of a canoe maker's career, though with varying emphases.

ENVIRONMENT, SOCIETY, AND CULTURE

THE NATURAL ENVIRONMENT

Location, geography, and climate.—In a process that may have lasted thousands of years, the Warao have adapted their culture to the difficult outer world of the Orinoco Delta. This area has become the heartland of tribal distribution in the delta, but over time some groups have settled in adjacent areas east and west of the delta proper, largely along the Orinoco's tributaries and branches running into the Gulf of Paria and along the lower reaches of delta rivers that empty into the Atlantic Ocean. Most of the Orinoco Delta is a vast tidal swamp lacking dry ground and stone and extending 50 to 100 kilometers inland (Liddle 1928, 20–24). The waters of the delta splinter the region into a multitude of islands of varying size that accommodate some 249 Warao settlements.[2] The Orinoco is subject to a four-season climate governed by the solstitial transitions (twice a year) of the intertropical convergence zone. More or less intensive showers occur throughout the year.

Botanical zones.—The Orinoco Delta may be subdivided into three major botanical zones: lower, intermediate, and upper. The lower delta is a coastal belt of mangroves growing at the edge of the swamp. Typically in such environments, the soil is almost always inundated, thus providing ideal conditions for the pioneering red mangrove (*Rhizophora mangle*). A mangrove forest grows on the periphery of the belt and dies at its core. This unusual feature is of prime importance to the Warao, for the central clearing created by the dying mangroves attracts such food producing palms as the moriche (*Mauritia flexuosa*), the manaca (*Euterpe* sp.), and the temiche (*Manicaria saccifera*), and many other useful trees and plants. Thus, within the coastal mangrove belt of the lower delta (and within the 60-kilometer-wide tidal zone of the intermediate delta inland), there developed the econiche of a palmetum which has long served the Warao Indians as an abundant food basket as well as a secure home.

Twice daily the tide inundates the intermediate delta, nurturing the palms. The annual inundations of the Orinoco are felt here only indirectly, and the flooding of the palm groves during the rainy season is actually caused by precipitation. In the dry season, when the waters

---

[2] Data are from the National Census of the Republic of Venezuela for 1960.

of the Orinoco recede, seawater runs into the intermediate delta, salinating the rivers and thus making water undrinkable.

Warao culture is especially adapted to life in this environment. If one were to single out the major factor facilitating the adaptation of Warao culture to the intermediate delta, it would have to be the moriche palm. The sago of this palm was the staple food for the preagricultural Warao during much of the year, and today, when most of the Warao practice subsistence agriculture, sago continues to be an important food for many local groups.

Several varieties of trees suitable for the manufacture of canoes grow in the intermediate and upper delta. The red cedar (*Colophyllum lucidum* Benth.) outranks all others in this respect; the white cedar (*Colophyllum* sp.) is second, and the *paramo* (*Symphonia globulifera*), *carapa* (*Carapa guianensis* Aubl.), and sassafras (*Nectandra* [?] *cymbarum*) are third.

Closest to the apex of the upper delta large portions of the gallery forest were cleared in colonial times for agriculture and arboriculture (coffee and cacao) by the predominantly Criollo population. But the area is subject to yearly inundations by the Orinoco River which, together with pests, have rendered the plantations inoperative.

The dense pluvial forest that covers many of the islands of the Orinoco Delta has played a major role in protecting the Warao from the intrusions of cannibalistic Cariban neighbors and enterprising Afro-Europeans. Until recently the Indians considered trees sacred, and Warao culture has imposed a taboo on the felling of trees. All trees, especially the larger species, except for the *sangrito* (needed for firewood), are protected by specific guardian spirits who inflict epidemic disease on the families of violators. The conflict between this perfect cultural goal and the necessity of felling palms (for food) and certain trees (for the manufacture of dugouts) demands a satisfactory solution. Many of the beliefs that surround canoe making serve the very purpose of maintaining the culture in a state psychologically balanced with the environment.[3]

---

[3] The wholesale felling of trees for timber, for swidden agriculture, for cash cropping (rice), or for the palmito industry cannot be reconciled with the traditional goal of forest conservation. Apparently the Warao, rather than allowing themselves to be torn apart by this dilemma, have accepted the white man's disbelief in spiritual guardians; whether their choice is for better or for worse, only time will tell.

Zoological characteristics.—The mammalian fauna of the Orinoco Delta is rather uniform. In earlier times the Warao were reluctant to hunt the nutritionally more valuable large species, such as *chiguire* (*Hydrochoerus hydrochoeris*), paca (*Cuniculus paca*), tapir (*Tapirus terrestris*), deer (*Odocoileur virginicus*), and peccary (*Pecari* sp.). Their attitude has changed, and now all these animals are eaten by commoners. Some priest-shamans, however, continue to abstain. Neither jaguar nor monkey is eaten, but among rodents the small agouti (*Dasyprocta rubrata*) is much sought after, as are birds such as wild turkey (*Crax alector*) and duck (*Cairina moschata*). Among the reptiles the Warao catch are turtles, caiman, *baba*, and iguana, but they ignore all snakes. Fish is the most important source of protein, especially small lagoon species such as *hoko* (*Rivulus* sp.) or river fish such as *morocoto* (*Collosama macropomus*) and several varieties of catfish. Crabs are an important seasonal supplement.

THE HUMAN ENVIRONMENT

The society.—Among the surviving tribal societies in South America, the Warao form one of the largest. They consider themselves a distinct people because of linguistic homogeneity and a shared common cultural denominator rather than for reasons of political federation. The largest social entity that is most meaningful and most functional to a Warao is the band, traditionally consisting of several extended uxorilocal families. Bride service is required for the lifetime of a woman who was married as a virgin. The bands average from thirty to fifty members who follow the advice and guidance of the paterfamilias.

Several bands recognize one another as belonging to the same subtribe, but beyond that unit group allegiance is weak. Subtribes are loosely held together by three types of religious practitioners who function as intermediaries between the community and a pantheon of supernatural beings. In more recent times missionaries and Criollos have introduced the political offices of *fiscales*, in charge of local groups; *capitanes*, for modern riverfront communities of more than one hundred inhabitants; and *gobernadores*, for larger aggregates. Besides these three political officeholders, religious practitioners holding three different offices are the Warao elite: the priest-shaman, the light-shaman, and the dark-shaman.

TABLE 2.1
WINIKINA VILLAGES AND POPULATION (1954)

Villages	Total inhabitants	Number of dwellings	Total dwelling space[a]	Number of other structures[b]
Yaruara Akoho	79	10	320 m^2	5
Naonoko Hanoko (a)	32	5	100 m^2	6
Naonoko Hanoko (b)	19	4	134 m^2	1
Hanoko Buroho (La Isla)	33	6	236 m^2	3
Bure Bureina	32	3	60 m^2	3
Total	195	28	850 m^2	18

[a] Occupied floor space in square meters, averaging 4.4 m^2 per person.
[b] Barns, kitchens, menstruation huts, temples. The house of the investigator at Yaruara Akoha is included in this category.

TABLE 2.2
SEX AND AGE RATIOS OF LIVING WINIKINA (1954)

Age category[a]	Total	Percent	Males	Percent	Females	Percent	Ratio of males to females
Infants	12	6	7	58	5	42	4:3
Children	75	38	34	45	41	55	4:5
Teenagers	19	10	12	63	7	37	4:2
Adults	78	40	36	46	42	54	4:5
Seniors	11	6	4	36	7	64	4:7
Total	195	100	93	48	102	52	9:10

[a] Infant, offspring below 1 year of age.
Child, prepubertal offspring between 1 and 10 years.
Teenager, bachelor.
Adult, married individuals of reproductive age between 18 and 49 years.
Senior, men and women approximately 50 years and over.

The kinship system of the Warao is of the Hawaiian type: all cousins are considered brothers and sisters. This typology reflects the customary marriage rule, inasmuch as first cousins seldom marry each other. Instead, marriage partners are commonly chosen from unrelated or more distantly related families of the subtribe, so that endogamy prevails as long as marriageable partners are available. Descent is reckoned bilaterally.

The largest concentration of Warao Indians is found in the littoral and intermediate delta, where 75 percent of the Warao inhabit an area of more than 10,000 square kilometers. The central sector of the zone is the home of the Winikina. In 1954 the Winikina, then numbering 195 individuals, lived in four settlements along the banks of the Winikina, the *caño* that gave the subtribe its name (table 2.1).

Judging from the demographic sample in table 2.2, the Warao are a young society with 54 percent of the population below eighteen years of age. The cycle of reproduction begins for the girls soon after they have participated in specific initiation rites that coincide with the onset of menstruation. Boys are usually somewhat older at marriage, and because of the existing uxorilocal rule of residence, a married man moves into the household of his parents-in-law. There he faces a closely related group of females who condition public opinion and exert considerable social pressure. Although both mates exercise free choice, final acceptability of a man by his future in-laws depends largely on his peaceful disposition and on his technical skill in the various activities essential to the young family's livelihood. The groom considers his in-laws as his new parents, and the father-in-law especially becomes an important new agent of enculturation. Depending on the number of marriageable daughters a man has, his association with his sons-in-law creates a formidable work force that plays a large role in enabling the co-resident extended family to remain entirely self-sufficient. The importance of this cohesion becomes especially apparent in tasks like canoe making which require teamwork. To weld a group of young men and women into a cooperative unit the culture has, of course, to provide adequate methods of enculturation, and Warao culture is fully programmed to accomplish that goal.

The culture.—The Warao speak a language that has been identified as either independent or of Chibchan affiliation. Should the latter turn out to be the case, Waraoan represents the easternmost extension of this linguistic phylum of northern South America and southern Meso–america.

The missionaries, who established themselves nearly seventy years ago among the Warao, were influential in bringing about a number of important cultural changes. For example, intensification and diffusion of subsistence agriculture spread throughout most of the territory. Although nonagricultural groups still exist in the intermediate delta zone, agriculture is now practically universal among the Warao. Among the main crops planted are taro, both bitter and sweet yuca, bananas, plantains, sugarcane, maize, and rice, a cash crop. Traditionally, however, most of the Warao were swamp foragers who relied heavily on vegetable and animal resources (mentioned earlier). Tobacco, their only psychoactive drug, was used mainly for magico-religious purposes and had to be obtained through trade with Trinidad or with some of the Criollo towns on the western fringe of the delta.

The Warao do not keep domestic animals for food. Hunting dogs are of considerable economic use in daily food-quest activities and as trade objects. Young birds and animals are also kept around the house to be exchanged for exotic items on periodic trade expeditions. Tame parrots, moriche birds, and monkeys are raised especially for this purpose.

Warao technology is little developed. Originally their only clothing was a fiber loincloth for women; pieces of wood, bone, and shell were made into necklaces, bracelets, and other ornaments. The ornaments are still made, but now most men and women have largely adopted garments of Criollo origin.

As containers for liquids the Warao use tree calabashes; for solids, they depend on baskets of various kinds. Iron pots of a casserole type are now used for cooking purposes, but traditionally the Warao lacked pottery as well as such other landmark crafts as weaving and metal-lurgy. Their original shelters were dome-shaped structures in which they slept in improvised leaf-stalk hammocks. The modern rectangular stilt dwelling with thatched saddle roof is a recent introduction that was adopted for living along riverbanks rather than in *morichals*. Simul-taneously, so it seems, the Warao also acquired the large net hammock of moriche fiber which has now become a characteristic feature of a Warao house; it is also one of the most sought-after Warao items in trade.

For hunting and fishing purposes the Warao rely mainly on lances, harpoons, bows and arrows, and hooks. In the early days they apparently made adzes of conch shell and axes of tortoiseshell, but the equivalent tools of iron prevail in modern Warao households, together with the inevitable multipurpose machete or bush knife.

By far the most complex and best-developed item of Warao material culture is the dugout canoe, the floating house of the traveling family. It is essential to the livelihood of the Warao because most life-sustaining activities in the delta require transportation by water. The Warao trade with it and sleep, cook, eat, and play in it. A person may even be buried in a canoe. As a consequence of its vital importance, the dugout became thoroughly integrated into the technological, sociological, and ideological systems of the society, a development that changed a severely limiting factor of the habitat—its dominant aquatic characteristics—into a distinct cultural advantage.

ENCULTURATION OF A CANOE MAKER

SKILL-TRAINING AND TECHNOLOGY

Technology is a major subsystem in any given culture. It enables man to adapt to his physical environment by producing specific goods and artifacts. Skill-training is the teaching of skills necessary to maintain a certain technology. The technology of the Warao, though of little complexity, is uniquely specialized to fit the conditions of their homeland. This adaptation was particularly valuable in earlier times, before the advent of Afro-Europeans, when food-quest activities of the Warao centered on arboriculture, lagoon fishing, and the catching of reptiles and shellfish. In those days the tool kit was meager: spears, bow, multipronged fowl and fish arrows, the sago hoe, the conch-shell adz, calabashes, and bell-shaped twilled baskets.

Under those circumstances the dugout canoe was then, as it is today, a major piece of equipment, especially adapted to the aquatic geography of the delta. Although the literature frequently refers to the giant Warao canoes that could accommodate as many as a hundred passengers, it is useful to remember that it is not the very large canoes that take care of the daily needs of these Indians. The oversized craft were often made to order for European patrons who needed them to ship bulk merchandise or substantial contingents of troops. But the Warao themselves employ large dugouts, for fifty or more passengers, only on an occasional overseas trading expedition. In the delta they make use of smaller dugouts, which often hold no more than the members of a nuclear family. The canoes are large enough to tackle the windswept waters of the major *caños* but still short and shallow enough to negotiate the narrow swamp channels. More important than the ability to cross wide expanses of water is the need for easy penetration of the boglands to distances of more than 10 kilometers inland, through the mangrove and hardwood belts clear into the heart of the life-sustaining palm groves.

The different sizes of Warao canoes correspond, of course, to the varying dimensions of the trees used to make them. Each type of Warao canoe is made from a single tree trunk, but canoes differ not only with respect to size. There are two classes of Warao dugouts which differ in construction and use: the plain canoe and the composite five-piece canoe.

The plain canoe ranges in length from 2 to 12 meters. A common medium-sized canoe averages about 6 meters. The shorter craft in this class have a maximum width of approximately 50 centimeters; longer ones range between 70 and 80 centimeters in width. They may be anywhere from 30 to 40 centimeters deep. The thickness of the hull is an even 2.5 centimeters in small dugouts and 4 centimeters in large ones. Along the inside of the gunwale runs a rim, 3 to 4 centimeters wide and one centimeter thick, which ends at bow and stern in an inverted triangular design. Bow and stern are about 10 centimeters higher than the straight body, and the approximately 1.5-meter-long pointed stem at each end is relatively heavy. The two ends look identical, although the Indians know how to distinguish between them (fig. 2.2).

The five-piece canoe has the same form and shape as the plain dugout, but it is invariably larger, measuring 12 meters or more in length, and is fitted with a plank on each side to heighten the gunwales. The planks are mounted on edge and lashed to each gunwale by means of lianas. At bow and stern these wash strakes are each connected by transverse prow boards which serve as escutcheons for painted symbols. The hull, two wash strakes, and two transverse boards are the five pieces.

Warao canoes of either class lack outriggers. The hollowed space of the vessel adds considerably to its buoyancy. Widening the hull by

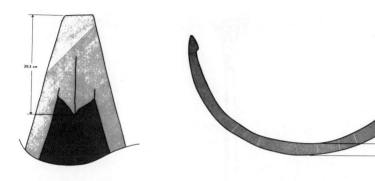

(1) Superior prow detail   (2) Cross section of hull

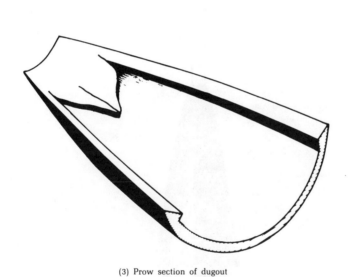

(3) Prow section of dugout

WARAO DUGOUT CANOE

FIG. 2.2.

Warao dugout canoe. (1) Superior prow detail; (2) Cross section of hull; (3) Prow section of dugout. Prototype in UCLA Museum of Cultural History (Cat. No. X70-36). (Drawings courtesy Raúl A. López)

Fɪɢ. 2.3.
Warao paddle. (Drawing courtesy Helga Adibi)

means of fire, hot water, and crossbeams increases the beam of the craft so that loads, even when asymmetrically arranged, do not easily cause rolling or capsizing.

Both classes of canoes are propelled by paddles with foliated blades and crescent handles (fig. 2.3). In the smaller craft the boatmen sit down in the middle and paddle from both sides while sitting on thwarts. In the larger craft the boatmen sit along both gunwales and paddle only from their own side. Sometimes, especially in the upper delta region, plain dugouts are also fitted with rectangular sails of leafstalk matting and triangular ones of cloth. The mast for the sail rests on a step mounted on the bottom of the boat in the forward section of the craft. The mast is further supported by two mast partners fixed above the step or by passing it through a hole in a benchboard. Nowadays, larger canoes of the same class are also equipped with outboard motors.

The plain dugouts are steered by varying the stroke direction of the paddle. Composite five-piece canoes are provided starboard with a large paddle lashed to the stern quarter as a rudder. In the center of these seagoing vessels is a railing of beams tied together in the form of a cross. This rack serves the shaman-captain of the vessel as support en route overseas to Trinidad: he holds onto the crossbeam mounted at elbow height. There may be as many as thirty boatmen in the large canoes.

Skill-training of the Warao boy and man has to satisfy the requirements for building canoes of all sizes in both classes. Techniques vary in certain respects according to whether a regular-sized or an oversized canoe is envisaged and whether the trainee is a child, a young man, or a mature adult.

SKILL-TRAINING DURING INFANCY

Infancy lasts from the day of birth to the end of the child's first year. The Warao recognize this initial period not as an age grade but as a period in which the baby passes through five stages of motor development and a series of concomitant levels of mental achievement and status progression (table 2.3).

Throughout the first two months the infant rests in a baby sling, practically glued to his mother's body. Mother and child rarely leave the family corner of the communal house, which is shared with two or

TABLE 2.3
STAGES OF MOTOR DEVELOPMENT IN INFANCY

Stage[a]	Designation	Ability
First two months	*Horoshimo*	Suckling, sleeping
Three to five months	*Hiota*	Grasping
Six to nine months	*Hiota kabuka*	Sitting
Ten to eleven months	*Kabayoro*	Creeping
Twelve months	*Kabaka*	Standing, walking

[a]Development stages are approximate.

three other matrilaterally related families. The platform of the stilt dwelling may offer a total living space of 40 square meters, with 10 square meters reserved for each nuclear family, an average of only 4.4 square meters per person (table 2.1). But the family corner is the most important to the infant as his first environment, not only during the first two months but throughout the entire year and even beyond.

Infancy is the period when the Warao baby is immersed in a world of women. Canoe making, in contrast, pertains mainly to the man's world in which he achieves progressively advanced status in his role as artisan. A woman's involvement in matters relating to canoes is more peripheral and is even hampered to some extent by negative associations attendant on her sex.

Yet, despite initial submersion in a female world, the presence of the male element soon breaks into the baby's sphere. Warao fathers frequently cradle babies in their arms and sing to them, especially when the infant has become a *hiota* and is able "to see and to laugh and to cry real tears." Sometime toward the end of this stage, the father may make a toy basketry rattle which he puts into the infant's grasping hand. The mother will also use the rattle thereafter to delight the infant during his longer waking hours. He is becoming frustrated with her because she leaves him behind more and more frequently while tending to her many chores. But if no baby-sitter is available, the mother or the parents jointly begin to take him along on short boat rides to the *morichal* or to the fields. By the time the infant has learned to sit up, he has taken many such rides, and the *hiota kabuka*'s familiarity with canoes, as an extension of the family corner, becomes very intimate.

Another circumstance that tends to increase the infant's contact with the canoe during the third stage of motor development is the Warao belief that an infant six to nine months old must be bathed frequently so that he learns how to stand up properly and how to walk rapidly. In fact, some mothers maintain that there ought to be several bathings a day. Thus, one frequently observes a mother carrying her baby to the river where she seats the screaming creature in the family dugout and subjects him to extensive washing.

Toward the end of the first year of life, it is difficult to confine the crawling, and eventually walking, infant to the small platform of the stilt house. Baby-sitting him becomes a full-time chore, and parents develop inventive ways and means to keep their enterprising child in safety. The landing place with its bobbing boats is an irresistible attraction for the child. He wants to play with the other children, and, like them, he wants to jump in and out of the moored boats. The father, seeking to keep the youngster contented while in the house, carves small toy boats out of light *sangrito* wood. Eventually he will cut a piece of the boardlike root of the same tree and put it down on the floor of the house, where it becomes the first "real" canoe for the infant, one he can actually sit in. Manipulating a miniature paddle with which his father equips him, he embarks on uncharted journeys, away from the house, through the fantasy land of infancy and childhood.

Among the many considerations of the parents is a concern for their infant's manual dexterity. Warao are right-handed as a rule, but some are left-handed or ambidextrous. This feature is no cause for alarm; left-handed children are not "corrected." On the contrary, naturally left-handed boatmen are appreciated on long journeys when the men paddle in rows along both gunwales of the canoe. There are also certain tasks in canoe making for which left-handedness is an advantage. Therefore, the parents of such a child let him be and teach him only how to hold the paddle properly. But little goading is required, for by the time a child can hold a paddle, he has observed his elders on so many occasions that paddle shaft and handle slide into the small fists almost naturally.

SKILL-TRAINING DURING CHILDHOOD AND ADOLESCENCE

This life period combines the ages from one to twelve (childhood) with those from thirteen to seventeen (adolescence). The Warao themselves make these distinctions between childhood and adolescence by using different terms to refer to individuals in the different categories and by changing the personal names of postpuberty boys and girls (table 2.4).

Warao children seem to prefer to play outside the house as often as possible. They play "house" below the platform of the pile dwelling and various games on the dancing platform if there is one in the settlement. But by far the most attractive playground is the landing place. There they enjoy themselves for hours diving off the platform of the house nearest the riverbank and climbing back into the boats. Small children bring their toy paddles; bigger ones pick up real ones lying in the canoes and pretend to be going on a real journey. They put in so much practice time on make-believe canoe rides that by the age of three all children, boys and girls alike, know how to maneuver a canoe perfectly. Parents cannot be too vigilant on such occasions, for on the flimsiest pretext—for example, a canoe "accidentally" gets loose and drifts away with the current, or temiche fruit comes floating by just beyond reach—the small children push off to take care of the "problem." When the parents finally give in and let their children venture forth in a canoe, the youngsters are euphoric. What they had been watching from infancy and had wanted so badly for themselves is finally attainable: they are able to get out onto the wide river all by themselves. It is truly breathtaking to observe a three-year-old child push off and paddle a canoe across a wide river in full control of the craft.

After a youngster has mastered the first step toward becoming a boatman, the drive to own his personal boat soon makes him eager for the time when he will be strong enough to develop his skills. In this

TABLE 2.4

AGE CATEGORIES OF CHILDHOOD AND ADOLESCENCE

Age category	Boys	Girls
1 to 12 years	*Noboto* (*nobotomo*, pl.)	*Anibaka* (*anibakamo*, pl.)
13 to 17 years		
a. Early teens	*Neburatu kabuka*	*Iboma hido*
b. Late teens	*Neburatu*	*Iboma*

respect, my informants consistently assured me, the process is actually a matter of imitation and copying, not of teaching. As one expert canoe maker explained, "Nobody teaches a boy how to make a paddle or a canoe." When asked why not he replied, "Because he is a boy. Boys learn from watching. Boys just have to watch carefully."

What the informant did not tell me (but what field workers, myself included, have observed) is that the canoe maker insists on having boys present when boats are being made. In other words, although adults may not give verbal instruction, they definitely require the presence of the learner when the opportunity for visual learning and instruction through demonstration presents itself. "The old Warao insist on performing this task [canoe making] in cooperation with their children, grandchildren, and sons-in-law" (Suárez 1968, 35).

I remember one occasion when the chief of the Winikina set out to manufacture a canoe for my personal use. His wives took the girls along to gather fruit and manaca shoots, but their nine-year-old son had to remain at the working place in the forest, although the prospect of eating fruit and palm cabbage strongly tempted him. Therefore, while it is true that, as one of my informants put it, "boys learn how to make canoes on their own initiative," the drive to learn must be fostered and the cue of "learning through watching" must be reinforced.

The son of the Winikina chief, despite his young age, had to perform several minor tasks connected with canoe building. There are also a series of precautions children have to take and taboos to observe, so that by insisting on a *noboto*'s participation the skill-training and social conditioning through which a Warao eventually becomes a master canoe maker are well under way at an early age. The paternal teacher is most understanding. Taking the relative physical immaturity of the apprentice into consideration, he is forgiving if the attention span of the child is not very long, owing to the many distractions offered by a jungle environment. In fact, when the chief's nine-year-old fell asleep on a temiche leaf right next to the hull, his father smiled and walked over to him once to chase a horsefly off his bare back.

This tolerance is not shown toward an adolescent. At the age of fourteen a boy ceases to be a child. He can handle an ax and a machete and now should participate more and more intensively in the actual production of a canoe; otherwise, he will be called lazy by his father and warned against growing up incapable of taking care of his future family. Postpuberty girls are denied the world of canoe makers for several reasons. For one, they are not considered clever enough to learn the art. They spend most of their time learning how to make hammocks and other tasks traditionally considered to be women's work. And, a young girl is especially dangerous to the canoe maker since she may unwittingly step into the dugout during menstruation. By so doing the girl would offend the patroness of canoe makers and provoke her devastating wrath.

Boys of fourteen, in contrast, make a decisive entrance into the world of canoe makers. One day the youngster will leave the settlement, ax in hand, to return with a piece of *sangrito* wood from which he carves his first paddle. When next the father goes into the forest to make a dugout, his son, now *neburatu kabuka*, accompanies him as his assistant.

A plain dugout canoe is manufactured in three stages. First, a suitable tree has to be located and felled, and its trunk has to be trimmed, hollowed out, and roughly shaped with an ax. The hull is then transported to the river and floated to the settlement. During the second stage the roughly hewn hull must be smoothed evenly inside and out by means of an adz. The third stage is the hardening and spreading of the hull with fire.

A fourth stage is required for the production of a composite five-piece canoe. During this stage it is equipped with the wash strakes to increase the vessel's volume and depth. Also two transverse prow boards have to be carved, painted, and fastened; the captain's rack is put into position midships, and the rudder is lashed to the stern of the boat. Life expectancy of a well-made canoe of either class is from three to five years.

The learning process to which a young *neburatu* has to submit during the four stages is best described by detailing the technical production of a canoe. Finding an appropriate *cachicamo* tree may take several days of searching in the forest. One young apprentice told me that his father always found a tree in a very short time. "He looks around a lot," he said. And, indeed, "looking around" is a favorite pastime of the men when out on boat trips or when walking through the bush. Traveling day after day by boat along the green forest edges becomes monotonous for a non-Indian. Not so for Indians. Travelers have often remarked upon the Warao habit of observing and studying the forest carefully as they go by. I personally have heard Indians comment more than once when a certain tree is missing from a particular spot. To know in general where to look for a good *cachicamo* is half the task of finding one.

The next step is to go out and fell the tree. This task has to be done during the early months of the dry season, and the boat maker who has no sons-in-law must rely on his son as helper. If he has no sons old enough, he must engage two men from among his brothers-in-law, his brothers, or unrelated friends, for he cannot fell and excavate the tree by himself. Hiring helpers, however, represents an expense, inasmuch as the "owner" must provide them with food during the days of labor. As every adult man probably wants to make a canoe for himself, it is not easy to find the necessary help. So a young father looks forward to the day when his son can be part of the team, and at fourteen that time has come.

Very likely the youngster will be one of three men who set out one fine morning to accomplish the first stage of making a boat. The *neburatu*'s most likely teachers are his father and his father's brother-in-law. So small a team does not usually set out to make a large canoe of 12 meters or more, let alone one large enough for overseas journeys. That requires a team of five or six men, usually made up of a father-in-law, who functions as the expert craftsman, and his sons-in-law, the workmen. The job of constructing a large canoe is performed with much ceremony and many ritual observances, most of which can be disregarded when a small dugout is being built.

Once the three arrive at the foot of the tree selected for the dugout, the first chore in which the *neburatu* participates is the cutting of trees growing around the *cachicamo*. The surrounding trees are felled in such a way as to form a grid on which the *cachicamo* comes to rest. This takes several days and serves to prevent the falling tree from plunging deep into the swamp. With neighboring trees and underbrush gone, the *cachicamo* can be inspected to determine in which direction it ought to fall. First, the flatter "back side" and the rounder "stomach side" of the tree must be identified. The father, if he is the more experienced of the two men, cuts a notch-shaped mark into the lower end of the back side of the tree, and then the men and the boy take turns cutting deep into the opposite stomach side so that the *cachicamo* will eventually topple on its back.

As I write this I have projected on my movie screen a tree that we filmed in 1954 during the process of making a dugout. From roots to crown, the tree measured some 20 meters in height. The father used as a measure the distance from the palm of his hand along the outstretched arm to the sternum, an extension I found to be 86 centimeters long. Applying this measure seven times consecutively along the trunk of the fallen tree, he marked with his ax the spot where his fellows would severe the crown from the trunk. Thus the boat was determined to become a craft of 6 meters in length. The base, which always becomes the stern of the canoe, measured 63 centimeters in diameter and the top, 59 centimeters. After trimming the tree the young assistant placed two pieces of manaca on each side of the trunk to brace it firmly and to prevent it from rocking while the work of excavating it was in progress.

The apprentice is permitted to excavate the trunk only after several seasons of experience. He is placed between the two adults and may excavate only the deeper layers, not the top ones. The first opening and the alignment of the various square excavations are delicate procedures which must be performed by an experienced craftsman. He starts at a point one meter from the bottom of the trunk and scoops out a piece 30 centimeters square and about 20 centimeters deep. From the farther side of this square he measures a distance the length of his ax handle at which point he excavates a second square and lifts out the section between the two. He repeats the same operation at the other extremity of the trunk, also approximately one meter from the end. After carefully aligning the squares at the extreme ends of the trunk, he then opens up the middle section. This first part of the actual task of hollowing out the tree is done while the craftsman is standing on the ground.

To perform the next step he stands astride the trunk with one foot on each edge of the shallow opening; he excavates the next layer of wood by striking diagonal blows zigzag from the middle of the trunk to the base and then from the middle to the top. Some of this work can be done in part by the young apprentice, as can the next step of scooping out a third layer of wood. This time the blows of the ax are directed laterally, excavating first a longitudinal groove through the middle of the trough from rear to front and then cleaving out the remaining shoulders. Two men can work simultaneously at these tasks, with the apprentice concentrating on the midsection of the boat.

The final step of excavating a tree has to be carried out by the hand of an expert. The partly hollowed out trunk is rolled on its side so that an experienced man can round out the interior of the hull. Next he tapers the ends for about 1.25 meters and rounds off bow and stern. This task, beginning at the stern, has to be performed with the utmost precision. Facing the stern the craftsman first tapers the left side. Ideally the right side should be carved by a left-handed person, but if no such person is available the same man must do both sides fore and aft. The following day he must rest so as to relieve the pain he suffers from straining unconditioned muscles.

While his father and the adult helper are resting from the strenuous five or six days of work, the young apprentice cuts manaca palms to prepare a 2-meter-wide corduroy road across the swamp from the workplace to the river. He is joined in this task by the women and children, who come to help by first placing the poles and then pushing the hull out of the forest into the nearest river. This procedure concludes the first stage of the manufacturing process.

The young apprentice has had a good opportunity to practice swinging his ax with precision. He has learned how to direct a falling tree and how to use his hands to measure the thickness of the hull between them. He has also seen how the excavated parts are visually aligned and how the ends of the boat are tapered. A seventeen-year-old *neburatu* has usually advanced far enough in his apprenticeship to go out alone or with a brother or a friend and try his luck with his first canoe. He often does so immediately after he has helped his father scoop out his boat and while the older man is busy by himself with the second stage of the manufacturing process. By the time a *neburatu* thinks of marriage he has participated as an apprentice to his father for four seasons. Under the guidance of an experienced man he carries out the procedures he has observed for ten or more seasons. Many a *neburatu* prides himself on owning his own boat by the time he marries and on having mastered the rudiments of boat making, though he would not yet pretend to be a full-fledged *moyotu* (boat maker). For that he needs more practice and, above all, a dream vision in which he receives a call to the office. Technological skill is a necessary but not a sufficient condition for becoming a craftsman.

The second stage of production is a task carried out by the owner of the boat himself without the aid of helpers. It requires thousands of blows with the adz, an implement consisting of a transverse blade on a short handle not much longer than the width of an adult man's hand, to smooth both sides of the hull. By rolling the hull from side to side and repeatedly gauging the thickness of the walls between the flat of the hands the task is finally accomplished; the hull is smooth and even and the internal rim along the gunwale is carved.

This work is done within the confines of the village, and the children have been watching the craftsman for weeks. The boys are frequently called to the site to observe the process, although they are not permitted to touch the tools, not only to prevent a child from damaging the hull but also to avoid provoking the spirit of a tool. Only men from *neburatu* up may pick up an adz. Thus, at least for the child, to learn how to handle the adz and how to finish the hull of a dugout is to learn through observation, never through practice. The adolescent will have to learn later under the guidance of his father. Again, there is little verbal instruction from father to son, but the father does correct the hand of his son and does teach him how to overcome the pain in his wrist from working with the adz. In another kind of explicit instruction, the son is taught how to use his outspread hands to measure the thickness of the hull. The father, after remeasuring the area, corrects his son's work if necessary.

Finally, the day comes when the carpentry work on the hull is finished. The next stage is to smooth the hull inside and out by fire. The canoe is laid on its side and the hull is packed with dry temiche leaves. It is for this moment that the children and everybody in the village have been waiting. The fire is lit and soon the hull is engulfed in a billowing bonfire. While the children jump carelessly around the fire, the boat makers themselves are busy directing the heat by adding or removing leaves at different places and protecting strategic parts by covering them with clay. After the fire has burned down, the men scrape off the charred portions with chips of wood. Then the other side undergoes the same treatment. This process takes care of smoothing the hull and removing all adz scars from the canoe. The hull is now jet black.

The next step is to widen the hull. The canoe is propped up at both ends on two short uprights which are notched in a V at the top. Each end of the hull is firmly locked between two uprights placed on either side and tied tightly together with lianas. This precaution prevents the hull from slipping off its props into the fire, a mishap that could cause it to crack and thereby ruin the entire job.

The hull is filled with water, and a new heap of temiche leaves piled underneath it is set on fire. From time to time the craftsman tests the water temperature with his hand. When it is at the right level he climbs into the hull and begins to widen it by inserting several crossbeams of varying lengths. Starting in the middle with the longest beam, he sets one end against the rim on one side. Then he pulls up the other end of the beam slowly until there is a certain degree of resistance. He inserts a series of crossbeams of decreasing length toward bow and stern. When he has finished that job he jumps out of the hull and runs to each end of the boat to check the symmetry of the intended longitudinal curve of the gunwale. If it needs correction, he climbs back into the hull and applies additional heat until the sheer is perfect. If it is, he tips the canoe and pours out the water.

After several seasons of helping his father with the simpler tasks in this third stage of the canoe-building process (maintaining and directing the fire, scraping off the charred parts, and the like), the apprentice is permitted to step into the boat and insert the crossbeams to spread the hull. The father still determines the correct temperature of the water and indicates how far up a particular crossbeam must be pulled to reach the maximum point of tolerance, but he remains on the ground and directs the operation from either end of the hull. That is how the *neburatu* gets a feel for each critical task: the evenness of the hull wall between the palms of his hands, the right water temperature, and the degree of firmness of the breaking point when the hull is spread. To see the boy eventually permitted to share in his father's pride in a job well done is a moving experience.

It takes one whole night for the new canoe to cool. The next morning branches are cut for the seats and the struts are put in place. The shiny black boat is then launched with the joyful participation of the entire village.

The technical aspects of converting a plain canoe into a seagoing five-piece vessel have already been described sufficiently for the present purpose. I return to the subject later to discuss certain nontechnical aspects.

TABLE 2.5
STAGES OF ADULTHOOD

Age category	Men	Women
Early	*Nebu*	*Iboma*
Late	*Aidamo*	*Tihidamo*

SKILL-TRAINING DURING ADULTHOOD

After his training as an apprentice, the *nebu* (young adult; see table 2.5) has little to learn about canoe making other than through experience and seasoning. By the time a man has made his own fourth or fifth dugout, his father-in-law and the master builder of canoes will ask him whether or not he has dreamed of Dauarani, the Mother-Goddess of the Forest. By now, a mature man of twenty-five or twenty-eight, he is about to embark on a new learning experience involving the supernatural and religious dimension of canoe construction.

SOCIALIZATION AND SOCIETY

The term "socialization" as used here refers to the various processes by which a man is integrated into Warao society as a full-fledged canoe maker. The integration "involves...the adaptation of the individual to the fellow-members of his group, the achievement of a position in relation to them that give him status and assign to him the role he plays in the life of the community" (Herskovits 1970, 38). More specifically, I describe how the Warao effect socialization of the individual during childhood, adolescence, and adulthood within the tribal environment, society, and culture.

SOCIALIZATION DURING CHILDHOOD AND ADOLESCENCE

Little need be added to what has already been said about the enculturation of the male Warao child. He is gradually socialized into the distinctly male domain of canoe making and encouraged to assume his place as a helper to his elder brothers and to his father. (I return to a boy's moral obligations in the section on "Moral Education and Ideology," below.)

The socialization process becomes much more apparent once the Warao youngster has reached his early and late teens and, especially important, once the adolescent has entered adulthood. A young teenager (*neburatu kabuka*) frequently becomes the "alter ego" of an elder brother in his late teens (*neburatu*). He will function as his elder brother's confidant, his go-between with his girlfriends, and his ever reliable cover. Several such pairs from the same group or from neighboring groups occasionally form single-sex gangs and roam through the territory, giving expression in various ways to adolescent *Sturm und Drang*. Whether such reactions are culturally conditioned or are natural, adolescent male and female Warao do not make their parents happy. The burden for disciplining a youth falls primarily upon the mother's shoulders and secondarily upon the society. Fathers rarely concern themselves with the behavior of their teenage sons and daughters.

From about his sixteenth year until the birth of his first child, a male adolescent adopts the identity characteristics of the tribal culture hero Haburi, the inventor of canoes. Like his model, the youth adorns himself with armbands made of bast and paints his face with two lines below the eyes and dots on his cheeks. His hair is cut short in the back with a crop left only on the forehead. Blowing on Haburi's flutes and playing the hero's drum, he leads the life of a restless wanderer, moving from house to house and from one settlement to another. A teenage girl finds his flute playing irresistible and both make use of the *neburatu*'s younger brother to exchange vows and gifts of food and to arrange for secret rendezvous. Eventually, taking advantage of his girlfriend's isolation during her menses, the young man and his sibling-companion pretend to go on yet another bird-hunting expedition, leaving the village for several weeks or months. Girls are known to have pursued their escaping paramours to beat them up and pierce the membranes of their expensive drums. All this behavior, so typical of the vicissitudes of adolescence, is routinely expected, and the young man moves on as did Haburi, whose very name means "he who roams about aimlessly." The reasons for Haburi's restlessness are explained below. Suffice it to point out here that he was tormented by remorse for having committed incest with his mother and that the dugout he

invented was transformed into the mother-goddess of restored sexual
order.

Fear of repeating the incestuous crime drives the adolescent youth
to visit the girls of neighboring groups. Chances are that among them
he may find some who are not consanguineally related to him. Under
a kinship system of the Hawaiian type (that prohibits cousin marriage
of any kind) and with prevailing subtribal endogamy, potential sexual
and marriageable partners are scarce. But the most pressing fear of the
youth and of his parents is that his heart might run away with his head,
that love and ignorance might trick him into an incestuous relationship.

What compounds these difficulties is the fact that endogamy and
uxorilocal residence may eventually force an adolescent to leave friends
and relatives to find a future consort among strangers in another
subtribe. Thus an adolescent's dilemma is that, although he has
considerable freedom in selecting sexual partners, his choice is severely
limited to a very few females in the bands of his subtribe because of
the constraints of social structure. For instance, of a total of twelve male
teenagers in our demographic sample of the Winikina subtribe, eleven
were bachelors; of the seven female teenagers only three were
unmarried (table 2.2). Thus the ratio of eligible male bachelors to
marriageable females is 0.6.[4] Moreover, the three unmarried girls were
consanguineal kin (hence forbidden) to several of the eleven bachelors.
No wonder, then, that the adolescent boy empathizes with Haburi,
whose only potential female partners were his consanguineal and
classificatory mothers. To avoid breaking the taboo he is required to
roam from band to band in search of a bride.

And that is how a young man succeeds in finding a young bride
instead of an older widow. To have his love returned by the girl is one
thing; to be accepted by the bride-to-be's father is quite another. Crucial
for the latter is the bridegroom's ability to handle the tools used by a
man. Does he know how to prepare a garden, how to hunt and fish,
how to build a house? Above all, does he know how to make a canoe?
If he is accepted by the girl's parents, the young man's father-in-law
may ask him to build a dugout for him, and it is understood by all

[4] Teenage boys usually remain unmarried several years longer than their female counterparts. Teenage girls wed soon after the onset of menstruation at about twelve. Men of high
status and rank often take a young girl as a second wife.

concerned that the canoe is compensation for a virgin bride. His firstborn child will seal the bond in accordance with the order established by Dauarani, the culture hero's canoe-serpent. With the birth of the first child the adolescent's Haburi behavior terminates, and he has successfully entered the world of adults.

SOCIALIZATION DURING ADULTHOOD

Marriage thus marks the boundary between adolescence and adulthood for a Warao youth. When his wife gives birth to their first child the young husband hands down the material evidence of *neburatu* status to his younger brother: the drum, the flutes, a necklace of jaguar bone, among other things. This gesture of passing on the paraphernalia of adolescence is associated with a good measure of trauma for the young man. It is the same trauma of separation which overshadowed his wedding day a few months earlier. In general, all bridegrooms in Warao society are required to leave their parents' homes and exchange the world of childhood for a strange physical and social environment. From that day a young man ceases to belong to the work team of his father, under whose tutelage he learned the basics of canoe making. He is a *nebu* (worker) now serving his father-in-law. He has to cooperate with his co-resident brothers-in-law, sometimes even in a new settlement, where he assumes junior status to those who have preceded him by marrying his new wife's sisters. Whatever remains to be learned about the art of boat making he will probably absorb from his father-in-law and brothers-in-law, the men of most consequence in effecting the enculturation of the newlywed.

This transitional period is an exceedingly critical time in a Warao man's life, especially if the uxorilocal residence rule should oblige him to move far away from his family of orientation, his cousins, and his friends. Fortunately, such removal is rarely required. With prevailing endogamy the settlements belonging to the same subtribe are usually not too distant from one another, and, under traditional circumstances, a man seldom has to move from one delta zone to another. This stability is of signal importance owing to the considerable differences in the physical and biological environments of the three delta zones. A man raised in the intermediate zone, for instance, knows best how to exploit the flora and fauna of that region. It would add considerably to the normal stress accompanying a change of residence if he also had to exchange his customary outer world for a strange one. Compliance with his in-laws and peers is the young man's best guarantee for happiness within the new family he has joined by marriage. (I have watched such a family grow over the past two decades, and I consider its members a good example for the present discussion.) To become accepted as an equal is the strongest motivation for education at this stage in life.

After establishing his family of procreation, the young family man is likely to be called upon during the first dry season to join his brothers-in-law and the "owner of the house," his father-in-law, in making a new canoe. According to the prevailing custom, however, he will learn of these plans not from his father-in-law or from any of the other men of the family, but rather from his wife. Of course, the initiative usually originates with the *aidamo* or *moyotu*, as the father-in-law is called, if he himself is a master canoe maker. But he speaks first to his wife, calling to her attention the need for a new canoe, one large enough for the women to transport firewood and for the men to use in transporting such building materials as sturdy house posts, manaca beams for construction and flooring, and temiche leaves for roofing. His wife agrees and, waiting for a good opportunity, draws her eldest married daughter's attention to the need. The daughter, in turn, communicates her parents' wishes to her younger married sisters, who then explain the situation to their respective husbands. Although there exists no avoidance taboo between father-in-law and sons-in-law, and although they usually communicate freely in daily life, the father-in-law would never speak directly to his daughters' husbands about labor that requires team work, such as clearing a patch of forest in preparation for a new field, construction work on houses and bridges, or making a canoe. He would feel "ashamed," as the Warao put it. For her part, each daughter makes sure that her husband agrees to respond to the *moyotu*'s wish by pointing out that the work of fabricating the hull would take no longer than a week if everyone cooperates.

Once the word is out that a new boat is to be built, it takes only a short time for the women to prepare a sufficient supply of victuals (like taro and sugarcane) and to pack the boats. Then one day all the brothers-in-law with their entire families set out in three or four boats, the youngest son-in-law and his wife among them. The small fleet travels up one of the *caños* several kilometers deep into the swamp until the boats come to the end of the waterway, where they are tied up. The men construct small shelters that will serve as living quarters while canoe construction is under way. The *moyotu* and his wife or wives do not depart with the younger family members. Instead, they allow one day for the young people to set up camp and join them there the following day, arriving early in the morning.

After breakfast the men sharpen their axes and fall into line to walk to the place where they have found a tree of the desired dimensions. As we shall see, this method of walking is ritually significant, for the sequence in which the men walk single file through the forest is determined by their status and rank. First walks the master. He is followed by his sons-in-law, who take their positions according to seniority, determined in this instance by the age of the wife. The man married to the eldest daughter of the master heads up the line of the *nebu*; our newlywed is at the end of the line. (There were four brothers-in-law in my sample family.)

The master walks with an air of solemnity, blowing a conch shell and chanting to herald each new phase in the process of felling and trimming the tree and scooping out the trunk. The workers depend on him to determine how the tree should fall; he marks the precise spot where the crown is to be severed from the trunk; he opens the first squares in the trunk and supervises the alignment of others. The actual excavation of the hull is then done by the workers. They line up along the edge of the trunk according to rank. The husband married to the eldest daughter puts himself in charge of the lower portion of the trunk, which is larger and tougher. Ranked on his side, according to their relative status, stand his younger peers. Thus their newlywed companion is assigned the last position at the upper end of the trunk.

If the trunk is, say, 14 meters long, it takes four men about seven days to complete the work of hollowing it out. They work for about six hours every day and, if too exhausted, sometimes skip a day. But each time they leave the camp or return to it after work, they proceed single file according to status. The hardest work is allotted the eldest son-in-law, who has the first chance to distinguish himself by earning the prestige commensurate with his rank. The youngest man is usually grateful for such formalities for he is under enough strain just to keep up with his older and more experienced companions. As word of his conduct will spread to the village of his parents, he labors conscientiously to protect his father's reputation. The quality of his work on the hull is there for everyone to judge; moreover, although nobody would dare criticize the young man publicly, there are more subtle ways to register dissatisfaction.

For the work of tapering the ends of the trunk the workmen team up in pairs. The senior pair takes the hind part and completes what will be the stern of the boat. The junior pair takes charge of the bow section. Should one of them be left-handed, he is assigned to the left side of each end point, and his contribution is greatly appreciated by his teammates for the reasons mentioned above. The junior son-in-law and his partner work more slowly on the hull and more deliberately than the senior workers at the stern. Therefore, as soon as the latter have completed their task, they relieve the younger men and finish the job for them.

The master builder does not participate in the hard labor of this phase of construction, but his advice is sought from time to time. He spends some time watching the men while they work and takes responsibility for all important ritual concerns. But a very specific task for him is to provide an abundance of choice foods, especially fish and meat. The women busy themselves with tending the small children and preparing the meals. They also assist at times with line fishing for the palatable lagoon fish which abound in the headwaters of the *caño*. Boys over seven or eight years of age go with their fathers to the construction site, where they watch the work in progress and perform small tasks, such as fetching drinking water or clearing away the chunks of scooped-out wood. In families boasting but one or two sons-in-law, the older boys, those of *neburatu kabuka* age, may be required to take an active part in hollowing out the trunk.

A more important task for the older boys, under the guidance of their youngest brother-in-law, is to fell a large number of skid logs for the corduroy road. Moreover, everybody has to pitch in to break camp when work in the forest is ended and the finished hull has been dragged to the river.

While perfecting his technical skills as a member of his father-in-law's work team, a young man also attempts to further his own career as a master boat builder. In the years when his father-in-law does not need a new boat, he tries his hand once again at fabricating a canoe for his own use. As the years pass, he will have seen four or five small canoes through all three stages of construction. He establishes a name for himself among his people as a man who has at his command all the basic skills. In fact, everybody realizes that the young man is on his way to becoming a master craftsman himself. His social status as a good carpenter is already established. Economically, he is also doing well. He owns one or two canoes and never has to borrow from his fellows. This self-sufficiency makes him independent in the sense that he can take care of his chores and his needs according to his own schedule. He is freed from obligation to the owners of canoes from whom he would otherwise have to borrow boat time.

A man owns the canoe he himself constructs, although large canoes are implicitly considered by the *moyotu* to belong to his senior wife. To run down to the village landing place and push off in a friend's canoe on a short errand is perfectly permissible, but for more extended trips a borrower must first obtain permission from the owner. Circumstances permitting, the owner lends the canoe with no thought of compensation. But it is one thing to borrow occasionally and another to do so consistently. Borrowing too often will soon severely undercut a man's prestige; people will refer to him as a *wayana*, an unskilled pauper who does not even own a canoe. Whenever he needs to go on a trip he has to rely on the favor of a relative who does own a boat. His wife is scorned because she is unable to get to the fields to bring in the vegetables. Firewood is chronically lacking in her household. As the borrower becomes more and more dependent, his fellows will start using him as a serf, one who has no choice but to comply with the whims and wishes of others.

I observed such a man who had married exogamously but still within the same area in the intermediate delta where the art of canoe making is not developed by all men. His band lived in the *morichals* away from the large rivers and the *caños*; there, canoes were of little importance in their moriche-oriented swamp life. The young man's in-laws, however, lived on the Winikina River, where life is insupportable without a river craft. Not only did the unfortunate *wayana* have to learn how to make a living as an agriculturist, but he also had to live a river-oriented life. He was forced to ask continuously for help from his fellows. I have seen this *wayana* live the life of a beggar, humiliated, jumping to oblige every man in the village who had done him a favor.

Even today he is still considered a man without the slightest chance of ever becoming a *moyotu*, in this world or the next.

In contrast, a good canoe maker, besides enjoying the prestige that goes with technical skill, may also become well-to-do. Warao canoes continue to fetch a good price, anywhere from the equivalent of U.S. $350 to $650, depending on size. Even if a young man sells one canoe only every second year, the sudden influx of wealth raises his family's standard of living far above the average. The wife of such a craftsman is well dressed and wears expensive bead necklaces which proclaim her husband's success as clearly as would a professional shingle. She owns an iron cooking pot, an ax, and kitchen knives, needles, and other metalware. He wears decent clothes and owns his own machete and ax, as well as a man's knife. These are just a few overt status symbols for gauging the level of prosperity of a competent boat maker, and there are many covert ones as well. For instance, a young boat maker does not keep for himself all that he earns by trading or selling a canoe. He gives some to his parents-in-law and his brothers-in-law. That everyone's wealth and prestige rise through mere association with such a man is a major motive for his striving to become an expert maker of canoes. Independent wealth and high status give him horizontal and vertical mobility.

The prestige accruing to a master craftsman who owns a seagoing five-piece canoe is incomparably higher than for anything else he may do in his entire life, and the enterprise of ultimate socioeconomic importance is an overseas trading expedition to the Island of Trinidad.[5] The best time of the year for such trips is the month of August, when the northern trades abate and waves are small. After being selected for the venture, about fifteen men and one woman then construct the large vessel as described.

On the last day before departure the men stow the boat with trade goods. In the 1930s, when such expeditions were still common, goods taken aboard included mainly dogs, birds, hammocks, and baskets. Naturally, the actual value of the goods received in exchange may have deviated considerably from the expected values as represented in table

---

[5] These expeditions are now almost wholly a thing of the past. Trade goods are more accessible in the delta and the Venezuelan government has prohibited island trips in order to curb smuggling.

2.6. For the Warao participants, however, these were actual values, equivalent to prices that the items listed would fetch in a Venezuelan market. The goods the Warao received in return, such as cotton cloth, men's clothing, and iron tools, were in their view equivalent to the same relative monetary value. Thus, if each of the fifteen men on board a trading boat had taken only one unit of each of the items listed, the total value, in the estimation of the sailors, would have amounted to roughly 2,000 bolivars, or U.S. $400 (according to the exchange at that time). I say "roughly" because there were probably fewer than thirty dogs involved and probably more than fifteen hammocks. In any event, a sum of this magnitude represented an enormous investment. The wide distribution of the returns among band members provided the motivation for the labor necessary to ready the boat and for mustering the courage to brave the dangers of the voyage.

The prestige of the man who made the expedition possible rose to new heights on these occasions. Thanks to the craftsmanship of the master builder, whose vessels brought the expedition to a successful conclusion, each family in the band was better off than ever before. Besides providing the canoe, the master would often take the rudder himself on such expeditions. He provided the rack and the tobacco for the shaman standing amidships to repel with abundant smoke both storm and malevolent spirits. Because the master builder was on good

TABLE 2.6
WARAO GOODS TRADED WITH TRINIDADEAN PEASANTS

Items	Value in 1930[a] (bolivares)
Hunting dog (young)	50
Hunting dog (old)	30
Amazon parrot	25
Cotorra	10
Hammock	50–60
Manioc press	10
Large basketry trays	10
Manare	10

[a]Prices according to Warao men who participated in trade expeditions. Payments were made in goods of equivalent value.

terms with the patroness of master builders, the steed of this goddess whose image was painted on the transverse prow board in the stern was sent out to speed the voyage of the vessel of her favorite servant. On the front escutcheon the master painted the oculus of the God of the North to guide their trip to the island. The God of the South pulled the boat back toward the mainland. In short, the master builder of canoes who achieved this technical and socioeconomic triumph had successfully been socialized as a master canoe maker of his society.

Contrast this exalted position with that of those Warao who fall into the kind of dependency relationship which parallels, in a sense, the informal serfdom resulting from general incompetence or from being a *wayana*. Almost equivalent to serf peonage, it entails the loss of a considerable degree of personal freedom. It originates in the following way. The three shamanic specialists of any Warao group expect to be compensated for their curing services. When summoned by a Warao in need, an agreement is entered into regarding the kind and the amount of compensation. If, however, the patient or his family is unable to come up with the necessary remuneration, it is agreed that the patient, should his health be restored, live the rest of his life in the service of his doctor. It means that he is expected thereafter to provide the shaman with goods and to do him favors. The shaman, in turn, is expected to look after him and his immediate family. A man too poor to pay for the services of a religious practitioner is known by a special name that proclaims his dependency. A relationship of this kind does not degrade him to an intolerable degree, but young men find the status undesirable because it curbs their social mobility to a considerable degree. It is a dependency that cannot befall the canoe maker. He always has sufficient tobacco in the house to make the shaman come when sickness strikes and to compensate the doctor for his services. Thus the members of his nuclear family and even his extended family are covered with sufficient health insurance, a benefit deeply appreciated.

To become a good family man who knows how to fulfill his obligations as husband, father, son-in-law, and brother-in-law is the goal of the young man who submits to the rigors of a canoe maker's life. Success in this respect makes all his effort and sacrifice worthwhile and provides the necessary motivation to excel at the specific role in which his culture has cast him.

For a substantial part of his adult life the young canoe maker continues to manufacture vessels, knowing perfectly well, however, that one important feature is missing from his career. He is not yet a *moyotu*, a master canoe maker. Of course, he enjoys the respect of his fellows for having acquired the technical skills of his craft. He also reaps the socioeconomic benefits commensurate with his expertise. But the prestige of an established *moyotu* transcends such material benefits because he has embraced the metaphysical. The true *moyotu* is chosen to become initiated as a workman of the goddess Dauarani, the patroness of the master builders of canoes. This initiation is the ultimate achievement in the career of a master, and much effort and time are expended to accomplish it.

There are, of course, several time-consuming prerequisites. The necessary mechanical skills have been mastered after approximately five years of marriage. Then will come the day when, while laboring on yet another boat, the apprentice has certain visions and goes forth to seek the help of an established canoe maker, the one who is to initiate him into the ranks of canoe craftsmen.

MORAL EDUCATION AND IDEOLOGY

I define moral education as the teaching of the concept of correct behavior. Canoe making, particularly the construction of a large composite five-piece vessel more than 12 meters long, is thoroughly imbued with the principles and considerations of those actions by which a person may be judged as being of good or bad character.

MORAL EDUCATION DURING INFANCY AND CHILDHOOD/ADOLESCENCE

During the initial stage of my first fieldwork among the Warao in 1954, it was dramatically brought home to me that a large canoe is not merely an item of material culture to these Indians. I had borrowed a 9-meter-long canoe from a Winikina who had reluctantly consented to let me outfit it with a twelve horsepower outboard motor. (In those days motors were still a novelty.) The boat had numerable cracks and an asymmetrical sheer but, as it was the only one available, aesthetic considerations had to take second place. The life history of this dugout was known to every adult male in the tribe, for it had been made by a man who had dared to cut down a large tree even though he was not a master builder. The bulging gunwales proved beyond doubt that his action had not been sanctioned by the patroness of *moyotu* craftsmen and that the spirit of the tree was angry.[6]

Then one day disaster struck. The chief had borrowed my canoe and gone with his family to the field, where they did their cooking. Unfortunately, the pot slipped from the burning embers, tipped over, and spilled its boiling contents all over the lower back of their nine-year-old son. The chief brought the child to me for treatment, explaining in rage and frustration that it was the canoe's fault. The restless spirit of the canoe had taken revenge on his child for having suffered construction by unqualified hands.

Warao children are held accountable for their conduct from their earliest years, or "as soon as they can think," that is, at the age of two or three. And it is such incidents as the one just recounted which keep them aware that canoes, especially large ones, are dangerous if not treated properly. Behavior offensive to the canoe, or rather to the spirit of the canoe, called Masisikiri, may occur as early as during a child's infancy. As the infant cannot yet be held accountable, it is not blamed, but some kind of disciplinary action may be taken as early as late infancy or early childhood. The child first learns to refrain from urinating or (worse still) defecating in or near the canoes. The toilet training of small children, I found, is not strict among the Warao, and nobody gets upset if the child soils the house. But both mother and father will not tolerate similar defilement of a large canoe, and the offending child is scolded severely. Usually children are told to stay away from the canoe at all times.

For the same reason mothers never use soap in or around the big canoes and call their children back if they notice them about to do so. To avoid all these complications the *moyotu* prefers to keep his canoes away from the busy landing place, where the children are bathed by their mothers, where they play, and where a young girl may inadvertently step into the vessel at the outset of her menstrual period. Women and girls are particularly dangerous for this very reason. In addition, they are also associated with other odors that are offensive to the boat's spirit, such as the smell of rancid coconut oil on their hair or the fumes from their kitchens. And so girls are taught to stay away from large

---

[6] I am afraid that the gasoline engine did not help to improve the reputation of the boat, although I was never openly criticized.

dugouts, especially as long as the canoes are new, lest their actions or even their mere presence cause harm, sickness, and death to themselves or to their kin.

Boys too must behave properly in the vicinity of a large canoe. Besides the restrictions pertaining to bad odors, they must learn a series of other taboos related to boat making and boat ownership. As they accompany the men to the building sites from an early age, and since the master builder chants the spells and liturgical texts aloud, boys become aware of the fact that more transpires during canoe making than meets the eye.

One of the first things the children are told is to stay away from the felled tree and the hull under construction. The Masisikiri-spirit is still all around the tree and will reside in the stump for all time. Children also learn that nobody may remain at the construction site at night, that even adults are afraid to face the jaguar that invariably comes in the dark to scoff at the tree that is "being devoured by the axes" of the men. Children learn to respect the jaguar as the chief haunt of their lives, for the jaguar who comes to jeer at the felled *cachicamo* tree is no ordinary jaguar but one endowed with supernatural powers.[7] The same is also true of other visible and invisible personages surrounding a construction site. Boys pick up fragments of this belief and value system in small increments, but by the time a young man follows a *moyotu* into the forest for the first time as a full-fledged workman he understands what the master has been chanting. He knows that below the technical level of canoe making there exists an ideational one, and that both together represent the true ethnographic reality of Warao canoes. Thus, when a man with full mastery of the technical skills who is desirous of becoming a *moyotu* approaches a master, he takes the decisive step toward articulating the technical, social, and ideational dimensions of canoe making in his own life and mind. Throughout his childhood he has been collecting the numerous pieces of this metaphysical mosaic. Now he seeks a guiding hand to help him fit the fragments together.

---

[7] This the children learn from listening to the chanting of the *moyotu* and the tales men tell about it in the evening. I imagine that the canoe is related to lunar symbolism and is mocked by the jaguar, a solar animal.

MORAL EDUCATION DURING ADULTHOOD

An apprentice is taught to become a *moyotu* in isolation. The initiation period may last the better part of the dry season, for learning some of the prerequisite (nontechnical) skills takes time. The teaching environment may be a temporary shelter in the forest or simply the house of the master, who usually concentrates on only one apprentice at a time. Both men abstain from food as much as possible but consume large amounts of tobacco in the form of cigars. They use only virgin fire[8] to light these cigars. Sexual intercourse is absolutely prohibited during the period of initiation.

The apprentice is not accustomed to smoking. According to traditional practice, only shamans and expert craftsmen like the *moyomotuma* may indulge in tobacco smoking. Consumption is strictly for magico-religious purposes. Tobacco is the food of the gods who inhabit many different sacred regions in the Warao universe, such as the cardinal and the intercardinal points, the zenith above the earth, and the nadir below it. Shamans placate these supernaturals by feeding them tobacco smoke from huge cigars. They hold a cigar in the direction in which the god is believed to reside, light it, and hold a lump of *caraña* resin (*Protium heptaphyllum*) to the burning end. They also mix granules of the same resin into the tobacco leaves contained in a consumable smoking tube made of the stipule of manaca. The resin smells like frankincense, a perfume most appreciated by the gods, and especially also by Dauarani, Mother of the Forest and Patroness of the master builders of canoes.

Smoking for the purpose of feeding the gods requires practice and a measure of physical stamina. Once lit, the cigar is smoked by hyperventilation. The tip is ignited and the resin-treated cigar is consumed so steadily that the small flame at the top is not allowed to die. The smoke is drawn into the lungs and gulped down into the stomach. As a consequence, the shaman exhales and belches up clouds of smoke, signs that the spirit in whose name the tobacco is consumed is satisfied.

Moyotu master craftsmen learn how to smoke exactly like shamans. Their smoke offering is intended to satisfy Dauarani and the ancestor-

---

[8] Virgin fire is produced with fire sticks through rotation; it is not taken from the kitchen fire, nor is it lit with matches.

craftsmen who reside on her world mountain. The apprentice unaccustomed to tobacco starts by inhaling less deeply; only toward the end of his schooling does he feed the goddess in the manner described. A major part of the curriculum concerns the origin story of Dauarani, a comprehensive and extensive myth cycle of Warao tradition (here presented in brief).

THE MOTHER OF THE FOREST AND THE FIRST CANOE

Long before man inhabited the earth there lived in the northwestern quadrant of the terrestrial disk the fishermen nation of the nutria. Two of their women, who were sisters to each other, married a hunter who lived in the southeastern part of the earth. The younger woman bore a son whom they called Haburi. Fleeing from an ogre who had killed their husband, the women and their infant son took refuge in the house of Wauta the tree frog (*Phrynohyas venulosa*[9] who lived in the southwestern quadrant of the earth and who was a farmer. The mythical frog-woman stretched the infant miraculously and made him grow instantly into a *neburatu*. Ignoring his origin, the young man unwittingly committed incest with his mothers who, in turn, did not recognize their son in the guise of the youth. Learning about his incestuous deed through his relatives, the nutria, Haburi and the betrayed women schemed their escape from the treacherous frog-woman.

Haburi invented the dugout canoe and escaped with his mothers to the northern world mountain, at the edge of the earth, which serves as the abode of the water-god, Naparima. The canoe, however, transformed itself into a giant snake-woman and the paddle into a man. They returned as the red *cachicamo* (canoe) and the white *cachicamo* (paddle) to the center of the earth, where the Warao had since come into existence.

The *cachicamo* woman became Dauarani, the Mother of the Forest. She was the first priest-shaman (*wishiratu*) on earth. Eventually, she departed from earth to take up residence on a world mountain at the end of the universe in the southwest (where her body lives) and in the southeast (where her soul remains). The paddle stayed in the center of the earth with the Warao; and the *moyotu* are to Dauarani, their supernatural patroness, as the paddle was to the boat. They are her lovers and serve her by creating boats in her image out of *cachicamo* trees.

This brief summary of the origin story of the canoe is related by the master during the initiation period of the novice *moyotu*. As the days of schooling under the rule of abstinence and incessant smoking

---

[9] Formerly known as *Hyla venulosa* or *Hyla tibiatrix*. The identification was made by Dr. Juan A. Rivero of the University of Puerto Rico from a specimen I collected in 1971.

pass, the candidate is admonished by his master to live in the future strictly according to the moral code of his trade. During the period of construction of a large canoe he must abstain from sexual intercourse, even though the project requires two or more months to complete, eat moderately yet smoke incessantly, offer tobacco and sago to the supernaturals promptly, hold in reverence finished canoes especially when new, and treat properly the tools used in carving the boat, especially the adz. All these taboos must be carefully observed lest the *moyotu* fall into disgrace with the goddess, thus jeopardizing the health and the lives of his kin as well as his own future happiness in this world and in the one to come.

After the preparatory period of learning, fasting, and excessive smoking, the spirit of the neophyte ascends one day in a trancelike dream to the zenith. Here he meets a black psychopomp who leads him to the beginning of a celestial bridge whose span reaches from the zenith to the world mountain of the Mother of the Forest in the southeast. The bridge is no ordinary bridge but an enormous snake whose head rests close to the zenith and the tip of whose tail reaches to the roots of the tree-mountain. The reptile always keeps its jaws open and hisses when the spirit or soul of the novice approaches. It has eight horns, four at each end. The two pairs on the right side of the body are red and green and those on the left side are yellow and blue. Flowers of the same color decorate each horn and chant the ceremonial songs peculiar to the profession of master builders of canoes. The entire body of the snake is decorated all over with colorful markings and is perfumed with the most agreeable smell of *caraña* resin.

Although this sky snake fills the novice boat builder with dread, he must step on its head, shake its horns, and then either pass through its body and exit at the anus or walk externally over its head and body. Should the snake swallow the novice while he passes through its body, the novice will die. Then in a most sublime moment the novice is allowed to pass his hands along both sides of the serpent's body, and in so doing he receives the proper measure for the conformation of a perfect canoe.

On the student's return from his initiatory celestial journey the master queries him about the details of his vision. If they correspond to what is expected, the master assures the new *moyotu* that his initiation was successful and that he has a long life ahead of him. At the same time, however, he warns the novice not to break any of the taboos. Both the goddess and the sky-snake carefully watch over their servant's conduct, as he makes his future canoe in the likeness of the great goddess's vulva. Also, the Masisikiri spirit of each *cachicamo* he transforms into a dugout will insist that he treat her in obedience to the promises of good conduct which she elicited from him before surrendering herself. Offenses against this code of honor bring about calamities such as accidents, ill health of children and adults, and even death of the offender's kin. The scalding of the chief's son reported above is an example of a calamity that can befall the unfortunate transgressor.

To officiate over the construction of his first large canoe as a full-fledged *moyotu*, the neophyte invites his fellow brothers-in-law to join him in the task of preparing the hull. Although he uses exactly the same technique as before, canoe making will never be the same after the initiation. He has now become an artist who manages the technical aspects of boat making automatically, so to speak, while at the same time his spirit roams freely and creatively, oblivious to the technology involved.

THE CEREMONIAL BUILDING OF A CANOE

The new master craftsman is not an ordinary man. He has been transformed during the initiation ceremony into a *moyotu* and is like the black psychopomp who accompanied him on his initiatory journey to the house of Dauarani. The body of this soul-guide is black like the newly fired canoe. In approaching a *cachicamo* the *moyotu* confronts, not a tree, but a female personage whom he must kill. This ritual death must occur only with the explicit consent of the victim. To obtain her permission, the *moyotu* engages the services of a priest-shaman who communicates with the spirit of the *cachicamo* in a special seance. She will tell the shaman whether she likes the master builder sufficiently to allow herself to be killed. But she surrenders only if the *moyotu* is a competent man, someone she knows will not abandon her once she has converted into a canoe. She also insists on being given adequate amounts of tobacco and sago while undergoing the metamorphic ordeal. A *cachicamo* tree who rejects a particular master may not be felled, lest sickness, death, and disaster befall the *moyotu*'s family and his entire village.

Even if the verdict pronounced through the shaman's mouth is positive, thus authorizing the *moyotu* to go ahead with his plans, he is still warned by the adult people of his group to proceed with utmost caution. They may recommend that the master restrain himself and not set his mind on too large a tree. "We don't want to suffer because of your mistakes," they say.

The men of his group draw his attention to the many precautions he must take to prevent evil consequences. They insist, for instance, that he adorn himself properly and prepare the necessary musical instruments and tools. So, while word of the pending project travels out through the mouths of the master's wife and their daughter to the workmen, the *moyotu* takes care of the various preparatory tasks with exquisite deliberateness.

First comes the inspection of the adz. The modern metal adz is the white man's version of an old Warao tool, the so-called *gubia*, made of the terminal spiral of a conch shell. It is considered to be a sacred and ritual implement. No child may handle it, and the adolescent girl or mature woman may not so much as touch it. Only women past their menopause may come in contact with it and then only when explicitly asked to do so by its owner.

The master, who must inspect the adz before embarking on a new project, walks to the eastern end of his house where he keeps the tool in a special basket. Here it "rests" quietly throughout most of the year, safe from the children and away from kitchen fumes. The people are very concerned as the master takes down the adz. They are afraid that he may be too hasty and fail to placate the tool when he removes it from its resting place.

A typical case of sickness caused by an offended adz spirit occurred among the Winikina while I was there. The young wife of a master canoe maker fell ill with high fever and pains in her back, side, and chest. Pain produced by the spirit of an adz is always "triangular," felt simultaneously in three different places. The most telling sickness caused by the adz is the stiffening of arms and legs into an L-shape. At the time the officiating shaman warned the *moyotu* to be more careful in the future and to treat the tool with consideration. Then the shaman, after assuring the offended spirit of the master's good intentions, cured the woman with his rattle.

Such is the responsibility of the master when he prepares the adz. "Look," he will address the adz. "Don't get upset. You were made especially for excavating trees. You must recognize this and not become angry now when I make you work." If treated with respect and awakened carefully, the adz will work of its own accord. The master simply holds the tool, which works by itself—"eating" the insides of the *cachicamo*.

Next the conch shell trumpet must be readied. So rare an instrument is hard to come by; if one is not available, a wooden trumpet made from the bark of a piece of mangrove aerial root may be substituted.

While the women prepare the food, the master twists moriche bast decorations around his upper arm, wrists, ankles, waist, and forehead. The yellow ribbons identify him with the tree whose body is also marked with natural bands of a similar kind.

Finally, the day to enter the forest to face the selected *cachicamo* tree has arrived. Shortly before daybreak the adorned *moyotu*, holding the trumpet in his hand, greets the sun with a chant:

"Sun, my grandfather, we are coming to you. We will take the right road at the fork, the one that leads to your house. It is dry like sand, and clean, and without danger. The left road is boggy, covered with thorns and infested with toads and snakes and jaguars. I have seen your house in my dreams," continues the chant. "I will come to talk in your house."[10]

The master sounds the shell trumpet while the workmen line up behind him. He smokes tobacco mixed with resin incessantly and then experiences a mystical levitation: he and his companions are lifted onto the horse of the patroness of the *moyomotuma*.[11] The spirit mount's left side is white and its right side is black. The forest opens magically in front of them like a curtain as they are conveyed on the back of the flying horse along a wide pass, at the end of which they behold the *cachicamo*. The *cachicamo* appears to the master, not in the form of an ordinary tree, but in the shape of a maiden. "Don't become upset," chants the master. "Be happy and smile at me. I am like your own

---

[10] The passages in quotation marks are free translations of the recorded chants.
[11] This animal may have been a jaguar before the horse became known to the Warao.

offshoot. I am the one you accepted. I am fond of you. I came to touch your body, to caress you lovingly."

The *cachicamo* maiden smiles. She has been expecting the master ever since her surrender to him through the voice of the priest-shaman. "You are a neophyte master builder," chants the *cachicamo*. "I can tell from your new ornaments. Do with me according to your vision: Kill me and thrust me down on the very soil that raised me."

The master is delighted, quite certain of the tree's benevolence and confident that the children will not have to suffer because of his actions. He says: "What I carry in my hand is called an ax. You will feel it at your waist, it will consume you." "So this is what you call an ax. It will eat my flesh, it will make me fall down to the ground that gave birth to me. Poor me," continues the *cachicamo* maiden. "Your hands will examine my body and my roots. Looking at my body, do you like what you see? You will notice that I also have adorned my body. I did it while awaiting your arrival."

Such is the dialogue developed through the master's chants while the work crew is approaching the tree. The maiden enters the tree before the men arrive, and her feet become its roots, her body, its trunk, her arms, its branches, and her head, the crown of the *cachicamo*.

The chanting continues all during the felling of the tree. "Now that it is done, come take my measure. You possess the measure in your hands." "Yes, indeed, I am the one with knowledge. I can tell you how long you are; your stretched-out body measures sixteen arms exactly. I make the mark so that the men can cut off your head."

The master builder continues his chanting all day while crouching at one side of the work site. He also chants most of the night after the crew has returned to the camp. The exhausted men are not particularly happy about his chanting, but they know that danger lurks all around them. Masisikiri, the maiden in the *cachicamo*, is upset and disturbed. Her home is now in the stump of the tree and she vacillates between it and the fallen trunk. The master must pacify her through his chanting. He has to offer her tobacco. Then the jaguar comes during the night to the camp and to the building site to jeer at the quartered tree maiden. The master's chant keeps him at a distance.

On the evening of the fourth workday, the *moyotu* requests virgin fire. He expects the visit of Moyotu, the sky-snake with eight horns, during the following night. She appears in his dream demanding moriche sago and tobacco. As soon as the vision disappears the master sits up in his hammock and narrates by chanting that the snake Moyotu will come to visit them in a day or two. Next morning an old woman accompanied by two or three children leaves the camp to collect stipules from the manaca palm. The boys have to cut the stipules from the top because those that have fallen to the ground are impure. But cursed be the master builder who neglects to have a sufficient quantity of tobacco. The snake will arrive to inspect the body of the *cachicamo* and look in vain for the gift of tobacco. Her revenge is swift. One of the master's children becomes the target of her wrath. Before the day fades the child will feel the snake penetrate his body like a cool breeze.

Through the medium of the priest-shaman, summoned by the frightened master to effect a cure, everyone in the camp will learn the real cause of the child's sudden illness. The horned serpent appears to the shaman during the seance and lets him know how disappointed she is. The entire work crew and their families begin grumbling about the master. They reprimand him for his negligence. "We have done everything according to the rules you laid down," protest the people. "But you don't see fit even to provide Moyotu with tobacco."

If it is the master's first offense, two cigars and a large basket of sago (about 150 pounds) may rectify the error and reconcile the sky-serpent. The offerings are placed beside the hull at the construction site. But it may take as long as three weeks to produce the necessary amount of moriche sago, a task that demands the strenuous efforts of the workers and their wives. The priest-shaman warns that nothing less will placate the offended spirit. The master builder must provide fish and meat for the families, while the men and the women work in the *morichal*. He also has to absorb the expense of a generous offering of tobacco, sufficient to roll at least ten giant cigars. These, together with the moriche sago, are presented to the serpent through the shaman.

A conscientious master builder will never begin his project before he has procured the necessary amount of tobacco. The *cachicamo* maiden realizes this requirement before she agrees to become his. The master's people also know about it because he takes his profession seriously. Conscientiousness, more than mere technical competence, is what distinguishes a good master builder.

From the moment of the serpent's visit the spirit will visit daily until the work on the hull is completed. She comes to contemplate, in company with the chanting master, the beauty of the work under construction. The men labor only during the morning hours in order to clear the site by one o'clock in anticipation of the sky-snake's visit. While serpent and master admire the balanced features of the hull, they smoke tobacco and chant through the voice of the master. The snake is also gratified to observe the large basket of moriche sago the master has placed as an offering next to the hull. She looks forward to the day when the work of hollowing out the hull is complete, for then the people will present the gift of sago to her. While construction is in progress, however, nobody dares remain in the vicinity of the hollow log after working hours.

On the last day of work on the hull, when the younger boys, the women, and the children are busily cutting and placing skid logs for a corduroy road, the master shaman begins the chant of farewell. In this beautiful song the *cachicamo* takes leave of her branches, of the many birds who formerly lived in her crown. She says good-bye to the animals and to the stump remaining behind as the abode of her soul. She also bids farewell to the bark and the excavated chips.[12] The master signals when his sentimental chant comes to an end and the arduous task of pushing the hull to the river is to begin. Chanting and forcefully blowing the conch shell trumpet, he walks ahead of the workers down to the river.

Months later, after the expert *moyotu* has at last finished the carpentry work on the hull, and after the families of his people have returned from the *morichal* with their baskets full of fresh sago for the launching, the day arrives when the master intones the chant for firing the canoe. It is a happy day for the *moyotu*. Not only did the adz in his hands work by itself, but also the hull has not buried him alive. It is common knowledge among craftsmen that hulls of large trees some-times rise erect before their masters and swallow them. A craftsman who has had sexual relations during the construction period is doomed, for the Masisikiri-spirit of the *cachicamo* does not tolerate intercourse

---

[12] The Warao have an ecosystemic approach to every physical and biological part of the earth. A tree does not exist in isolation. Like everything else in the environment, it functions as one part of a system of associated parts. Together they form a characteristic unit in which each part is interdependent; hence, removal of any one part disrupts and destroys the system. The farewell song of the *cachicamo* expresses the philosophy of partnership with nature rather than helotism.

at that time. The *moyotu* is her lover and she jealously wants to keep him, especially before he opens her with fire.

The swallowing of the master by the boat occurs in the *moyotu*'s dream. The victim finds himself imprisoned in the dark, as if he were in a coffin.[13] He hears a voice from the outside directing him to escape through a knothole in the hull. Since these events transpire in a dream, the spirit of the *moyotu* may eventually escape through the hole. If not, it is taken as a sure sign that the master has committed a moral offense and that he will therefore soon have to die.

To cohabit with one's wife during the period of smoothing the sides of the hull with the adz is taboo. But if the wife of a craftsman should visit her husband in a dream, that is a good sign because the *moyotu* gently separates the woman's legs and has coitus with her, as he will separate the legs of the *cachicamo* maiden when he warms her body with fire. He offers her the tobacco and the sago flour in payment for consenting to have him so treat her. The master concentrates on the carved rim along the edges of the boat walls. They are two pairs of legs and the triangular signs in the bow and in the stern are the vulvas of the maiden. The feet of both pairs of legs touch midway along both sides of the canoe, forming the rim. The craftsman inside the boat inserts each crossbeam, which the men refer to as a penis. Only the *moyotu* may open the legs of the *cachicamo* maiden and behold her organ, but he must not contemplate intercourse with her. Being in the boat, however, means being inside her womb. From where he stands the boat has the shape of the vulva of the goddess.[14] In the presence of their wives, especially their mothers-in-law, the men call the "penises" of the boat simply "seats." The "vulvas" they call "stars."

On the morning of the day when the boat is burned, the master orders the women to begin baking sago cakes. He intends to invite the sky-serpent to an agape of moriche bread and tobacco and then to send her back to her celestial home. Six women are selected to build a virgin

[13] The Warao traditionally bury their dead in scooped-out tree trunks.

[14] Opening the hollowed-out *cachicamo* by fire symbolizes the defloration of her maiden spirit. As long as the boat is new, the deflowered maiden visits the craftsman in his sleep to make love to him. She is extremely jealous and seeks to possess him to the exclusion of any other woman. A man, in order to break free from this possession, may have to imbibe a quart of rum and thus become intoxicated. The spirit lover dislikes the smell of alcohol and leaves the craftsman.

fire in a fireplace for baking the cakes. The gifts are offered by the priest-shaman. In fact, he and the master builder arrive at the workplace early in the morning before anyone else in order to start calling the sky-snake and the spirits of all the predecessors of the master who have died. It is they who have spent their lives in the service of Dauarani and now, after death, enjoy their afterlives in her divine company. All the *moyomotuma*—that is, the serpent protector-spirit and the souls of the defunct master craftsmen—respond to the invitation extended by their young colleague. They come to admire his boat, to eat the sago, and to smoke the ten cigars he offers them for their pleasure. "Are you satisfied?" asks the shaman. "Yes, this is the right way. We are very pleased." Then the shaman urges the spirits to leave the clearing and to return to their home. Soon many women and children will be arriving, and spirit presences could be harmful.

After the *moyomotuma* have left, the entire population comes to admire the beautiful new boat and to praise the art of the master. From chief to smallest child, everybody receives his share of moriche bread. All the people, young and old, are beautifully adorned for the festival of launching the new canoe. The actual launching, however, does not take place until the following day. During the night the master sings the final chant of farewell to the *moyomotuma*-spirits who have permitted him to complete the arduous task of successfully making a large canoe.

In the years that follow, a master boat builder will enjoy many such occasions. If he lives by the moral code of his profession throughout his life, he leaves earth wholly confident that his soul will again pass the snake bridge unharmed and that he will be received in the celestial village of canoe makers. Only the souls of those who have offended the patron goddess by violating her ethical standards are devoured by the sky-snake and are lost.

After the craftsman has died, the people on earth ponder the outcome of this final decision for five or six days. A black soul-guide has come to take his soul to the zenith, where he is allowed to rest and is furnished with his final cigar. Several days later the soul departs with lightning and thunder to its final destination in the southeast. "Rest now," the artisan's wife or someone else close to the deceased will say. "You have made many big canoes."

The soul hears this benediction and may become sentimental, but he must avoid doing so. Rather, he must hasten on through the sky-snake without ever looking back to earth. If he passes his final test and exits via the snake's rectum, he will find the abode of the Master Spirit of Canoe Making, a rectangular windowless house that boasts but one arched entrance, which faces west. Nevertheless, its interior is bathed in a blaze of light and never darkens. He finds a bed and a table on which rests a bowl of water perfumed with incense. The roof of the house is beautifully decorated with six pairs of flowers at the four corners and at the center of the long sides: blue and yellow flowers at each of the eastern corners, green and red flowers at each of the western corners, and yellow and red flowers on each of the lateral sides of the roof. The stalks of the flowers, which are hooked on top, are the same colors as the leaves and petals. The flowers chant the same song as, and synchronized with, the song of the eight horns on the sky-snake. Their perfume of tobacco smoke and incense is most agreeable to the arriving soul, who is given a similar house for his own use. In it he finds a complete new outfit, which he puts on after taking a bath in incensed water. He has reached his heaven in proximity to the patron deity he has served so diligently throughout his adult life.

PSYCHOLOGY AND SYMBOLISM
OF THE CANOE MAKER

A Warao embarked upon the career of master canoe maker engages in a learning process from which he emerges as a technician of the secular as well as the sacred aspects of his profession. He achieves the former during adolescence and early adulthood, but he commences a voluntary vision quest only as a mature individual. In making this personal decision he aims for an encounter in dream and trance with the spirit world so that he may transcend the profane physical condition and attain an exalted spiritual status. This metamorphosis is patently shamanistic and distinctly reminiscent of the initiatory complex of shamanism. He is, nevertheless, not actually intent on becoming a shaman, a sorcerer, or a medicine man. Rather, he undergoes the initiatory ordeal and subjects himself to the hardships of a *moyotu*'s life strictly for reasons of personal advancement.

Although not unique, the presence of an initiatory complex for nonreligious practitioners among the Warao is certainly remarkable, especially because it involves an almost complete scheme of shamanic initiation with most of the characteristic features of shamanism anywhere in the world. I have described the ecological, sociological, and ideational circumstances under which a Warao man becomes a master canoe builder; now I explore briefly by way of dream and trance symbolism some of the psychological conditions attached to the learning process. This discussion may not only satisfy our intellectual curiosity; it may also furnish pragmatic guidelines for people concerned with the future welfare of the Warao Indians.

I have retraced the technical stages of boat construction in order to experience each one through the mental eye of the sublimated *moyotu*. Now I turn to the symbolic features of the initiatory complex to reveal certain covert psychological dimensions of the boat maker's world inherent in the specific milestones on his journey to his origins, his return journey to the womb.

The driving force at work in the psychological process of learning is the boat maker's desire for personal sublimation. He chooses to engage in a vision quest that will help him transcend his human condition and interact with the supernaturals, the patron goddess, and the souls of the ancestor shamans. The perils lurking along the way are devouring monsters, the self-erecting canoe hull, and especially the sky-snake. It is believed that Warao culture has placed these devourers on the path because of the original incest committed by the culture hero Haburi. The *moyotu*'s fear of failing in his quest and of being devoured by the mother guardian motivates him to excel and to adopt the ethical code that rules the psyche on its pilgrimage from one cosmic plane to another. In short, the ophidian sky monster is the "symbolic representations of the fear of the consequences of breaking the taboo and regressing to incest" (Jung 1967, 259). Thus the Warao sky-serpent functions as guardian and defender of the maternal treasure just as snakes and dragons do in other cultures of the world. The serpent's main threat is to swallow the unworthy trespasser, but for the worthy neophyte it functions as bridge or tunnel by means of which he reaches Dauarani, the Mother.

To foster the proper climate for the test the master candidate must repress his human condition through fasting and exertion. On this minimum level of physical existence, when his body falls into a deathlike state, his psyche reaches its stellar hour of ecstatic levitation. The novice's soul is sped on its celestial journey to the zenith and the sky-bridge by tobacco mixed with *caraña* resin. This is the moment of transcendence and judgment, of ascent to power, or, conversely, of dissolution and death. During the preparatory period of learning the novice has been cued to the requirements for the realization of his upward impulse. In pushing his physical endurance to an existential minimum—how to chant and to smoke "properly"—he has responded positively to the cue and has accepted the challenge of the symbolic journey, the ascent to the sky.

From the zenith the path directs the neophyte's soul to the tunnel of darkness, of unconsciousness, and of possible death. Usually it is not the first time the master's psyche experiences this fearful symbol. He has frequently before been "swallowed" by the unfinished hull of a canoe under construction. The hull is made from a tree that the sky-snake, during her visits, says is shaped like her own body; in other words, it is ophidian. Thus we see a blend of the tree-symbol with the serpent-symbol on the one hand and, on the other, an amalgamation of the dragon with the water and the boat. In both instances, the devourer is a snake and initiation of the candidate is effected by his penetration into the snake's body.

Being enclosed in the darkness of the boat is analogous to being inside the womb of the *cachicamo* woman. Canoes and hollow logs are used by the Warao as coffins in which a corpse is reduced to a skeleton. The bones are reburied. Lying in the hollow envelope of his tomb, the novice contemplates his own death and his own skeleton. He has reentered the womb of his primordial life in the expectation of mystical rebirth. Only if he successfully clears the "clashing-doors passage" through the serpent's jaws will the novice be regenerated in the germinal darkness of the monster. Within he faces annihilation, but he hopes to emerge as before through a "knothole" in the boat, this time through the rectal opening, and to proceed from one world into a new world.

The sky-monster appears to the novice as a rainbow serpent, with colorful stripes on her rigid body and colors on her arching horns which mark the strata of the sky-bridge. The heroic neophyte may step on the serpent's head, pass the threatening horns, and walk over the rainbow into the world beyond.

Having passed the guardian spirit, the soul of the *moyotu* reaches his goal; a transtemporal existence in the house of the great Mother

Dauarani. He is allowed to enter this boxlike house, symbolic of the maternal body, holding in his hands the secret of boat making. Thus he is called to enjoy his reward: life in the dazzling light and splendor of his new existence. The *moyotu* has completed the journey back to his origins.

After his ecstatic initiatory dream the young master spends the rest of his earthly life in repeated approaches to his maternal home with every large canoe he makes. It is similar to the mystic's yearning *ex tenebris* for the light he has experienced in one sublime blinding moment of ecstasy. And it is a spark of the same creative energy of the mystics of Eastern and Western traditions which powers the psychic energy needed for the perpetuation of the art of canoe building among the Warao. The black and white horse that Dauarani sends him to be his mount while he is still on earth symbolizes the *moyotu*'s life between his temporal existence in the darkness of this world and his transtemporal existence in the otherworld. It also symbolizes his position in the arena between good (white) and evil (black), a position forcing his decision at the crossroads on the path to his *cachicamo* maiden. Perhaps the black and white horse of Dauarani may be just another symbol of the great Mother. Its black (female) and white (male) halves are possibly indicative of the goddess's androgynous nature, which corresponds in turn to the hermaphroditism of the *cachicamo* tree, another symbolic double for the Mother.

Many other symbolic meanings related to the psychological process of becoming an expert canoe maker are beyond the scope of the present context, such as the spiritual marriage to the *cachicamo* woman which prohibits (incestuous) fulfillment in sex and restricts the sex life between the possessed master and his wife with a jealousy characteristic of such "celestial fiancées." Nevertheless, I hope that my sketch of the psychological and symbolic areas of canoe making among the Warao supplements the technical, social, and religious data in a significant way. To me the psychic experience reveals what I believe to be the profoundly vital matrix of the canoe making complex of the Warao. Certainly the desire to achieve technical competence, socioeconomic status, and religious bliss is a prime mover in the learning process of a canoe maker. But the mystical yearning of the *moyotu*, as he attempts with each canoe he builds to recapture the light that may once more dispel the "dark night" of his soul, could well be the most dynamic motivation of all.

CONCLUSIONS

In this chapter I have focused on the processes that pertain specifically to the development of a Warao canoe maker in order to illustrate the question of global enculturation. By way of summary I propose now to scan the ethnography here presented for an answer to this complex question.

Skill-training of a canoe maker takes place in three distinct ways: through general conditioning, by the teaching of technical skills, and by the transmission of esoteric skills.

The general conditioning of the Warao male toward navigation begins during infancy. The daily routine of child care introduces him to life on the water. His first toys are model boats in the family corner of the communal house. A child's playground is the landing place with its moored canoes. By the time a child of either sex is three years old his familiarity with canoes, paddles, and currents is so intimate that he can be trusted to go out on the river by himself.

From the age of three on, the conditioning of boys toward canoe construction becomes more intensive; it is quite different from the training of a girl who will be required as an adult woman only to maneuver a canoe, a task she has learned how to perform as a child. In the canoe-building process the woman plays at best an ancillary role. The father requires his prepubertal son to witness the different phases of canoe construction over and over again. In addition to being exposed to the necessary technical processes, the child also develops the realization that boat making requires esoteric skills on the part of the master craftsman. As technical skills are mastered, the emphasis shifts during adulthood to concentration on the esoteric skills. A man's aptitude for the career of craftsman which, according to the Indians, is a "natural" concomitant of being male is the result of such pervasive attitude conditioning. Casual though the general conditioning may look to the outside observer, it is for the most part planned intentionally.

Technical skill-training predominates during postpuberty and early adulthood. The boy of fourteen swings his machete and ax with precision, participates progressively in the selection of an adequate tree,

TABLE 2.7

DISTRIBUTION OF INHABITANTS BY AGE CATEGORIES:
SETTLEMENT OF YARUARA AKOHO (1954)

Age category	Number	Percentage	
Infants	12	11	
Children	41	38	} 54
Teenagers	5	5	
Adults	48	44	} 46
Seniors	2	2	
Total	108	100	

and is permitted to try his hand at cutting and excavating the trunk. The young adolescent also knows how to prepare the corduroy road along which the excavated hull will be dragged to the river. Approximately five years of in-service training creates skills sufficient for the eighteen-year old to fabricate his own first canoe from start to finish. His technical proficiency improves over the next six or seven years; thus skill-training per se can be said to terminate by the time a man is twenty-five years old. Training in esoteric skills commences at this point for the properly conditioned, now technically competent, Warao. Under the guidance of a teacher he internalizes a complex curriculum of ritual and metaphysical knowledge. Among the skills he must acquire are chanting, verbalization, and the ability to function in altered states of consciousness.

Socialization of the canoe maker takes place in four different social contexts: his nuclear family and extended family of orientation; the community of his childhood; his family of procreation and the community of his in-laws; and the subtribe of which these various groups are a part. I use the village of Yaruara Akoho as an example (table 2.7). A child may find as many as four "mothers" (matrilineally related women) and four uncles living either in the same house as his own parents and grandparents or in close proximity. One or two teenage consanguineal or classificatory brothers and sisters also live in the house. All the males in the house are engaged in canoe craftsmanship, either as full-fledged *moyomotuma* or as aspirants to that status. Chances are that children also live in the house and that for the two or three males among them it is natural to relate to their father's team of boat makers.

Once a child is old enough to venture down to the landing place he finds himself in the company of more than fifty infants and children, most of whom play and travel with him in and around the canoes. With more than half the quasi-permanent population of the settlement below the age of eighteen, the importance of the youth group as a socializing agent cannot be overemphasized.

A particularly powerful socializing force is the male teenage gang made up of pairs of brothers from various settlements. For a period of three or four years the adolescent seeks acceptance among his peers and the rest of the society by identifying himself with Haburi, the culture hero, projecting onto himself Haburi's fame as an irresistible lover, accomplished hunter, and, above all, the maker of canoes par excellence. During childhood the youngster may have been called "Ax Swinger" or "Machete Man." Now is the time to prove his competence. With the arrival of the canoe-making season the adolescent anxiously seeks a place on his father's work team. The problem is that a truly meaningful position for him exists only on the team of his future father-in-law. Nevertheless, some of the uncles on his father's force, who are not much older than he is, serve as models for his future role.

The work team of boat makers is the strongest socializing force experienced by the Warao adolescent and young adult male. On the team of his father the adolescent son has the opportunity to establish his personal identity as his technical competence increases. On the team of his father-in-law, however, the young adult is assigned a rank and is expected to fulfill the role attached to that rank. He must perform well for the sake of his own nuclear family and the community to which he now belongs. His status will rise with the addition of new brothers-in-law, as he assumes increasing responsibility for each successive work role.

The ultimate socialization force in a canoe maker's life is composed of the elite of the band and the entire community of ancestor artisans so closely associated with them. The elite of his own band includes several religious practitioners as well as several political officeholders. We have seen how the shamanic elite controls the craftsmen completely. What would happen if the artisan was forbidden by the priest-shaman to cut down the desired tree? What would the result be if the priest-shaman allotted only mediocre trees to the canoe maker? He would have no opportunity to enhance his social and economic position by building large canoes and would thus be forever barred from the ranks of the elite. With his prestige as a canoe maker undermined and ultimately destroyed he would further be branded as potentially dangerous to the entire band.

By the time an adult experiences the socializing pressures exerted by the elite he has reached the age of thirty-five and has found his social identity as a canoe maker. He now gradually assumes the role of leader of his own work team. One of the imperatives of Warao culture is that canoe making is to be conducted, not merely as a secular business enterprise, but rather as a religious activity. Esoteric lore as expressed to the team workers by the master craftsman is acquired by the artisan through association with the tribal elite, a social setting in which he submits himself to the rigors of his profession. Accordingly, he aspires to align himself with a particular deity and a certain world direction. As a career man he seeks to become destined after death to reside on a world mountain with the ancestral canoe makers. And, like the shamans, he wants to adopt from the supernaturals a special metaphoric language attesting to his elevated status. Acceptance by the band's elite is an essential prerequisite for the attainment of both temporal and eternal goals.

The moral education of the canoe maker starts during childhood when he and his playmates are taught respect for the spirit of the *cachicamo* tree, which lives on in the craft. Even during the construction of a canoe children are required to show respectful behavior. They may not sit on the stump that harbors the spirit of the tree, and they must refrain from interfering with the ritual aspects of the making of a large canoe. From experience recounted frequently by adults, children know that they may be smitten with disease, may suffer accidents, or may even meet death as a result of misbehavior. It is also known that children are the first to suffer punishment for any sin committed by the artisan and his crew.

The master canoe maker receives his instructions for proper conduct during the initiation and promises to abide by the ethical code of his profession. He must not engage in felling a *cachicamo* tree without first having obtained permission from the Mother of the Forest. He must not use the adz without propitiating it properly. The supernaturals, including the ancestral canoe makers, must receive offerings of tobacco smoke and sago, and sexual intercourse during the months of construction is taboo. Any careless disregard of the prescribed set of rules governing the entire process of making a canoe, especially a large craft, is punished supernaturally: wrath is visited upon both children and adults in the band, and even the artisan himself is "swallowed."

Thus skill-training, socialization, and moral education are lifelong processes of enculturation for the Warao boat maker. Skill-training begins with an informal conditioning during childhood, develops into postpuberty and early adulthood in-service training for practical skills, and is complemented during a man's prime and old age by esoteric skill-training. Skill-conditioning takes place in the house, the neighborhood, the forest, and on the river. At no time is instruction given within an especially assigned area or building. The form of instruction is visual learning, demonstration, and participation in real-life situations. Verbalization during conditioning and technical skill-training is either nonexistent or exceedingly rare. Esoteric skills, in contrast, are transmitted and learned in the context of initiation schooling. A special room may be set aside for this purpose and a curriculum of esoteric lore underlies the training process. Instruction is predominantly verbal.

Socialization is effected by seeking and finding acceptance in a number of different social groups, ranging from the small nuclear family through large children's cohorts and adolescent gangs, to adult work teams and finally to the tribal elite. In all these groups the artisan has to achieve the social status prescribed by the culture and play the role society expects.

Moral education is the result of lifelong conditioning controlled mainly by parents, father-in-law, and tribal mythology. Nonformal (noninstitutional formal) education in ethical standards and moral conduct is provided by a hired expert during a ritual initiation for canoe makers. Fear of supernatural punishment serves as the primary reinforcement for proper moral conduct. There are also indications that strict alignment with ethical standards may bring mystic experience as a reward. Such an experience will make the artisan pine for repeated encounters with the Mother Goddess, a yearning that turns him into a harsh proponent of the canoe maker's code lest he jeopardize his transcendental personal (and collective) purpose of life.

Three recognized modes of education are well described in the literature. Coombs and Ahmed (1974, 8) define informal education as "the lifelong learning process by which every person acquires and accumulates knowledge, skills, attitudes and insights from daily experiences and exposure to the environment." Nonformal education is defined by the same authors as "any organized, systematic, educational activity carried on outside the framework of the formal system to provide selected types of learning to particular subgroups in the population, adults as well as children." Finally, formal education is defined by them as referring to the "institutionalized, chronologically graded and hierarchically structured 'educational system', spanning lower primary school and the upper reaches of the university." Although formal education does not apply to the Warao, the definitions of the first two modes are clearly applicable but must not be understood as mutually exclusive. All preliterate societies, the Warao included, have been found to practice simultaneously informal and nonformal methods of cultural transmission. The skill-training, socialization, and moral education of a canoe maker evolve on a continuum of informal and nonformal education. As modes of enculturation they occur in parallel rather than in staggered fashion. Furthermore, informal education overlaps with nonformal education. La Belle suggests (1975, 20) that the three educational modes be viewed as "modes of emphasis or predominance" rather than as discrete entities. We have seen, for example, that the conditioning and skill-training of the prepubertal Warao are directed and regulated. In turn, the novice artisan in the bush school, now a recipient of nonformal education, benefits from far more than the verbal instruction given him by his teacher. The informal education experiences acquired by the candidate through association with his fellow canoe makers and from the chants and interpretations of the master, heard year after year, are a vital input to the nonformal learning process. A good example is again the novice canoe maker who believes that he is the recipient through a dream of the revelation of esoteric lore and especially its chants coming directly from the supernaturals. The teacher's role is only to correct the "spontaneously acquired" knowledge and to help the student put the various passages together. Clearly, the novice has prelearned the texts through many years of association with the master artisan prior to undergoing nonformal education. The sessions with the teacher are designed to help him internalize them according to a preconceived plan. Thus we see both informal and nonformal modes of education existing side by side, with emphasis shifting from one to the other on different occasions throughout the course of the artisan's career. The informal mode is never quite free of nonformal characteristics just as the nonformal is scarcely ever encountered without traces of the informal.

It will come as no surprise that informal and nonformal modes of education perform the function of interpreting for the Warao roles and symbolic meanings as each new identity crisis occurs. Bear in mind that canoe making represents an unconditional imperative for Warao survival and that the culture has to provide effective stimuli to prompt the males in society to respond with the desire to undergo such identity changes. It is the genius of Warao culture that enculturation along informal and nonformal channels succeeds so well in motivating the developing craftsman by holding out new goals each time a change in personal identity becomes desirable. The culture is adequately programmed to recognize publicly the signs of accomplished growth and thereby to make the learner conscious of his new identity (Goodenough 1961).

Despite rather traumatic experiences when the youth changes from residing with his intimate kin to living among his wife's people, the enculturation process of an artisan is continuous. It is conducted by people of the same basic culture, and adult knowledge builds organically on that of earlier life stages. Because a boy is expected to learn canoe making as a natural byproduct of being male, the learning process itself remains largely free from anxiety.

This discussion leads me to a final comment. The informal education figuring so prominently in Warao enculturation is particularistic, affectively charged, and tradition bound (Cohen 1971). It follows that enculturation in preliterate societies is highly culture-specific. Our knowledge of cultural procedures can certainly yield important insights into the educational process per se. But the transfer of the actual technical, social, and ideational content of the curriculum from one society to another will be possible only to the extent that the societies in question are culturally similar. Furthermore, because canoe making occurs in a culture-specific framework, transfer within the same society of knowledge of the canoe-making process to the fabrication of some other product is problematic. In the Orinoco Delta I have heard of plans for such a transfer. People have assumed that the Indians' proven ability to build canoes can be redirected toward a successful program for fabricating Western furniture. Needless to say, such plans are doomed to failure. The Warao culture is completely unequipped to handle such a transfer. Nothing in the environment demands such Western products; within the society there is no economic benefit or social status associated with the products; and there exists no traditional heaven for furniture makers. If such transfers are promulgated anyway, new markets created, and modern values established in the name of progress, the changes will be at the expense of the autochthonous culture. I am afraid that such changes will be the lot of the Warao and all the remaining indigenous societies of South America. Complex and teleologically functioning educational systems, the combined wisdom of untold generations, will crumble in the process of incorporating the Indians into the ambit of modern states. Any intention to "develop" these systems ought to be predicated strictly on the Indians' terms. The assumption that since these people already practice informal and nonformal education, all they really need is Western schooling is fallacious.

Even though the transfer to other processes of the curriculum content of indigenous enculturation systems is highly problematic, generalizations made on the basis of the processes involved will prove invaluable for the study of international education and for the understanding of the problems of education as a whole. To have described the intricacies of the system developed by the Warao represents the Indians' contribution to the bedeviled educators in the civilized world and remains our only solace.

Chapter Three

Eschatology in a Participatory Universe: Destinies of the Soul[1]

The Warao have an anthropocentric worldview. They conceive of themselves as living in the center of the terrestrial disk and at the foot of the world axis that connects the earth with the zenith and the cosmic vault. Thus, when a Warao baby emerges from the womb of his squatting mother, it falls right into the heart of the universe. Throughout a person's entire existence, and especially during adulthood, he or she shares this universe not only with his or her fellow tribesmen but also with a host of spirits who expect him or her to interact with them according to time-honored patterns of reciprocal behavior. There exists a relationship of compelling mutuality between humankind and the supernaturals, and neither the gods nor the mortals are free to disengage themselves from this entelechial purpose of life. The gods are forever affecting humankind, while humans exist perennially before the curtains of eternity. In this chapter I describe the Warao universe with its different places of ultimate destiny of the human soul, and at the same time I explore the dynamics of interaction between heaven and earth.[2]

---

[1] "Participatory universe" is a concept I borrow from Princeton Professor John A. Wheeler, who, as a physicist, believes that "we are going to come to appreciate that the universe itself in some strange way depends on our being here for its properties" (Helitzer 1973, 32). This belief is, from an ideological point of view, essentially similar to Warao thinking about the interdependence or mutuality that exists between man and the supernatural world.

I am grateful to Dr. Donald W. Lathrop and Dr. Irving Rouse for commenting on this chapter and to Dr. Peter T. Furst for editing it.

[2] The data for this chapter were gathered in the course of repeated fieldwork (since 1954) among the Winikina-Warao. While I use the generic tribal designation "Warao," it is well to bear in mind that regional variations in cultural patterns do exist among the many local groups of the tribe and that the facts as described in this chapter best fit the Winikina. Furthermore, the information in this chapter was obtained by interviewing many different religious practi-

CONCEPT OF THE UNIVERSE

According to the Warao concept of the universe, the earth is saucer-shaped with a flat surface, and humans—more specifically, the Warao themselves—live at its center (figs. 3.1, 3.2). The earth is surrounded by water that extends to the horizon and to the very ends of the world. Submerged in the ocean and encircling the earth is the Snake of Being, a sea monster that adopts a *uroboros* position, with its featureless extreme ends approaching each other east of the earth. In a cylindrical world below the earth and the ocean exists the earth-monster, a four-headed serpent. According to some Warao, this *quadricornutus serpens* is a huge snake with deer horns on each of her four heads. There is supposedly no passage from the underworld to the surface of the earth, although others maintain that this Goddess of the Nadir can leave her world in the form of a woman, via a passage along the world axis, and manifest herself before human beings with her torso sticking out of the earth. She has also been encountered by wanderers in the forest who saw her from behind as she sat astride a fallen tree.

GODS OF THE CORNERS OF THE WORLD

At the cardinal and intercardinal points of the universe there are world mountains that are believed to be gigantic petrified tree stumps. These mountains are the abodes of certain deities to whom the Warao refer collectively as *kanobotuma* (Our Grandfathers). Included also are the gods of the zenith and the nadir.

Uraro, the cardinal god of the south, lives at the end of the world (*aitona*). He has a companion by the name of Karoshimo who resides on a lesser mountain at the edge of the earth (*hobahi akari*). The two gods resemble each other to so high a degree that either one can be invoked with the other's name. Nevertheless, Uraro is the senior of the two gods of the south and the most powerful in the Warao pantheon. It is noteworthy that the left sides of the bodies of these gods resemble the skin of a toad. Their right sides also have a toadlike, warty surface, but they are fiery red and shriveled, as if seared. The Toad-God of the

---

tioners, none of whom would necessarily know all the data presented here. As much of this lore is based on dream experiences of individual shamans, it differs in descriptive detail from informant to informant.

south, like the other major gods, may assume a corpulent, light-complexioned human form. Together with their wives, the gods of the south dwell in huge mansions, own golden horses, and reign supreme over many subjects.

Their counterparts are the gods of the north. Here on the highest of two world mountains, on the very edge of the world, resides Warowaro, the Butterfly-God (*Calligo* sp.). His companion, who lives on a smaller

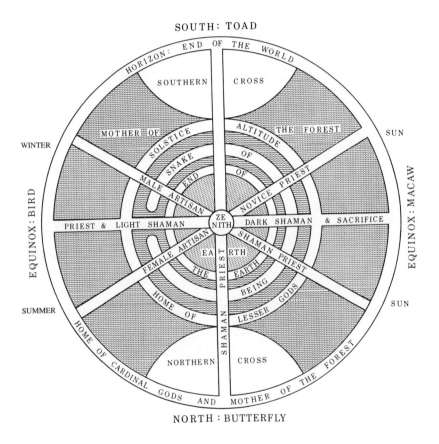

FIG. 3.1.
Top view of the Warao universe showing the celestial pathways of the soul.
(Drawing courtesy Noel Diaz)

mountain on the edge of the earth, is known as Nabarima (Father of the Waves). The gods of the north are surrounded by the same fine things as are the gods of the south, but the Warao consider them slightly inferior to their southern counterparts. Warowaro appears at times as a gigantic owl-faced butterfly with a huge eye on each wing. An enormous cave on the mountain of the Father of the Waves harbors Haburi, the culture hero, and his mothers.

Residing on the world mountain in the east is Ariawara, the God of Origin. He is described as valiant and vigorous and as having qualities of greatness. He is of avian form, like the Creator-Bird of the Dawn, his companion who lives in a cave on a mountain in front of the God of Origin. Many things originated through the powers of the latter god, while the Creator-Bird of the Dawn is particularly responsible for light-shamanism.

Finally, the Macaw-God of the West is one of the cardinal gods of the Warao universe. The Scarlet Macaw (*Ara chloroptera*) rules over the underworld, an abode of darkness, and is called Hoebo. The Macaw-God is Hoebo's body; his soul resides at the zenith. While the supreme spirits of the south, north, and east are free to travel along the horizonal boundary of the world and down the world axis to earth, the Macaw-God of the West cannot visit his fellow gods, nor does he

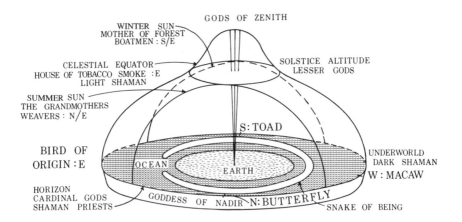

Fɪɢ. 3.2. Profile of the Warao universe. (Drawing courtesy Noel Diaz)

descend to earth. Instead, ever since the connection between the underworld and the rest of the universe was severed in primordial times, he has remained confined to his part of the world, where he rules as the lord of dark-shamanism and death.

Although in general the sex of supernaturals is ambiguous, the gods of the cardinal directions are usually considered male. But there is also a goddess of the same rank, Dauarani, Mother of the Forest. Like Hoebo, she is divided into a soul, which resides on the world mountain on the southeastern horizon, and a body, which lives on a mountain in the southwest. The locations of these intercardinal mountains seem to coincide with the observable points of midwinter sunrise and sunset, respectively. Body-Dauarani is the patroness of canoe makers. Dauarani is the only female deity on the edge of the world. She is one of four supreme deities of the world of light, whereas only one cardinal god, the Scarlet Macaw, reigns over the world of darkness.

Opposite the Mother of the Forest, at the place of summer solstice, are the world mountains of sustenance and fertility deities: the Mother of Moriche Sago (Aruarani) is at the rising point of the midsummer sun in the northeast, and the God of Dance (Oriwakarotu) is at the point of midsummer sunset in the northwest. The winter solstice is also identified, among others, with the Natue, "Our Grandmothers," patronesses of the moriche palm, which in view of its high nutritional and material value has rightly been called the "tree of life" for the Warao Indians.

GODS OF THE MIDDLE OF THE WORLD

The zenith is inhabited by three lesser gods who direct the traveling spirits and souls to and from the earth via the *axis mundi*, as well as along the paths that connect the zenith with the various world stations described.

First, in ancient times the god Yaukware ascended to the zenith by means of his sacred rattle. He is recognized as the God of the Center of the World. His companion spirit is his own son, whom he has taken along on his celestial journey. The two live in a beautiful adobe house, with a banner in front and furniture such as tables, chairs, and beds, within. They also keep ritual paraphernalia in readiness, among them various kinds of rattles, trumpets, clarinets, necklaces, and, above all, tobacco. Everything up here—the god, his son, the instruments, the house, and its inventory—is white and bright with light. Yaukware is a contented god who, since his ascension, has never left the zenith. Originating at the threshold of his house is a network of paths that interconnect the cardinal and intercardinal points of the universe, excluding the underworld in the west.

A second spirit lives at the zenith whose features are not disclosed but who guides traveling spirits and souls across a white bridge with colorful flowers to the House of Tobacco Smoke southeast of the zenith.

The third spirit in the center of the world is Soul-Hoebo (the Scarlet Macaw at the world mountain in the west being Hoebo's body). The black adobe house of Soul-Hoebo is a dark and dreadful structure. Filled with the stench of rotting cadavers and filthy with a blood-soaked floor, it heralds doom for all souls passing through on their dread journey to the Lord of the Dead. Soul-Hoebo's house is furnished with chairs made of human bones and skin. There are also hammocks of coagulated human blood inside the house. Hoebo's one-year-old son, lying in one of them, is rocked by his mother so as to keep him from crying. One solitary path, slippery with human blood, leads from Soul-Hoebo's house straight to the underworld.

Looking at the Warao universe in profile, one pictures the cosmic vault as bell-shaped rather than rounded like a dome (fig. 3.2). The upper rim of the depression occurs roughly on the imaginary level marked by the maximum altitude of the summer sun. From here to more or less the lower third of the bell-shaped vault exist such gods and spirits as the minor companion gods of the south (Uraro) and the north (Nabarima), the food-related gods of the northeast (Aruarani) and the northwest (Oriwakaroto), the snake-goddess of boat builders and priest-shamans in the southeast and the southwest, as well as several others beyond the scope of this discussion. Below the earth and the ocean is the dark, almost featureless realm of the Goddess of the Nadir. This realm is solid; it supports the earth, serves as the bottom of the ocean, and carries the world mountains. On the latter rests the cosmic vault which is supported in its center by the world axis.

ALIGNMENT OF HUMANS WITH THE SUPERNATURALS

A Warao Indian's alignment with the metaphysical world begins the moment he makes his appearance on earth. In fact, it commences when the baby's first cry echoes across the earth and the sea to the world mountain of the God of Origin. Soon after the "new cry" has reached his distant abode, the deity can be heard acknowledging the baby's cry by crying himself.

Another supernatural personage is eager to confirm the arrival of a new human being—the Snake of Being, the womb of all life on earth. A Warao myth explains the nature of this *uroboros* snake:

There were male voices to be heard, and many women were heard talking in Warao. Children were crying, and all kinds of animal voices reached the surprised Natue's ear. "What are all these voices in your body?" she asked Hahuba. "There seem to be many people and animals living inside of you." "You are right," answered Hahuba. "These are my grandchildren. I am the grandmother of them all."

The serpent's acknowledgment of a baby manifests itself on the third day after its arrival, when she embraces the entire village with a balmy breeze.

Finally, the mythical turkey-bird, Shiborori, has his permanent residence at the foot of the eastern world mountain, but he also has a resting place at the top of the world. He comes to the meridian at noon and at midnight to chant for the boys and girls on earth whom he considers his brothers and sisters.

From this early age on, the individual Warao remains engaged in a relentless tug-of-war between himself and the supernaturals, a contest that may not be settled even by a man's physical death. He must weigh his every action to remain on good terms with the gods and to be protected against attacks or defeat. There is no pardon in this struggle, mistakes are intolerable, and disengagement is fatal, for the entelechial cause that forces upon life a proposition of mutuality and participation is governed by the very dictates of survival. The gods need humans to provide them with food, and humans need the gods to protect their lives and their goods. The gods demand moriche flour, honey, and, above all, tobacco, which calls for major inputs of human energy and time. Worse still, the Lord of the Underworld requires human flesh, blood, hearts, and livers; he destroys a person, body and soul.

Much of a Warao's life is therefore spent fulfilling his part of the bargain. In doing so he avails himself of the services of three different religious practitioners who know the way through the maze of celestial stations and who are experts at arranging a modus vivendi among all parties concerned. These practitioners are the priest-shaman, who

mediates between humankind and the *kanobo*-gods, including those of
the zenith and nadir; the light-shaman, who stands between his fellows
and the powers of the Land of Light; and finally, the dark-shaman, who
communicates between this world and the Land of Death. The shamans
serve as media in this dialogue between mortals and the supernaturals,
anxious to negotiate a quid pro quo that makes life a little more livable
for their fellowmen. The Warao, however, do not engage in self-
deception; they have no word in their language for living, only for
dying. If one asks a Warao who is suffering from a generalized feeling
of indisposition how he is doing, he answers, *wabaia sabuka*, "somewhat dying." A sick person is *wabaia* (dying), a corpse is *waba* (dead)
and buried in a *wa* (dugout canoe). Thus the various forms of illness
are simply different stages of death, and both states are referred to by
one and the same term, *waba*. The dugout canoe (as is explained in
chapter 2) is the vulva of Dauarani, Mother of the Forest, so that life,
according to Warao symbolism, can clearly be recognized as a process
of dying by returning to the womb. Death occurs almost exclusively
through the intervention of dark- and light-shamans, as well as of
several supernatural powers. How and through what agent is of
secondary importance; what matters to the Indian is the survival of his
soul, *mehokohi*, the light in his breast. All Warao hope for a life after
death and arrange their affairs teleologically toward an existence in the
heaven of their predilection.

JOURNEYS OF THE SOUL

The Afterlife of Shamans

Warao shamans die with the relative certainty of an afterlife in the
company of their patron gods. During their lifetime the spirits of
shamans travel routinely to their respective heavens in trances and in
dreams. The shamans are familiar with the roads and are confident that
they will survive their final journey, as did all the others who came
before.

The priest-shaman.—The priest-shaman, for example, listens in the
falling night of his approaching death for the beating of the hoofs of
the golden horse dispatched by his patron-god to carry him to his eternal
home. He sits on this winged spirit mount and rides upward to the
zenith, where, in the house of the God of the Center of the World, his

soul rests for four days. Yaukware queries his guest concerning his final destination. If a particular priest-shaman has served the God of the South, his soul will go to reside with him. If he has served the God of the North, or the God of the East, he will proceed in the appropriate direction. On the fourth day, the God of the Center provides him with his final cigar. Again he mounts the winged horse and sets out on his final journey. The souls of shamans travel like shooting stars, comets, or lightning bolts to the houses of their respective patron-deities. While traveling, they always face toward the end of the world, never backward toward the center. The shaman arrives with a thundering noise that resounds throughout the world, and when he alights, hot and perspiring, the companion god hands him a fan with which to cool himself. The priest-shaman also receives beautiful clothes, a hat, and shoes, and he is taken to his own dwelling which, like the residence of the god himself is furnished in gold and is surrounded by a garden of beautiful white flowers. He keeps looking at his god and begins a restful life in the company of the peers who preceded him. Theirs is a life of peace and contentment; no sickness reaches their beautiful city atop the mountain; their supply of delicious tobacco smoke, provided by their fellow shamans on earth, is always plentiful. The latter invite them periodically to feast in their temples and send up smoke offerings to keep them warm and contented. Nothing disturbs the tranquility of this heaven so long as man provides ample supplies of tobacco smoke. Man, being in possession of fire, is the only source of this divine sustenance.

Among those who attempt to become priest-shamans are many who fail. Their fate is sealed when, on their initiatory ecstatic journey, they have the misfortune to succumb to one of the twelve tests or ordeals along the way. The pathway of this maiden voyage into the otherworld must be traversed by all novice shamans during initiation. It leads from Yaukware's house, at the zenith, to the world mountain of the Mother of the Forest in the southwest. Multitudes of men have perished on this hazardous pilgrimage, their bodies having been devoured and their souls destroyed.

The light-shaman.—The accomplished light-shaman also dies confident of the immortality of his soul and of a blissful life in the company of his patron deity and of fellow shamans. For the light-shaman, as for the priest-shaman, dying is only the last of the numerous occasions when he embarks on the celestial journey typical of his profession. The soul of the light-shaman ascends to the top of the sky to rendezvous with the invisible psychopomp who resides to the east of the zenith. After resting there for several days and being provided with a final cigar, he follows the soul-guide to a bridge made of thick ropes of solidified tobacco smoke, which commences a short distance from the center of the world. Beautiful flowers border the bridge: a row of red and a row of yellow flowers on the left and lines of blue and green flowers on the right.

At the end of the bridge is a white ovular house, also made of tobacco smoke. It is the residence of *Kanobo* Mawari, the patron deity of light-shamans. In primordial times this birthplace of light-shamanism originated through the will of the Creator-Bird of the Dawn. It is inhabited by a hierarchy of four powerful spirits—Black Bee, Wasp, Termite, and Honey Bee—each of whom occupies a chamber along the eastern wall of the house and incessantly chants the song of light-shamanism.

Inside the house is a table draped in white and set with four dishes in a row; also on it are a bow and two arrows. Through the floor of this sacred mansion there emerges from time to time the head of a serpent with four colored plumes on its head: white, yellow, blue, and green. The plumes chime a musical note like a bell. Rhythmically, the snake produces from within its mouth a glowing white ball on the tip of its forked tongue. A novice shaman who ventures into the presence of this snake during initiation instantly receives the entire wisdom of his profession.

Ever since the first light-shaman ascended to live in this sacred mansion, the souls of light-shamans have followed his example. Also, just as with the primordial light-shaman, the wives of light-shamans follow their husbands. The male light-shaman is the father of the tutelary spirits in his breast; his wife (through a ritualized sexual union) becomes the mother of these same spirits. Some women are known to have received the power to cure seizures. Again, as with the cardinal and intercardinal gods, the souls of light-shamans and those of their wives live exclusively on tobacco smoke supplied by their colleagues on earth.

Besides the souls of light-shamans and their wives, yet a third category of souls come to live on Mawari's mountain—the souls of basket makers (of whom more is said below).

The dark-shaman.—Of the three different religious practitioners, we finally consider the fate of the dark-shaman, whose soul belongs to the Macaw-God of the Underworld. The Warao underworld, situated on a world mountain in the west, engulfs in its darkness the entire region between the setting points of the summer and winter suns. Ruled by the Scarlet Macaw, this Land of Death has existed from time immemorial; it was originally connected with the earth through an umbilicuslike artery that reached from the west along the curvature of the celestial vault to the zenith, whence it dangled down to the dancing platform in a Warao village. The end of this duct was provided with a brilliant ball of light which at night sought out and penetrated the heads of sleeping people in order to drain their hearts of blood. The blood flowed through the artery to the underworld, where the spirits drank it from an enormous canoe made of bone or ironlike rock. In the mythical past, in a violent act of jealousy, the blood duct was severed and the artery snapped back to the west so that the flow of nourishment for the spirits of the underworld was interrupted. Since then it has fallen to the dark-shaman to guarantee the survival of these spirits. By means of his magical arrows he kills fellow Warao, preferably those of neighboring villages, and carries them head down on his back to the *Hoebo* house at the zenith and beyond to the Land of Death. Besides two tutelary spirits in his breast, the dark-shaman also carries a sling below his sternum which assists him in sacrificing his victims by throttling them. The pathogenic bolt is carried by tobacco smoke he blows from his reversed cigar that, searching for the heart, enters the individual's rib cage to perform the sacrifice.

The Land of Darkness is the final destination of many souls, those of dark-shamans and those of the common people, but especially of children. In their final journey the souls of dark-shamans, the Warao believe, depart immediately after death for the Soul-Hoebo, west of the zenith. From the time of his initiatory journey the dark-shaman has become thoroughly familiar with the road and its two major stations: the black house at the top of the world (with its Hoebo-Family, the crying child in the hammock of dried blood, and furniture of human skin and bones), and, of course, the underworld itself. Here on the western world mountain stands the house of the Macaw-God, completely dark except for a faint white light and a yellow light. The house is surrounded by innumerable smaller houses inhabited by the souls of dark-shamans who have come to live near their master. The houses, built with posts and beams of iron, stand on top of the bald mountain. The soil is a blood-soaked black morass, and the air is heavy with the stench of putrefaction which serves the approaching soul as a guide. Also, big black flies fill the air and thickly cover every land surface.

The supreme Hoebo spirit has the appearance of a man with long blood-clotted hair, but he is also the Scarlet Macaw with fiery-red plumage covering his entire body, a black beak, black feet, and black streaks on his cheeks. His voice is harsh and his beak is sharp and strong. He uses it to attack his victims by the neck and to tear off their heads.

The approaching soul of the dark-shaman smokes a cigar which from earth looks like a falling star. He listens to the continuous hooting of the trumpet of the Macaw, which, in this instance, is made, not of a conch shell, but of a human skull. The piercing sounds of a clarinet can also be heard. The instrument is made of long human bones and has a skull as its resonance chamber. Upon his arrival, the soul is greeted by his patron god, who allows him to drink blood from the canoe and eat as much human flesh as he pleases, a food that was denied him in life. He is given a necklace of human rib bones, similar to the one the master wears, and proceeds to occupy his personal dwelling in the joyful company of his fellow dark-shamans. Like them, he assumes a body that is half parrot and half human, with the tail of a monkey.

THE AFTERLIFE OF THE COMMON PEOPLE

The sacrifice for the underworld.—Not so joyful is the lot of victims sacrificed as food for the inhabitants of the underworld. Nothing awaits them but the death of body and soul. Although the congregation of shaman souls is numerous, even larger is the number of souls that end up in this dark world without ever being able to enjoy the gift of immortality.

When an ordinary person succumbs to the magic arrow of a dark-shaman, he dies in the knowledge of having been singled out as a sacrifice for the Macaw-God in the House of the Dying Sun. (The underworld is identified as the place where the sun sets, but it is not identified with the Macaw itself.) His flesh is to be eaten by the spirit shamans, his blood will be their drink, the god himself will relish his heart and liver, and his bones and skin will serve as raw materials in this sinister world. No wonder that this death is the most dreaded imaginable for a Warao Indian. As the spirits of the underworld demand a steady supply of human flesh and blood, no one is safe from the magic arrow of the dark-shaman. "One cannot imagine what would happen if our dark-shamans were to stop providing nourishment for the spirits of the west" is a common reply to a field-worker's query. "The world would probably come to an end. All children would die and so would the gods."

Meanwhile, the infant son of the Soul-Hoebo at the zenith continues to cry over the earth, and his crying is the chanting of dark-shamanism. A novice on his first ecstatic journey learns his chant by listening to a crying baby. The infant is hungry, and the novice shaman pledges to contribute his share.

The artisan boat maker.—Fortunately, not all people end up as sacrifices for the underworld. Instead, with some wit and luck—that is, by not offending the gods and the shamans—a person, male or female, can succeed in living a full life, learning to perfection the skills of his or her sex, and joining his or her respective patron deity after death.

That is the lot, for instance, of the soul of an expert canoe builder. Throughout his adult life the artisan practices his trade with diligence and careful observation of the ethical code that governs it. He knows that only utmost dedication will please the Mother of the Forest in the southeast and guarantee him a place on the sacred mountain with this patroness of the boat builder and his fellow artisans.

Accomplished canoe makers die with the certainty of eternal life because, as apprentices, they have successfully completed their initiatory journey to the house of Dauarani, Mother of the Forest. After a preparatory period of fasting and much smoking, and the completion of four trial dugout canoes, the spirit of such a neophyte ascends to the zenith where a black psychopomp leads him to the beginning of a celestial snake-bridge that connects the zenith with the world mountain of the Mother of the Forest. The snake's body smells very agreeably

of *caraña* (*Protium heptaphyllum*), the *caranna* of the Orinoco.[3] The
reptile never coils up and never turns; it simply crawls forward and
then a little backward, back and forth, in either direction.[4] As described
in the preceding chapter, boat makers observe many taboos to serve
Dauarani throughout their lives and to reach her world after death.

Weavers of baskets and hammocks.—Basketmaking is practiced by
both sexes among the Warao. Some old men and women, on achieving
a high degree of proficiency as weavers, become known as *uasi*. The
hands of an expert weaver are identifiable by the permanently damaged
nail on his left index finger, but the *uasi* himself sees a vastly more
significant change in his hands: the gradual whitening of the palms.
Weavers believe that a small hole will eventually appear in each palm.
Through continuous handling of the reeds, the spirit of the plant
converts the *uasi* into a light-shaman of the *sehoro*-reed. The spirit
appears in the artisan's dream and hands him or her a cigar and a set
of tutelary spirits. This gift makes the *uasi* of either sex equal to a light-
shaman. It is believed that the maggot that can often be seen in the
pithy core of the reed burrows a tunnel leading from the artisan's chest,
where the nascent tutelary spirits reside, through each arm to the
opening in each hand. In other words, the weaver is aware that the reed-
spirit is at work in his or her body, and one day, upon noticing the
supernatural holes in his or her hands, he or she knows that the
transformation from ordinary person to light-shaman has been accomplished. Henceforth the basket maker has to live by the same rules
as the light-shamans who came to office through a long process of
initiation. If the artisan complies, his or her soul will go to live after
death with the Creator-Bird of the Dawn in the east.[5]

Hammock making is an exclusively female occupation. "The women
belong to the Mother of Moriche," who lives on the summer solstice

---

[3] Priest-shamans use the same resin for incense, burning it at the tip of their ritual cigars
or in braziers in the temple. The fragrance of the incense is most pleasing to the spirit world
they communicate with, and is, therefore, of great ritual significance in connection with the
cult of the cardinal gods. I am indebted to Dr. Richard Evans Schultes of the Botanical Museum of Harvard University for the botanical identification of the resin.

[4] This way of crawling may simulate the moon's risings in the course of a lunar month.

[5] Métraux (1948, 129) found that the Tupinamba called those who had achieved fame
karai or *pay-wasu* (great medicine men), a possible terminological and conceptual parallel.

in the northeast. She makes the palms fertile each year, thus providing an abundance of fruit and moriche flour for the people.

A woman who becomes a *uasi* in making hammocks will find the Mother of Moriche waiting for her soul upon death. The same is true of the expert music master who is in charge of playing the sacred trumpet (clarinet) during the annual moriche sago harvest festival. His soul goes to a place next to the Mother of Moriche, where the spirit of the sacred trumpet lives. This spirit is the Mother of the Sacred Trumpets on earth and, when the Mother of Moriche hears the master tuning his instrument for the festival, she releases her fertilizing energy and thereby guarantees food in abundance. To be the player of the sacred trumpet of a particular group is an exacting office, but he will reap the reward for his service when his soul finds eternal happiness on the mountain of these sustenance goddesses.

NO HEAVEN FOR CHILDREN

Since the turn of the century, and especially since 1925 when the Capuchins established their first permanent mission in Warao territory, the Winikina have become increasingly more riparian, moving out of the moriche-palm forest to the banks of the large rivers. Before that time, local bands, each consisting mainly of a matrilocal extended family, settled in a cluster of houses deep inside the *morichals*. Several such bands congregated periodically for ritual purposes as a predominantly endogamous subtribe. The gathering place was a ceremonial center in the moriche forest, with a simply constructed temple or shrine on the eastern side of the clearing and a single or double row of houses on the western side. Separating the two areas was a large dancing platform made of juxtaposed poles or strips of moriche bark, which served as the plaza where most of the ceremonies were performed (fig. 3.3).

For several months each year the members of the subtribe worked together to prepare the moriche-sago festival to propitiate the directional gods. The patron god of the subtribe, either the Toad-God, the Butterfly-God, or the Bird-God, to whom the members had pledged allegiance, was represented in the temple in the form of a sacred rock. Even today several, but not all, of the Warao bands possess such a sacred stone and believe it to be the son of either one of the mentioned supreme spirits. The highest-ranking priest-shaman is regarded as the father of

FIG. 3.3.
Ceremonial center of a Warao subtribe. The dancing platform separates the
temple (background) from the settlement. (After Barral 1964, 41).

the rock spirit. He addresses it as his son, whereas the congregation calls it "Grandfather." Whenever the band moves to a different location the rock is carried in a basket on the back of an apprentice shaman.

It is probably safe to say that more than half of the men of any local group are religious practitioners of one kind or another, with their final destinations well defined. There is more than one shaman of a kind, some senior and accomplished, others junior and beginners. Several of the men who have not embarked on religious careers are probably expert artisans, basket makers, or boat makers, aiming for the heaven that corresponds to their profession. The souls of the undistinguished rest are believed to roam perpetually through the neighborhood as invisible dwarflike spirits. Similarly, the women aspire to some kind of life after death, either as shamans, wives of light-shamans, artisans, basket or hammock makers, or herbalists. Of course, some adults would be accounted for as victims of dark magic, and again, some common women's souls would remain on earth as companions of the souls of the undistinguished men. But it is conceivable that all adult members of a local group believed that they had a future life as long as they succeeded in escaping the curse of sorcery.

Not so the children. Looking, for example, at the demographics of the Winikina subtribe in 1954, in the entire subtribe there were 172 children, of whom eighty-seven were alive and eighty-five had died; infant mortality was a high as 49 percent (tables 3.1 and 3.2). The living

TABLE 3.1

INFANT MORTALITY AMONG WINIKINA (1954)

Sex	No. of Living	Percent	No. of Dead	Percent	Total	Percent
Male	41	43	54	57	95	55
Female	46	60	31	40	77	45
	87	51	85	49	172	100

TABLE 3.2

DECEASED PREPUBERTAL OFFSPRING OF WINIKINA (1954)

Age Category	Total	Percent	No. of Boys	Percent	No. of Girls	Percent	Ratio of Males to Females
Baby	69	81	41	59	28	41	4:3
Child	16	19	13	81	3	19	4:1
	85	100	54	64	31	36	

prepubertal offspring accounted for 45 percent of the total Winikina population (table 2.2).

These genealogical statistics of children pose an interesting question: What did parents think had caused the death of their eighty-five deceased youngsters? If the children were believed to have souls, there is certainly no obvious place within the Warao universe where they might have gone—except, of course, to the underworld. When I asked the parents this question, I was told that, to the best of their recollection, twenty-two children had died of dysentery, twenty-one of *hoa* (the magic arrow of the dark-shaman), twelve of *hebu* (spirit sickness), five of measles, and the rest of bronchitis, vomiting, and several other specified and unspecified causes.

Interpreting these figures in eschatological terms, I believe they point to the fact that many of the twenty-two children who died of dysentery and the twenty-one who died of *hoa* were believed to have been claimed as food for the spirits of the underworld. (I include dysentery because, to the parents, the symptomatic loss of blood often associated with this disease is indicative of *hoa* sickness. Some or most of the deaths caused by vomiting could probably also be included.) Bloodless dysentery is *hebu* disease caused by directional gods other than *hoebo*. The twelve children who died of *hebu* perished through the magic of the directional gods, and the five deaths from measles were specifically caused by the Toad-God of the South (whose head, it will be recalled, is covered on one side with the warty skin called *borabora*, the Warao word for measles). Bronchitis, too, probably falls into this category of causes of death, interpreted by the people as such because of the fever frequently associated with the illness. Some of the less well defined deaths can most certainly be ascribed to the magic of malevolent light-shamans.

What this discussion of the cause of death amounts to, I suppose, is that if those dead children had souls, as many as half of the eighty-five possibly had theirs destroyed in the underworld. I assume that the belief is that the directional gods also destroy the souls of their victims, just as the Goddess of the Nadir, for instance, is believed to kill the bodies and steal the souls of babies whose mothers are careless enough to spill their milk on the ground where the goddess can lap it up. The remaining souls of diseased children continue their existence on earth, as do the invisible souls of undistinguished men or women. Some

Warao also believe that the souls may reenter the wombs of their mothers to become reborn. Others say that some of the children's souls can be sent by the priest-shaman to a spot in the cosmos where any one of their relatives abides. Finally, the figure of 49 percent infant mortality reflects the stakes involved in this tug-of-war between the Indians and the supernaturals, as more than half the population is believed to perish in the struggle.

RITUAL PROTECTION FOR CHILDREN

To the Warao of a local group the rate of child mortality does not present itself statistically through retrospective calculations spanning entire generations. These Warao experience the total number of children at any given time, carrying their dead offspring in a seemingly unending procession to the cemetery, and, in some years, when the waters swamp their islands with foul debris, as many as two-thirds of the entire infant population of the band may die (Barral 1964, 69). Supernatural protection on a continuous and daily basis was, therefore, an absolute necessity for the children. Such protection was won by holding frequent sago festivals and through Shiborori, the Bird of the Beautiful Plumage.

The constellation of the Southern Cross is believed to be a mythical turkey-bird with a green head and a green body and tail. Its yellow tongue has a blue ball on its tip. Its crest, eyes, beak, right wing, and right leg are red. The left wing and left leg are blue. The red right wing (female) is polka-dotted with three rows of blue, green, and blue dots; the blue left wing (male) has three rows of green, yellow, and green dots. On its chest the turkey-bird has a bone-colored emblem in the shape of a coat of arms.

Every evening at nine o'clock, so goes the myth, this bird rises in the southeast to fly to the meridian. Here its blue (male) wing chants to protect the newly born girls on earth.[6] In return, an older woman of the settlement, upon hearing the turkey's call, shouts back and encourages it to fly on and not to resign itself to the idea that the cardinal gods, who perennially pursue it, will eventually capture and

---

[6] The issuance of a peculiar chantlike sound is characteristic of the *pauji* turkey, as Schomburgk (1922–23, 1:327) observes. The *Crax tomentoso*, identified by the Guiana Indians with the Southern Cross, begins to sing at the beginning of April, just before midnight, which is, supposedly, when the constellation reaches its highest point.

rob it of its feathers. If a baby girl has been born to the group that night, the old people may also sing a special chant. Shiborori needs this encouragement by a Warao mother because he knows that she understands the predicament of the hunted, which is similar to that of the children. The bird, who calls the Warao children his siblings, knows that the gods pursue them as tenaciously as they pursue it. Reinvigorated by the mother's compassion and encouragement, the bird continues on its journey to reach its home at 3:00 A.M. After resting there, the bird then returns to the meridian where, at twelve o'clock noon, it will chant with its red (female) wing for the protection of the male children, especially the newly born. Thus women belong to the night hours and men to the day hours, and again, if a male baby has been born that day, the old men will also chant with Shiborori for his protection. Thus a powerful chorus is produced when the people sing and the bird creates its song by shaking its wings and projecting the song through the blue ball on the tip of its tongue.

Shiborori learned its chant from the flowers of the Creator-Bird who originated sui generis as a pair of male and female birds in a cave at the foot of the world mountain in the east. Here the couple planted a square garden of four beds of flowers: the male bird grew one black and one green bed; the female, one white and one red bed. Only the female flowers know how to chant; the male ones are mute. Each time the Bird of the Beautiful Plumage returns from the center of the world, it enters this flower garden to rest in the house. From there it has direct access to the house of the Creator-Bird since it is situated in the middle of the bifurcation of pathways that lead from the house of the Creator-Bird to the male (left) and female (right) flower beds.

Should Shiborori one day fail to return and be caught by the pursuing directional gods, he will lose his feathers, his song will never be heard again on earth, and the supernatural hunters will fall upon the village, spreading sickness and death among the children and other people as well. The Warao know about Shiborori because their priest-shamans can see the beautiful bird in dreams and trances. Neither the ordinary people nor the dark- and light-shamans ever see him. They may listen to his chanting only at noon and at midnight, when it never sounds quite as beautiful as it does when it comes straight from the blue ball on the bird's tongue in the priest-shaman's vision.

Only one other bird can match Shiborori's pleasing appearance and his beautiful song—his twin, the Northern Cross. The northern spirit-bird, Akuehebu, flies to the meridian, just as the southern one does, and performs the same magic for the children as does his counterpart. But the two birds must never look at each other lest they lose their song and their power.

Searching the sky at night for the beautiful birds that are so important for the survival of half of the Warao, the Indians are quick to point out the constellation of the Southern Cross, which they call *yaromu* (*pauji*) or simply *domu* (bird). It dominates the southern sky from April to June, and the hunters pursuing it so relentlessly (α and β Centauri) are also clearly visible (Heinen and Lavandero 1973, 11). But in Warao country (at lat. ±9° N) the Southern Cross never quite seems to reach the meridian by midnight when it rises at 9:00 P.M., as it spends ten hours rather than six above the horizon.

For this phenomenon to occur according to the specifications of the myth, one has to instruct the machine of a modern planetarium to change latitude so that the Cross remains visible for only six hours. If in addition one follows the earth's motion of precession back in time until the Southern Cross appears at exactly 1200 hours right ascension, the day of the year on which the Cross reaches the meridian at midnight will be precisely the first day of spring instead of about a week later, as at present. As it turns out, at certain latitudes on earth the constellation can rise at 2100 hours, transit at midnight, and set at three o'clock in the morning on one day each year.

In conducting this experiment at the planetarium of the University of California, Los Angeles,[7] we had to go back in time about five hundred years and move northward from the Warao country to a latitude between twenty and thirty degrees north. An ideal position from which to observe this phenomenon of stellar movement is somewhere between these two latitudes, and one is persuaded to fix one's observation point at 23.5 degrees north latitude, the Tropic of Cancer, where at noon on the first day of spring the sun stands vertically

---

[7] I gratefully acknowledge the assistance of Mr. T. Ericson, a student at the California Institute of Technology, and Mr. Stephen Lattanzio, a graduate student at UCLA, for having helped me with the astronomical interpretation of the data. Lattanzio operated the planetarium at UCLA, and I express my sincere thanks to the Department of Astronomy for permitting me to make use of their fine facilities.

overhead at the zenith. But the Tropic of Cancer cuts through Meso-america, not through the land of the Warao.

From this vantage point and on the day when the sun is at the vernal equinox, the first day of spring, one can also observe the Northern Cross rising in the northeastern quadrant at about 2:00 A.M., when the Southern Cross is about to set in the southwestern quadrant (fig. 3.4). Both constellations appear as mirror images; in fact, there are scarcely any other two constellations that resemble each other to the same

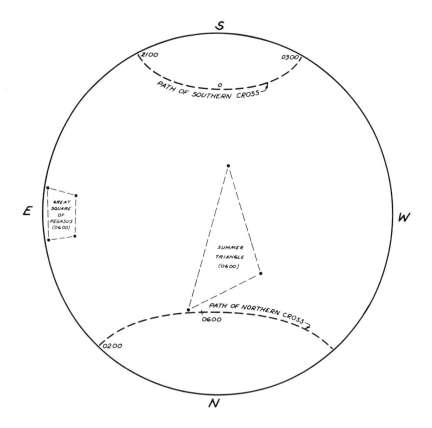

Fig. 3.4.

Reconstruction of stellar position on 21 March A.D. 1500, at ±23.5 degrees north latitude. The Southern Cross rises at 2100 hours, transits at midnight, and sets at 0300 hours; the Northern Cross rises at 0200 hours and reaches 55 degrees (Deneb) altitude before sunrise at 0600 hours. The great square of Pegasus becomes fully visible at 0600 hours. The Summer Triangle's position at 0600 hours is also shown.

degree. The similarity is in shape and size and in the brightness of the particular five stars in the two constellations, as well as in the fact that they are mirror images. Each cross has three bright and two fainter stars, and the fainter stars in both crosses are closer to the horizon at this point in their trajectory. In addition, both constellations are in the Milky Way. In their only dissimilarity, the Northern Cross is tilted a little closer toward the horizon than its southern counterpart.

As the sun on that day is up exactly twelve hours and down exactly twelve hours, the two crosses can be seen together for about one hour before the Southern Cross sets. The Northern Cross remains visible three hours longer, approaching the meridian to about fifty degrees up from the horizon before daylight blots it out. In a more southerly latitude, then or today, the period of time in which both crosses are visible simultaneously would be longer.

Thus, in A.D. 1500, at ±23.5 degrees north latitude, the celestial bird could indeed be observed carrying out its mandate to fly at midnight and during the day to the meridian, shake his beautiful wings, and sing for the protection of the children on earth. At night Shiborori could soar toward the meridian as the Southern Cross and, during the day, as the Northern Cross. At present, because of the change in latitude, the Warao can no longer observe this phenomenon; the Southern Cross requires ten hours to complete its journey. Because it follows a higher arc in the sky, at 9 degrees north latitude, it can never rise at 2100 hours and transit at midnight. Nor, even at 23.5 degrees north latitude, does it now do so at the spring equinox.

It also happens that on the day of the midnight transit of the Southern Cross, the last star of the great square of Pegasus rises synchronously or heliacally on the eastern horizon as, according to my interpretation, a brilliant square flower garden at the foot of the eastern world mountain, where Shiborori rests from his flight. The sun rises exactly to the east on this day, and the square appears a little to the north but right next to it. The house of the beautiful bird is situated within the triangle formed by the pathways that connect the flower patches with the house of the Creator-Bird. This triangle of pathways, the summer triangle, is visible in the sky, with the apex star close to the zenith and the northern star, α Cygni, popularly known as Deneb, connected with the Northern Cross.

It should be pointed out that the Warao, with a cosmological atlas of eschatological significance strongly reminiscent of Aztec and Mayan concepts, trust the well-being of their offspring to a stellar bird that cannot be observed in its full mythical context from their present habitat but was observable in Mesoamerica and was recognized in a similar fashion by the Aztecs around A.D. 1500.

According to Durán (1971, 418–19), during the third month of the Aztec year, the Indians venerated "a beautiful bird with a bone piercing its body."[8] He "understood it to refer to a star formation that appears in the heavens like a bird." The main feast was held on the first day of the month, April 10, at the beginning of the rainy season, when the fields were planted. On April 20 "all children under twelve were bled, even breast-fed babies,…in honor of the coming feast, which involved the general purification of the mothers." Soothsayers went from house to house to inquire about the children and to see whether their ears had been pierced and whether they were fasting on bread and water as prescribed. If so, the soothsayers decorated them by fastening red, green, blue, black, or yellow threads to their necks, strung with snake bones, beads, or small figurines. Obviously, then, the month of the beautiful bird was taken by the Aztecs as an occasion to petition the supernaturals for the gift of abundant crops and healthy children and for their protection from evil and dark magic.

In addition to these characteristics, clearly reminiscent of similar concepts related to the Warao protector bird of children, the Aztecs "also made bouquets with flower buds in order to revel in them on that day…. This ceremony constituted the offering of the first flowers to the gods,"[9] and there were great masters skilled in the craft of flower arrangements (ibid., p. 419).

Turkeys are important during the New Year ceremony of the Chorti-Maya at the beginning of the rainy season (Girard 1969, 106–7, 111–12). After a ritual banquet a pair of turkeys is sacrificed, a male on the northern side of the altar and a female on the southern side. Four priests take their places at the corners of the altar according to their positions in the cosmic quadrant. The blood of the decapitated birds runs into a hole in the ground, and the carcasses are opened so that the hearts and intestines can be removed and thrown into the holes and stamped underfoot. The birds are then plucked and their feathers are sacrificed

---

[8] One is at once reminded of the white breast emblem of Shiborori in the form of a coat of arms.

[9] The *pauji* (*Crax alector*) eats flower buds.

as well. The sacrifice takes place under the supervision of a high priest, who starts the ceremony at twelve o'clock midnight and ends it at 3:00 A.M.; the actual sacrifice takes place at about 2:30 A.M.

Among the parallels between this Maya ritual and Shiborori of the Warao are the connection with fertility, the northern (male) and the southern (female) birds, the directionally positioned priests (probably representing the equivalent gods of the world quarters who sacrifice the feathers of the bird), and the timing of the ceremony, which begins at a time when, in A.D. 1500, the Southern Cross appeared at the meridian and which ends shortly before it set.

Shiborori's real prototype is probably the ocellated turkey (*Meleagris ocellata*). The coloring of this rare bird with its beautiful plumage corresponds largely to the specifications of the mythical Shiborori. What is of far greater significance here, however, is the fact that the ocellated turkey with "polka dots" on its tail and wing feathers is found only on the Yucatan peninsula, where it is endemic to the tropical forest of southern Mexico, the Petén of Guatemala, and the adjacent areas of Belize (Thomas R. Howell, pers. comm.).

These striking analogies, together with the startling ethnoastronomical data, seem to be persuasive indications of contact between Mesoamerica and northern South America. Did these Mesoamerican influences reach the Warao via the Antilles through Cariban tribes, that is, along the east and north sides of the Caribbean Sea? Or are these parallels between Mesoamerica and South America best accounted for within Lathrop's model of a Colombian hearth for proto-Mayan culture, that is, along the western and southern sides of the Caribbean? There is, however, also reliable evidence that the Caribbean functioned for at least two thousand years as "a wide-open avenue of trade and intercommunication among all points on its shore" and that "the bulk of the trade was in the hands of peoples of Arawakan speech" (Lathrop, pers. comm.).

These and still other lines of diffusion deserve careful ethnographic and ethnohistorical examination. Not only are they of interest from a purely historical point of view but they also promise, as Peter T. Furst has correctly observed, insights into the importance of nonphysical, supernatural manifestations for a society's ecological adaptation and survival.

Chapter Four

Tobacco and Shamanistic Ecstasy[1]

Tobacco (*Nicotiana* sp.) is not generally considered to be a halluci-
nogen. Yet, like the sacred mushrooms, peyote, morning glories,
Datura, ayahuasca, psychotomimetic snuffs, and a whole series of other
New World hallucinogens, tobacco has long been known to play a
central role in North and South American shamanism, both in the
achievement of shamanistic trances and in purification and supernatural
curing. Even if it is not one of the "true" hallucinogens from a botanist's
or a pharmacologist's point of view, tobacco is often conceptually and
functionally indistinguishable from them.

We know that Indians from Canada to Patagonia esteemed tobacco
as one of their most important medicinal and magical plants and that
some of them employed it as a vehicle of ecstasy. We also know that
everywhere, and almost always in prehistoric and more recent historic
times, its use was strictly ritualistic. Its increasing secularization among
Indians is a modern development, adopted from Europeans (to whom
tobacco was of course unknown prior to the first voyage of Columbus).[2]

[1] I am indebted to several colleagues, including Dr. Peter T. Furst, Dr. Michael Coe, and
Dr. Floyd G. Lounsbury, for discussions that helped to clarify some of the theoretical implications of this chapter; to Ms. Karin Simoneau for her efficient research assistance; and to
Franklin L. Murphy, Jr., for his assistance in the field. Field research on which this paper is
based was funded through the Venezuelan Indian Project of the University of California, Los
Angeles, and was cosponsored by the Centro Latinoamericano de Venezuela (CLAVE). Fi-
nancial assistance rendered by the Creole Foundation of Caracas has greatly aided the research
work. I also gratefully acknowledge the logistic assistance of the Capuchin mission in Guayo,
Orinoco Delta. But most of all I am indebted to the shamans of the Winikina-Warao, who
gave me their trust and their friendship.
   [2] In view of the many parallels between Siberian and American Indian shamanism,
Wasson's remarks (1968, 332) on tobacco are of interest: "Among Europeans and their descendants elsewhere it became a habit and an addiction but played no role in religion. But
after tobacco reached Siberia, probably also in the latter part of the sixteenth century or at the

Nevertheless, ancient ritual meanings associated with native tobacco persist; in many tribes the tobacco they themselves cultivate or collect in the wild state is reserved for ritual and ceremonial use, whereas the white man's tobacco, or "Virginia tobacco," a hybrid domesticate of *Nicotiana tabacum*, is freely smoked.

Tobacco may be one of several vehicles for inducing ecstasy; it may be taken in combination with other plants to bring on narcotic trances; or it may be the sole psychoactive agent employed by shamans to transport themselves into the realm of the supernatural, as it is among the Warao. That Warao shamans smoke enormous cigars that may be 50 to 75 centimeters long has been known since early contact times, but the meaning of tobacco in Warao intellectual culture has often gone unnoticed. Such a failure is not surprising; few outsiders can expect to penetrate a culture meaningfully in the limited amount of time usually available for fieldwork. My own experience is instructive. In 1954, after an initial period of fieldwork, I dimly perceived the religious complexity of the Warao culture with its three types of shamans and a temple-priest-idol cult (Wilbert 1956b). After 1954 I worked intermittently for more than fifteen years (at the time of writing) with the Warao shaman to whom I owe much of what follows in these pages. At first we communicated through an interpreter, in Spanish, and finally in his own language. Only in 1969, however, did he finally consent to lead me step by step beyond the outer fringes of Warao religion into that complex supernatural world that opens up for the shaman through the act of intensive smoking.

THE SHAMANISTIC WORLD OF LIGHT AND DARKNESS

The Warao believe they inhabit a saucer-shaped earth surrounded by a belt of water. The bell-shaped celestial vault covers both earth and ocean and rests on a series of mountains situated at the cardinal and intercardinal points. Much of a Warao Indian's life is spent in propitiating a number of supreme spirits (*kanobo, kanobotuma*, pl.) who

---

latest in the seventeenth century, it is astonishing how quickly the tribesmen adapted it to shamanism, thus recapturing for it the religious meaning that it always had for the American Indian." (Commentary by Peter T. Furst.)

inhabit these mountains at the ends of the world and who require nourishment from the people in the form of tobacco smoke.

The priest-shaman (*wishiratu*) visits these spirits in his dreams or in a tobacco-induced trance and, on returning from such a visit, transmits the message of the supreme spirits to the community. One of the four major spirits is usually present among the people in the form of a sacred stone. The annual moriche festival, called *nahanamu*, over which the priest-shaman presides, is celebrated in propitiation of the supreme spirits who request that the ceremony be held and who will protect the community if their command is heeded. Sickness is believed to be caused by one or another of the deified *kanobotuma*, who thereby expresses his dissatisfaction with humans and sends his *hebu* (spirit) to do harm or even to kill. Children especially are subject to such attacks. The priest-shaman is the only one who can intervene as curer because only he can relate directly to the supreme *kanobotuma*.

In addition to the priest-shaman, the Warao have two other important religious practitioners. The light-shaman is known as *bahanarotu*. He presides over an ancient cult of fertility called *habisanuka*. As we shall see later, the *bahanarotu* travels in his dream or tobacco-induced trance to the eastern part of the cosmic vault. The celestial bridge of tobacco smoke between his community and the eastern Supreme *Bahana* (spirit), which he maintains and frequents, guarantees abundance of life on earth. In their aggressive shamanic role, *bahanarotu* shamans spread illness and death among their enemies by hurling magic arrows at them. Only a friendly *bahanarotu* can assuage such misfortune, which he does through the use of tobacco and the widespread traditional shamanic technique of sucking out the illness-causing foreign bodies magically introduced by the malevolent sorcerer.

The dark-shaman, known as *hoarotu,* maintains the connection between the Warao in the center of the universe and the powers of the west. This connection, severed in ancient times, can be reestablished only by the *hoarotu*. The spirit beings in the west subsist through their medium, the dark-shaman, on the blood and flesh of humans. To procure this human food for his masters, the *hoarotu* "kills" his victims by means of magic projectiles, again through the medium of tobacco smoke.

Thus there exist among the Warao three religious practitioners who derive their shamanic power from three different cosmic sources. All three are ambivalent and may adopt either a benevolent or a malevolent role: the *wishiratu* can cause and cure *hebu* sickness; the *bahanarotu*, *hatabu* sickness; and the *hoarotu*, *hoa* sickness. Further, all three kinds of shaman use tobacco smoke as their principal ecstatic and therapeutic vehicle. In spite of the regionalism that exists with regard to underlying concepts, it is generally true that shamanic initiation, ecstasy, and curing are unthinkable among the Warao without the aid of tobacco.

The overwhelming magical importance of tobacco is all the more remarkable in view of the fact that originally tobacco was absent from the Orinoco Delta. As even today it is not widely cultivated, it must be acquired through barter or purchase. Until very recently, smoking was the prerogative solely of religious and magical practitioners, who obtained their supply from Creole settlers in the western delta and from the island of Trinidad. *Wishiratu* and *bahanarotu* shamans require considerable quantities of tobacco to feed the *kanobo* and *bahana* spirits by smoking their extraordinary cigars. Because propitiation of these spirits by means of tobacco smoke is an absolute sine qua non of Warao intellectual culture, and because shamans must use tobacco to achieve the required trance for travel to the otherworld, it is likely that procuring the sacred plant provided the principal impetus for Warao excursions into the hazardous frontier regions and onto the open ocean.

In the old days ordinary mortals hesitated to smoke for fear of precipitating an undesirable encounter with tobacco-craving spirits. Nowadays cigarettes and tobacco in every form are smoked frequently by most Warao; even the women indulge more or less freely as evening falls. But the long indigenous "cigars" are exclusively shamanic. (Strictly speaking, the Warao "cigar" is really a long tubular wrapping made of the stipule of a manaca palm, called *winamoru* in Warao, into which plugs of tobacco are inserted and which is consumed along with the tobacco, rather than a true cigar whose wrappings as well as contents are made of tobacco.) Warao shamans must never attempt to feed the supreme spirits with "Virginia blends," because the foreign "perfumed" aroma is offensive to the spirits. (Unaware of this prohibition, on one ceremonial occasion I deposited a Camel cigarette as an offering in the sanctuary of the *kanobo* spirits. The officiating priest-shaman immediately asked me to replace it with a piece of "black" tobacco. Not only would it be more suitable for the *kanobo-*

tuma, but also its smell would be free of the offensive odor of burning cigarette paper.)

THE *WISHIRATU*

At the ends of the universe (*aitona*) reside four supreme spirits, three male and one female, called *kanobotuma* (Our Grandfathers). The *Kanobo* Supreme, named Uraro, lives on the world mountain of the south, *Kanobo* Ariawara on the world mountain of the east, and *Kanobo* Warowaro on the mountain of the north. The female *kanobo* is called Dauarani, the Mother of the Forest; her serpent body lives in the southwest and her spirit in the southeast.

Generally speaking, all four *kanobotuma* are benignly inclined toward humankind, so long as people propitiate them with tobacco, moriche flour, fish or crabs, and incense. The Grandfathers accept these offerings gratefully before returning everything except the tobacco to be ritually consumed by the people. The tobacco the spirits keep for themselves, for tobacco smoke is their proper nourishment. They appreciate it especially when it has been perfumed with incense. If neglected for a long period of time by the priest-shaman, the *kanobotuma* may become vindictive and send *wishi*-pains and death down to earth. Pains, though invisible, are still materially conceived agents of the *kanobotuma*, who endow the priest-shaman with the power to control them; his name, *wishiratu*, means literally "Master of Pain." This control over pains represents the actual power base of the *wishiratu* as shaman.

The Warao recognize lower- and higher-ranking *wishiratu*. The most prestigious *wishiratu* of any Warao community is always the keeper of the sacred stone image. This stone, said to measure no more than 30 centimeters in length and 10 in width, with an irregular surface, is variously called "Grandfather" and "Son of *Kanobo*." Though wholly unsculptured, it is conceptualized by the Indians as a head with a recognizable face. On the lower back of the head there is said to be an open sore, constantly oozing blood. The Indians are convinced that if an ordinary person, whether a member of the tribe or an outsider, were to lay eyes on the sacred stone he would instantly be struck blind. The mythic origin of the image goes back to a primordial "first time," when an ancestral shaman, anguished by death and pain in his community, undertook an arduous pilgrimage to one of the sacred mountains at the end of the cosmos to ask the *kanobo* for an end to the dying. The shaman begged him to come and live in the midst of his people rather than far away on the mountain. The *kanobo* agreed to do so, but only in the form of the sacred stone image. He also promised to advise the shaman in the future and to refrain from sending pains if an initial sacrifice of ten men was made and the people agreed to continue to make offerings of tobacco smoke. By the act of residing in the cult house or temple of the community in the form of the image, the *kanobo* effected the actual transfer of control over pain to the first shaman and, by extension, to all future *wishiratu*. The ten men selected for the primordial sacrifice were laid side by side and killed by the *kanobo*'s jumping over them.

Ever since that first contract between the ancestral *wishiratu* and the *kanobo*, Warao communities have identified themselves as "People of *Kanobo* Uraro," "People of *Kanobo* Ariawara," or "People of *Kanobo* Warowaro," respectively, depending on which of the three male *kanobotuma* was visited on the primordial pilgrimage in the tradition of the local group. The temple of the *kanobo*-image is a small hut set apart from the dwellings and screened on all sides with palm fronds or walls of folded temiche leaves.

To fulfill the primordial promise of abundant sacrificial tobacco smoke, *wishiratu* shamans smoke incessantly. Their "cigars," as we have noted, are between 50 and 75 centimeters long and contain several tightly rolled leaves of black tobacco sprinkled with the fragrant resin (*caraña*) of the *curucay* or tacamahaca (*Protium heptaphyllum* [Aubl.]), called *shiburu* tree by the Warao. Incense is offered either in special incense burners or together with tobacco smoke. Small granules are wrapped into the cigar with the tobacco or else a ball of the incense is held to the burning tip in the course of smoking.

The *wishiratu* is not only obliged to "feed" the *kanobo* whose rock-spirit is housed in the village temple; he must also offer tobacco and incense to the other *kanobotuma* living at the ends of the world. The *wishiratu* carries out the "feeding" of these spirits by holding the long cigar vertically and pointing it in the direction of the supreme *kanobotuma*, all the while inhaling with hyperventilation or swallowing the smoke.

The *kanobotuma* travel over well-conceived roads: from the dancing platform in the middle of the village they ascend to the zenith, where a lesser *kanobo* by the name of Yaukware, who supplies them with fresh tobacco, lives. From the zenith the roads lead along the curvature of the firmament to the cardinal and intercardinal points of the *aitona*, the end of the Warao universe. The roads of the major *kanobotuma* all end on top of sacred mountains which look like giant tree stumps and which support the cosmic vault, reminiscent of the well-known Mesoamerican concept of world trees supporting the sky. *Kanobotuma* also travel along the *aitona* circle at the end of the world to visit one another.

A *wishiratu* frequents the same celestial roads but mostly visits the mountain inhabited by the patron-*kanobo* of his community. Here the shaman has his own house. If he wishes to confer with his *kanobo*, he travels in the smoke of his cigar to the zenith. There, after more intensive smoking, he mounts a flying horse (*behoroida*, literally, big dog) which takes him to the *aitona*. It is understood that only well-prepared and established *wishiratu* shamans—that is, those who carry three pairs of pains (*wishi*) in their breasts and who have successfully completed their initiatory trance journey to their *kanobo*—are able to do so.

Yaukware, the *kanobo* of lesser rank who lives at the zenith, was also once a *wishiratu*, the first shaman ever to make the celestial ascent. This *wishiratu* lived peacefully on earth with his mother, brother, wife, and son, until one day he came upon his wife and his brother committing adultery. Deeply grieved, the *wishiratu* took his shaman's rattle, called his son, and sat with him on his shaman's box. He lit a long shamanic cigar, and, ignoring the pleading of his mother, slowly ascended with his son to the zenith within the smoke of the shaman's cigar. From the zenith Yaukware sent pains to kill the adulterers and to make other Warao ill.

Nowadays, novice *wishiratu* must be taught how to ascend to Yaukware's house in the zenith by means of smoking tobacco. After undergoing instruction in the special knowledge of a *wishiratu*, the novice chants and fasts for several days. Then the master *wishiratu* hands him a long cigar charged with *wishi* spirits. These are to become the young *wishiratu*'s spiritual *kanobotuma* and special familiars. The candidate falls into a deep trance and in this state finds himself embarking on his initiatory journey across the "Road of the *Wishiratu*" to the end of the world.

This maiden voyage into the otherworld is the most crucial ecstatic flight the *wishiratu* will ever undertake. Not only must he overcome many obstacles, but his very life is threatened by the ever-present possibility that his dream will be interrupted so suddenly that his roaming soul will not have time to return to his body. A novice suffering this fate will never become a practicing shaman and will soon die.

Once the *wishiratu* in his ecstatic tobacco trance has left *Kanobo* Yaukware's house in the zenith, he sets out on one of the roads that lead to a *kanobo* at the end of the world. It is a difficult journey and he would surely fail were it not for an invisible psychopomp, or soul-guide, who leads the way and advises the young traveler. The first station he reaches is a manaca palm. As noted, it is from the epidermis of the manaca leafstalk that the Warao make the *wina*, or tube, for their cigars. This palm is the shamanic tree of all *wishiratu* shamans, who come here to carve their mark into its bark. The novice, who is advised to follow the example of his predecessors, is told that his mark will remain fresh as long as he lives.

Next he and his soul-guide come to a place with many water holes, where each living *wishiratu* finds his own reservoir of water for drinking and purification. Only upon his death will his water hole dry up forever. Farther along the road, the novice shaman encounters another manaca palm, and here he rolls his first shamanic cigar (the initial one having been presented to him by his *wishiratu*-teacher).

Then the young *wishiratu* has to clear an abyss filled with hungry jaguars, snapping alligators, and frenzied sharks, all eager to devour him. A vine hangs down over the abyss, and the novice, grasping it firmly, swings himself across. But still his ordeal has not ended, for he soon reaches another obstacle. The path becomes extremely slippery, so that he can hardly keep his balance. To make matters worse, on every side are threatening demons armed with spears, waiting to kill any novice who falls.

Next there are four stations where the novice is tested by groups of people barbecuing the meat of boar, deer, tapir, and alligator, respectively. He is offered the meat of all, but no matter how hungry he is and how strong the temptation, he must reject all the proffered meat except the venison. Greatly tempting also are the women he meets next;

he sees them making bark cloth for pubic covers but must not linger with them, much less have sexual intercourse with them.

Escaping the powerful lure of these women, the novice reaches the terrifying place where, stretched out on its back before him, he encounters the giant hawk, devourer of young *wishiratu*. Its beak snaps, its claws grasp, and its wings flap open and shut. Without betraying fear, the novice must step over the rapacious bird and pass by a huge pile of bleached bones, sad reminders of his less fortunate predecessors.

Finally the candidate shaman has to pass through a hole in an enormous tree trunk with rapidly opening and closing doors. He hears the voice of his guide and companion from the other side of the trunk, for this spirit has already cleared the dangerous passage and now encourages the fearful novice to follow his example. The candidate jumps through the clashing doors and looks around inside the hollow tree. There he beholds a huge serpent with four colorful horns and a fiery-red luminous ball on the tip of her protruding tongue.[3] This serpent has a servant with reptilian body and human head whom the candidate sees carrying away the bones of novices who failed to clear the clashing gateway of the tree. The novice, hurrying to get outside the tree, finds himself at the end of the cosmos. His patron *kanobo*'s mountain rises before him. Here he will be given a small house of his own, where he may sojourn in his future tobacco trances to consult with the *kanobo* and where eventually he will come to live forever upon successful completion of his shaman's life on earth.

After this initiatory encounter with his patron *kanobo* at the end of the world, the young *wishiratu* awakens from his tobacco trance a new man. He carries with him six *wishi*-spirits to assist him in curing patients who suffer from spirit sickness. This sickness is caused by a hostile *wishiratu* who blows a "pain" into a victim. In his shaman's rattle, the *wishiratu* carries additional spirit helpers in the form of quartz crystals. These too assist him in curing by extracting sickness-causing *wishi* pains. As time goes by, the young *wishiratu* will become more and more familiar with the complex world of the *kanobotuma* and will acquire wisdom in maintaining a contractual partnership between them and his people. This monumental spiritual obligation, which weighs

---

[3] Reminiscent of the well-known and very ancient Chinese and Indian motif of the sky dragon with the wish-fulfilling pearl.

heavily on him, involves a never-ending cycle of ritual observances and tobacco-induced ecstatic journeys to the ends of the cosmos.

THE *BAHANAROTU*

The "history of consciousness" of the Warao as a people has its origin in the House of Tobacco Smoke, created *ex nihilo* by the Creator-Bird of the Dawn. The House of Smoke is the birthplace of light-shamanism, called *bahana*. Its materialization by means of solidified tobacco smoke took place through the conscious act of a bird-spirit, who at the beginning of time arose as a young man in the east. The radiant body of this youth, his weapons, and his shamanic rattle are all made of tobacco smoke.

A young man who has decided to embark on the road of the *bahanarotu* takes a gift to the house of an older and respected *bahanarotu* whom he has chosen to be his teacher. If the gift is accepted, the master prepares a cigar charged with four wads of black leaf tobacco.

"Smoke this," he says. "It contains four *bahana* who come to open your chest."

These four *bahana* are Black Bee, Wasp, Termite, and Blue Bee. Black Bee hits hard when the smoker inhales the first charge of tobacco. Then Wasp, Termite, and Blue Bee tear painfully into his body. It is said that the smoke does not reach the stomach. *Bahana*-spirits reside around the heart. They cleanse the novice of polluted foods.

"Smoke it slowly, very slowly," advises the master *bahanarotu*. "You had better be cleansed thoroughly."

The smoking of this first cigar introduces four days of fasting. After successfully completing this period of purification, the novice *bahanarotu* undergoes four additional days of abstinence, during which he incessantly smokes cigars lit from a virgin fire (i.e., a fire on which no cooking has been done).

The novice falls into a trance; the Indians say, "He dies." And in this state, "All of a sudden it happens." The unconscious apprentice perceives the sonorous vibrations of the four *bahana* insect-spirits. Louder and louder they grow, until the trees of the forest are transformed into gigantic rattles, swinging and swaying and emitting sounds that are most agreeable to his ears. He feels exalted and, euphoric from the marvelous sound, embarks on his initiatory journey across the celestial bridge and its rainbow of colors. Buoyant as a puff of cotton, he is wafted by the breeze toward his encounter with the Supreme *Bahana* in the House of Tobacco Smoke.

Awakening at last from his ecstasy, the new *bahanarotu* clutches his chest which encloses the gifts of *bahana*: White Smoke and White Rocks. Still small and feeble, the spirits require much care. The young *bahanarotu* eats little but smokes a great deal. For more than a month he observes celibacy and avoids the touch of blood and odors like those of roasting fish, onions, lemons, and rancid oil. In the palms of his hands small brown spots appear which grow proportionately to the growing *bahana* in his body. Nowadays, unlike the first *bahanarotu*, *bahanarotu* shamans have only one *bahana* exit in each of their hands, through which their spirit-sons leave them to assist during trances or curing sessions.[4]

"Now swallow this small stick," orders the master. "Let your *bahana*-spirits transform it."

The stick travels past the spirit in the chest and through the arm of the new *bahanarotu* and is "born" white through the mystical hole in the palm of his hand. A second stick that is swallowed exits as a white stick through the other hand.

"Now swallow the white sticks," orders the master.

This act produces the final proof of a successful initiation. Now the white sticks travel past the *bahana* in the chest and through the arms, this time to be born as white crystal beads.

"The *bahana*-spirits are beginning to play," observes the teacher. He is satisfied. He blows tobacco smoke over the arms of his young colleague and bids him go, with this warning: "Should you take a bath now, you would drown. Should you cohabit with your wife now, you would die. Your spirit-sons would return to me, whence they came. Do not send your arrows to cause evil."

---

[4] All this, of course, is how it appears to the Indians, who see the shamanic phenomena through the eyes of faith and apprehend them as religious reality. I am reminded of the time when I was told by Sanemá Indians in Venezuela that their shamans fly, or at least walk a foot or so off the ground. When I remarked (intentionally naïvely) that I could see shamans walking just like ordinary people, I was told, "That is because you do not understand" (Wilbert 1963, 222). P. Martin Dobrizhoffer, who worked among the Abipon in Paraguay in the mid-1700s, had much the same experience when he tried in vain to convince the Indians that there was no such thing as shamans transforming themselves into jaguars. "You fathers do not understand these matters," was the Indian's answer (Dobrizhoffer 1822, 2:78).

But of course many *bahanarotu* do emit magic arrows to kill or cause illness; all *bahanarotu* have this capacity. *Bahanarotu* can see these projectiles fly through the night like fireballs. They know that somewhere a malevolent *bahanarotu* has swallowed a piece of glass, a twig, a human hair, a rock, or some other object and sent it on its way to enter the body of a victim and make him or her sick. The procedure is as follows: the *bahanarotu* ingests the chosen object and lets it pass by his *bahana*-spirits in his chest and through his arms to the wrist. Here it waits, moving slowly toward the exit hole in the hand. Now the *bahanarotu* takes a deep pull at his cigar, lifts the hand with the magic arrow to his mouth, belches out a ball of smoke, and sends the projectile on its way. A *bahanarotu* shooting magic arrows of sickness in this fashion is known as a *hatabuarotu*, "master of the arrow." He works his malevolent magic during the night, when he can follow with his eyes the glowing puff of tobacco smoke in which the arrow travels. The impact of a *bahana* arrow is painful. It may hit any part of the body and only a benevolent *bahanarotu* knows how to extract it.[5]

If summoned to treat a patient, a *bahanarotu* waits until evening, when the heat of the day has diminished. He places his hand on the affected part of the body and his *bahana*-spirit helpers diagnose the nature of the arrow of sickness. The healer then sucks it out, inhales large quantities of tobacco smoke, and lets the magic arrow travel through his arm and through the exit hole into his hand, where it is "born" for the patient and his relatives to see. During the night the malevolent *bahanarotu* appears to the curer in his dream. He tells him what it was that provoked him to send an arrow of sickness and warns

---

[5] Warao beliefs concerning the ability of shamans to shoot sickness projectiles through a tube in the arm from an exit hole in the hand with the help of tobacco smoke are closely paralleled among the Barama River Carib of Guyana (formerly British Guiana). According to Gillin (1936, 173), these techniques are taught to the neophyte shaman by his teacher, who "places a spirit stone in the novice's mouth and draws it from the mouth through the shoulder and through the arm three times, in order to make the tube in the arm through which the shooting is done." Elsewhere (p. 140) Gillin writes: "It is believed that a tube somewhat like the barrel of a gun extends from the piaiyen's [shaman's] neck to the elbow joint, and from the latter point to a small opening between the bases of the first and second fingers. . . . With the 'shots' held above the elbow joint, the piaiyen, when ready for action, takes a long inhalation of tobacco smoke and extends the right forearm in the intended direction. The force of the smoke is believed to be the physical agency necessary for the ejection of the shot."

the victim not to offend him again. The following morning the message is conveyed to the convalescent.

Since *bahanarotu* shamans can see *bahana* in the dark, they sometimes get together for a tobacco seance to play the supernatural game of *bahana* before the eyes of the awestruck villagers. Exhaling puffs of smoke, they send the four pieces of their *bahana* game one after the other to travel like luminous bodies through the dark house. The quartet of *bahana*-spirits delights in this game. Generally they are said to be the aforementioned "power objects"—rock crystals, hair, rocks, and puffs of tobacco smoke—but a bullet, a piece of glass, or a button will also serve as a magic projectile. They drift through the air, seeking out one or the other of the spectators, but as this is only a game, they do not enter his body. The people in the room are fearful of this supernatural demonstration of shamanic power, but the "fathers" of the roving *bahana* always call their "sons" back if the game threatens to get out of hand. They blow tobacco smoke to intercept the flight of the spirits and put them back in their baskets.

Bahanarotu shamans travel frequently to the House of Smoke in the east, and when they die they go to live there forever.

The *Hoarotu*

The Scarlet Macaw (*Ara chloroptera*) is the Supreme *Hoa* spirit who rules over the Abode of Darkness, called *Hoebo*. This place is situated at the end of the world to the west. Here live all the souls of deceased dark-shamans, the *hoarotu*, as beings half man and half animal. The stench of human cadavers and clotted blood saturates the air, and the stream of *hoarotu* shamans who come from all parts of Waraoland, with cadavers hanging head down from their shoulders, is endless. It has to be endless if the Supreme *Hoa* and spirit companions called *hoarao*, are to continue living, the former by eating human hearts and livers, the latter by devouring the bodies. All *hoarao* in the *Hoebo* drink human blood from a gigantic canoe made of human bones.

The Abode of Darkness has existed since the beginning of time. Originally the Supreme *Hoa* and his companions sustained themselves with human blood supplied through a long umbilicuslike artery reaching from the end of the world in the west across the water to the Warao village on earth. The artery was connected in the *Hoebo* to a gigantic structure of rock (or iron), where it was illuminated by one yellow and one white light. From there it followed the curvature of the celestial vault to the zenith and dangled down from the heavens over the dancing platform in a Warao village. The end of this duct was provided with a brilliant ball of light which at night sought out the heads of sleeping Warao in order to penetrate through the skull down to their hearts and thus drain their blood. The blood flowed through the umbilicus to the *Hoebo*, to nourish its spirits. No one could see this cosmic artery, nor did the Warao die after being thus drained—they felt weak but they recovered.

One day this arrangement was changed through a violent act of jealousy. The bridge of blood in the sky disappeared and *hoarotu* shamans became the sole providers of the spirits in the western world of darkness. This change came about in the following way:

There was an old man by the name of Miana (Dimmed Vision). As his name implies, he had impaired sight. He lived alone in the zenith and begot a son whose name, like that of the Abode of Darkness, was Hoebo. Hoebo had learned to sing like his father in order to activate the search for blood by the celestial umbilicus. One day Hoebo wanted to visit the Supreme *Hoa*. Father and son set out on their journey. They heard the humming chant of the Spirits of the West when they had gone only halfway. They also beheld the bright lights of white and yellow penetrating the darkness of the *Hoebo*.

"See the *hoa ahutu* artery," said Miana to his son. "Listen to its humming."

The youth became very anxious to reach the Supreme *Hoa*. Then his eyes fell upon a beautiful girl below him in the Warao village. He decided to marry her. But when he lowered himself headfirst from the *hoa ahutu*-umbilicus to the dancing platform in the center of the village, a jealous rival for the girl cut off Hoebo's head. The sphere at the end of the blood duct fell to the ground and disappeared. All the people present suddenly felt sick with a sharp pain in their stomachs. The elastic blood duct snapped back to the west.[6]

Thus was severed forever the connection between the Warao on earth and the *Hoebo* at the end of the world in the west. Hoebo's soul

[6] A remarkable parallel to this concept was recorded by Tozzer (1907, 153) among the Maya of Southern Mexico: "According to the information obtained from the Mayas in the vicinity of Valladolid, this world is now in the fourth period of its existence. In the first ep-

still remains above the village, a short distance in a westerly direction from the zenith. But the umbilicus has gone, and from the zenith to the *Hoebo* there now leads only a black road. This path is taken by the *hoarotu* shamans who have to carry their human victims along it to the west in order to feed the hearts and livers to the Supreme *Hoa* and the bodies to the *hoarao* who inhabit the *Hoebo*. The victim is always carried head down, dangling at the *hoarotu*'s back from his knees, in order to express extreme mockery of and ridicule for the victim. *Hoarotu* dislike having to kill their fellowmen with magic arrows. But what would become of humankind if they stopped providing human blood and flesh for the Supreme *Hoa* and the *hoarao* in the western world of darkness? All would come to an end, so there must be *hoarotu* shamans who provide this service.

THE *HOA* SNARE OF TOBACCO SMOKE

To become a *hoarotu* shaman, a young man has to submit to severe initiatory ordeals. He feels bitterness within himself for a long time before he finally decides to ask an accomplished *hoarotu* to teach him how to make malevolent *hoa* magic and how to cure it. If accepted, the novice is taken by the master to a small hut in the forest, where the two men remain secluded for five days. Smoking incessantly, the candidate waits to be taken to the zenith to visit the *Hoebo*. But first he must learn the many *hoa* songs—one kind to cause sickness, another

---

och there lived the Saiyamwinkoob, the Adjustors. These composed the primitive race of Yucatan. They were dwarfs and were the ones who built the ruins. The work was all done in darkness before there was any sun. As soon as the sun appeared, these people turned to stone.... It was at this period that there was a road suspended in the sky, stretching from Tuloom and Coba to Chichen Itza and Uxmal. The Pathway was called *kusansum* or *sabke* (white road). It was in the nature of a large rope (*sum*) supposed to be living (*kusan*) and in the middle flowed blood. It was by this rope that the food was sent to the ancient rulers who lived in the structures now in ruins. For some reason this rope was cut, the blood flowed out, and the rope vanished forever."

It may also be noted that in the Maya area and elsewhere in ancient Mexico the Scarlet Macaw is the Sun Bird, a concept that seems to survive in attenuated form in sacred mushroom rituals of Oaxaca, for which the Scarlet Macaw feathers are considered indispensable. Both the *wishiratu*-temple-idol complex and the *hoa* complex of the Warao are in fact strongly reminiscent of Mesoamerican religion and ritual. In the context of this chapter it is impossible to include an analytical discussion of these interesting and, from an ethnographical point of view, puzzling parallels. (Commentary by Peter T. Furst.)

to cure it. Finally the master lights a long cigar, turns it around with the fire in his mouth, and blows into it. Now the cigar contains two *hoa* spirits ready to enter the body of the apprentice and become his "sons." The master hands the *hoa* cigar to the apprentice, and one after the other the two *hoa* tear violently into his body. The pain is excruciating. Now comes the first test: Do the *hoa* want to accept him as their father? Has he kept his body strong? Will he be a good provider?

If he proves acceptable to them, the two *hoa* sons remain in the young man's breast. While he continues to sing the *hoa* songs, he experiences increasing pressure at the base of the sternum, where his *kaidoko*, the *hoarotu*'s snare of tobacco smoke, begins to grow. From now on, the *kaidoko* tendrils will snake from the corners of his mouth each time he begins to chant or to speak ritually with a loud voice. To increase the effective length of his *kaidoko*, the *hoarotu* novice has to fast and smoke incessantly for approximately a month. During this period he is repeatedly asked by his teacher, "Did anything happen to you last night?"

Finally one night something does happen. In his ecstatic dream state induced by tobacco, the novice meets a spirit who beats him across the neck with a heavy club.

"I felt as if I were dead," reports the novice. "But I did not die." His teacher is very pleased with this dream.

A second dream follows. This time the murderous spirit kills the novice and places him in a hollowed-out tree.[7]

"But I was not really dead," explains the novice. "I was lying there in my coffin when I discovered a small hole in the palm-leaf wrapping. Through that hole I escaped."

Then the novice *hoarotu* has a third dream. This time the demon leads him to a human cadaver. "Eat this," he commands. But the novice finds it repulsive and impossible to swallow the piece of human flesh he takes to his lips. The demon proffers a cup of human blood but the novice is revolted by it also. He lifts the blood to his lips, but he cannot bring himself to drink it. The master *hoarotu* is also pleased with this dream.

---

[7] Warao traditionally bury their dead in dugout canoes or hollowed-out tree trunks.

"You will never die," he tells the agitated novice. "You will live forever."

Finally the novice has a fourth dream, but sometimes weeks pass before he embarks on it. His body is so emaciated that he can hardly move or perform the most essential functions. He is truly near death. In his trance the demonic spirit appears once more to lead him to his grave, which this time is made of stone slabs. Inside it is very cold and pitch black. The foul stench of decay and putrefaction is nearly unbearable. The novice feels like fainting and is terrified that he might wake up—because if that happens he really will die and remain in his grave. Day breaks and with the rising sun he discovers a crack between the stone slabs that cage him. Again he makes his escape.

The master *hoarotu* is pleased. He calls for his wife, who feeds the novice slowly and patiently to bring him back to life. The community has a new *hoarotu*, who will handle the *hoarao* of the west prudently, propitiate them, and provide them with sacrifices only when absolutely necessary.

The *kaidoko* snare of a powerful *hoarotu* is infinite. The two front ends emerge slowly from the corners of his mouth. First they appear as short white tendrils, but they continue to grow and to travel toward their victim.[8] Invisibly they wind themselves around his neck and begin to weaken him by strangulation. The Indian falls ill. When he has become sufficiently debilitated, the *hoarotu* prepares to kill him, so that his organs and his body may be fed to the spirits of the west.

---

[8] According to an editorial comment by Peter T. Furst, *kaidoko*-like tendrils also appear in the ceremonial art of the Maya, where they are identified as characteristics of the Sun God, and in Veracruz. Earlier still they appear on certain Olmec face masks, such as one, believed to date to a Late Olmec period, in the Peabody Museum at Harvard. Here the tendrils in the corners of the mouth are associated with a triangular toothlike projection in the center of the upper jaw. This same association is found on certain tall cylinders depicting the Sun God of the Night from the Classic Maya site of Palenque, Chiapas. Michael D. Coe, in a letter, points out that one of the Maya names for the sun deity is *Kinich Kakmoo*, literally "Sun-Eyed Fire" (i.e., Scarlet Macaw). Is the triangular projection perhaps a stylized frontal view of the macaw's beak? If so, it would strengthen the correspondence between the Warao and the Maya. Long ribbonlike tendrils are also associated with the Maya bat. Barthel (1966) discusses the composite Maya glyph *"Schleifen-Fledermaus"* (ribbon or tendril bat) in connection with an anthropomorphic bat demon depicted in a Chama-style Classic Maya cylinder vase. Long tendrils emerge from his mouth. Barthel suggests that glyphs associated with this supernatural being may signify drilling or boring into or sucking from the head, reminiscent of the function of the *kaidoko* in Warao shamanism. The Maya associated the bat with the East (the rising sun) and death, and Barthel suggests that it may have been conceptually linked by them with the Scarlet Macaw, the Sun Bird of the West.

"*Miana warao akuamo saba*," he sings. "Dim-visioned, it is going for a Warao's head!"

He smokes six long cigars while singing, and with the final word of his chant he puffs out a cloud of smoke and pulls the snare shut. It takes the entire next day for the *kaidoko* to contract and completely return to the breast of the *hoarotu*. Then, during the night, the sorcerer smokes again and throws the (living) soul of the victim over his shoulder to carry it to the zenith and from there to the *Hoebo* in the west. Here the soul is clubbed to death, bled, and dismembered.

It is impossible for a *hoarotu* not to kill. For example, when the two *hoa* "sons" who live in his breast approach him in his dream and beg for food, he can delay and propitiate them at least four times with tobacco smoke and moriche palm starch. But when they come a fifth time and demand their proper food—human blood—he can no longer turn them away unsatisfied.

The following day he goes alone into the forest. In complete solitude he sits down on a log and lights a cigar. The cigar contains his *hoa* sons. While smoking, he chants his *Miana* song, and as he does so the ends of his *kaidoko* snare of tobacco smoke slowly begin to emerge from the corners of his mouth. The *kaidoko* travels toward its victim, be he near or far, and when it arrives at its destination the *hoarotu* pulls heavily at his cigar, turns it around, and, holding the fire in his closed mouth, blows into it. Out come ribbons of smoke, and these now transport the *hoa* arrow over the treetops to the intended sacrifice. The magic arrow enters below the rib cage and searches for the heart.[9] And, at the instant the *kaidoko* snare of smoke closes, the *hoa* enters the heart to kill.

It is excruciatingly painful when the *hoa* enters the chest of the victim. And people are well aware of what is going on. They have observed the *hoarotu* depart alone for the forest. So, when someone in the village or in a nearby community starts complaining of a sharp pain in his breast and falls ill, he, like everyone else, knows why.

Only a friendly *hoarotu* can prevent death when a person has been struck by *hoa*. His *hoa* sons know all their fellow *hoa*. He begins to smoke and sing the curing chants, and as soon as he divines the nature

---

[9] Reminiscent of the flint knife with which the Aztec priests opened the breast of the sacrificial victim in order to tear out his heart, which, like the blood, organs, and bodies of *hoa* victims, was fed to the gods to give them strength.

of the illness-causing *hoa* (e.g., the *hoa* of a particular species of tree, an animal, or the like), his own *kaidoko* snare of tobacco smoke pries it loose from the victim. The intrusive sickness-causing object jumps into the massaging hand of the curer who blows it into the forest in a puff of tobacco smoke. This action effects the cure.

Some *hoarotu* "kill" a person each time their *hoa* "sons" come and ask for flesh and blood. This kind of *hoarotu* kills more people than he cures. Because other *hoarotu* are almost constantly occupied with curing victims of *hoa* magic, however, a kind of equilibrium between negative and positive forces is established. In some communities there is nearly perpetual competition between *hoarotu* that kill and others that cure. A village is indeed lucky if it can rely on a powerful *hoarotu* who knows how to keep the Scarlet Macaw and his spirits of the west appeased with a minimum of sacrifices, while maintaining the strength of his own group by saving his fellows from the *hoa* snare of malevolent *hoarotu*.

Throughout their lifetime *hoarotu* shamans travel often to the *Hoebo* in the west, always using tobacco as their means of ecstasy. They too have a house in the otherworld in which they will dwell forever after death. But while the house of the *bahanarotu* is in the east, the land of light, that of the *hoarotu* is in the west, the realm of darkness.

As far as I have been able to determine, tobacco is the only psychotropic substance available to the three kinds of Warao shamans. The *caraña* resin employed by the *wishiratu*, and to some extent also by the *bahanarotu*, seems to lack hallucinogenic properties. All three supernatural practitioners—*wishiratu*, *bahanarotu*, and *hoarotu*—employ tobacco extensively to put themselves into ecstatic trances. They achieve such states exclusively by smoking, rather than by other routes of ingestion, as do novice shamans in some other Indian groups (Wilbert 1987).

It will have become apparent that the various forms of shamanism practiced today by the Warao with the aid of tobacco occupy a central position in tribal culture. They seem to me to constitute true survivals of a more ancient shamanistic stratum with roots in Mesolithic and even Paleolithic Asia, introduced into the Americas 30,000 to 40,000 or even more years ago. Although attenuated and certainly overlaid with more recent features, including some characteristic of more advanced social systems in Mesoamerica and western South America, they seem to belong to what some anthropologists, including La Barre, Furst, M. D. Coe, and myself, have come to see as an archaic shamanistic substratum underlying, and to some extent uniting, all or most aboriginal American Indian cultures.

Chapter Five

The Calabash of Ruffled Feathers

The origin of the shaman's sacred rattle of the Warao Indians of Venezuela goes back to the legendary "first times," when an ancestral shaman ascended to the sky to visit the great spirit of the south, one of the four sacred quarters of the Warao universe. In the course of this primordial encounter, the Indian was given the first *hebumataro*, literally, "spirit calabash," the sacred medium of communication with the supernatural. He was also taught how to fashion it from the fruit of the calabash tree, so that he and his kin might never lose contact with the gods of the north, the south, the east, and the sacred center.

Ever since, the *hebumataro* rattle has been the hallmark of the *wishiratu*, "Master of Pain," the shaman-priest of the Warao. For the people as a whole it has been the center of their universe and the hub of the world axis. In the shaman's hands, especially in the rituals of curing, the rattle summons the lesser and greater spirits, including the gods of the cardinal and intercardinal points, the single exception being the god who resides in the west and who is outside the *wishiratu*'s sphere.

To the Warao, the fruit of the calabash tree, *Cresentia cujete*, from which the sacred rattle is made, is a "head," that is, the seat of the life force of a supernatural being, a great *hebu* of ancient times. One is at once reminded of an old Maya tradition of the origin of the calabash tree and the sacred shamanic rattle that came to be fashioned from its fruit. As recounted in the Popol Vuh, the sacred book of the Quiche Maya of highland Guatemala, the *Cresentia cujete* tree bore no fruit until the Lords of Xibalba, the Maya underworld, cut off the head of Hun-Hunahpu, 1 Hunter, one of two supernatural hero brothers whom they had defeated in a sacred ballgame, and placed it in the tree's branches. The tree was immediately covered with round calabashes, among them the dead hero's head. Ever since, says the Maya tradition, the fruit has been called "head of Hunahpu."[1]

As supernaturally sanctioned in primordial times, the fruit of the calabash tree must be large and perfectly ellipsoidal to qualify as the Warao shaman's rattle. The harvesting and all the work, of course, must be done by the shaman himself; the touch of anyone else, then or later, would be an act of desecration, fraught with extreme danger not only to the shaman but to the entire community. (In the Maya story, the Lords of Xibalba forbid anyone to touch the fruit or even to approach the tree.)

After selecting and taking the proper fruit from the tree, the shaman grinds off the woody pericarp and, through holes he carves at either end, removes the seeds and the spongy interior. Next he cuts four narrow slits on opposite sides of the wall, one juxtaposed pair is longitudinal and the other is transversal. These slits are called the mouths of the head of the *hebumataro* rattle. Frequently the "mouths" are bordered by bands of triangular or rectangular designs, representing its teeth. Some rattles are also decorated with symbols representing humans, animals (especially insects), and the sun.

Then the shaman blows tobacco smoke impregnated with a fragrant resin over scores of small quartz crystals and places them one by one in the hollowed-out gourd, invoking for each a particular ancestral spirit believed by the Warao to be embodied in the stone. These quartz crystals are his familiar spirits who assist him in curing and other ritual endeavors; indeed, he refers to them as his "family." Obviously, the larger the number of crystalline spirits, the more potent the instrument. It should be noted that stones of any kind, and especially quartz, are hard to come by in the wooded swamplands and open watercourses that are a large part of the Warao environment.

Once his spirit family is assembled inside the "head" of the rattle, the shaman inserts a central shaft through the openings at either end of the fruit. The handle is called the rattle's "leg," but the insertion is actually a symbolic union of male and female symbols. And the union, in turn, is related to the fertilizing power believed to adhere to the

---

[1] I am grateful to Dr. Peter T. Furst, the original editor of this article, for drawing my attention to the various Popol Vuh parallels mentioned herein.

completed instrument. (Here there is yet another contact point with the Maya tradition, for the calabash tree of the Popol Vuh is barren until the divine hero's head is placed in its branches. Only through the head's magical presence does the tree become covered with fruit. This aspect of fertility is further emphasized by the fact that the calabash skull of 1 Hunter impregnates the daughter of Blood Chief, one of the lords of the Maya underworld, with his saliva as she stands beneath the tree.) As a final act the Warao shaman decorates the tip of the rattle shaft with a long band of bird feathers, which become its "hair." Warao rattles have parrot feathers, and the proper hair of a *hebumataro* rattle consists of the red median tail feathers plucked from a live *cotorra* (*Psittacidae*).

Established priest-shamans of the Warao own two sacred rattles. The one destined for ordinary shamanic use and for most curing rituals is less elaborate. The other is the real seat of sacred powers, fashioned with special care and richly decorated with crisp plumage. It is reserved for the most solemn occasions, such as the annual festival celebrating the harvest of wild vegetable foods, especially the nourishing food prepared from the starchy pulp of the moriche palm. The Indians also call this rattle *marimataro*, Calabash of Ruffled Feathers. "The gods feel secure in the presence of this sacred instrument," I was told. For this reason, the two supernatural jaguar helpers of the priest-shaman, who guard the entrance to the Warao community's temple hut and who have their counterparts far to the west in Andean Colombia and elsewhere in the Andes, keep careful watch over the rattle and the sacred quartz crystals within its walls.

THE RATTLE AS INSTRUMENT OF FIRE

One important purpose for which the sacred rattle is indispensable as the instrument of direct communication with the supernaturals is to serve as a healing wand for certain illnesses. In this context, fire, universally recognized as an element that both purifies and reinvigorates, is the main agent enabling the rattle to function as healer.

The word *wishiratu*, designating the Warao priest-shaman, translates literally as Master of Pain. When the shaman speaks of *wishi*, however, he is referring specifically to pain caused by poison, which the Warao believe to contain fire. Thus, the shaman's name can also be read as

Fig. 5.1.

Warao priest-shaman's Rattles of Ruffled Feathers and his secondary rattles in their baskets inside the sanctuary. (Photo Johannes Wilbert)

Master of Fire, an attribute virtually universal in shamanism all over the world. It also explains the magical powers and sorcery so often associated with smiths and the forging of iron and other metals in the traditional world. As masters of fire, the priest-shamans of the Warao cure only *hebu* sicknesses. A *hebu*-afflicted person suffers from heat, because *hebu*-spirits, related to the gods of the cardinal points, are essentially heat and light. As soon as they invade a human body the individual falls sick with a generalized sensation of overwhelming heat. As the noun *hebu* carries the meaning of heat and fever, the sacred *hebumataro* rattle becomes a heat or a fire calabash. In the hands of the Master of Fire, the shaman, it attacks the pathogenic heat of the patient through sympathetic magic; that is, it fights fire with fire.

The fire associations of the sacred rattle, however, far transcend mere semantic symbolism. For one thing, the central staff of the rattle— its leg and, in another dimension, the axis of the universe itself—is carved of *himaheru* wood. This species is employed exclusively by the priest-shaman as the source of the fire sticks he uses to kindle the virgin fire for his brazier and to light the long ritual cigars whose smoke he "eats" in order to attain a state of ecstatic trance. As with fire-containing poison, fire is believed actually to be burning within this wood which, as laboratory tests have proved, has an unusually low flash point.

Closely related to this attribute, and indeed central to the fire symbolism of the sacred rattle, are the quartz crystals, embodiments of the spirit-helpers of the shaman as he seeks to divine the origin of a *hebu* sickness and effects its cure. Like all Warao, the patient, lying prostrate at night in his hammock under the physical and metaphysical ministrations of the shaman as curer, is of course well aware of the fire symbolism connected with both shaman and rattle. How much more profound must be the effect on his fevered mind, and on his kinfolk who attend the healing seance, when the rattle actually begins to emit a shower of glowing sparks as it whirls ever more rapidly in the shaman's hand to summon the denizens of the spirit world to his assistance! The actual process by which this magic fire is produced has been analyzed by David Weide of the University of California, Los Angeles (pers. comm.): through rapid rotation and shaking, the pebbles within the calabash shave off fine meal from the highly combustible wood of the central shaft. These particles ignite in the heat generated by the whirling crystals and fly out as glowing sparks through the rattle's four mouths. But the technology hardly matters. What counts is the visible validation of the shaman's attribute as master of fire and of his rattle's power as instrument of fire, as both purifier and healer.

It is from this essential role in curing that the rattle also derives yet another name, *kanobo arose*, literally, "wand of *kanobo* (supreme spirit or god)." After localizing the intrusive supernatural pathogen through massaging, blowing of tobacco smoke, and chanting, the shaman brings the heavy instrument down to the affected area as though he were swinging a club. After he has done so three or four times, the helping spirits inside the rattle are believed to have vanquished and expelled the spirits of fever.

THE FEEDING OF THE RATTLE AND OF THE GODS

Basic to Warao religion—and also to the worldview of the ancient civilizations of the New World—is the conviction that humanity must give sustenance to the gods of the cardinal points if they in turn are to feed and protect humans. If neglected, the gods appear to the priest-shaman in his dreams to reprimand him for causing them to suffer starvation and cold. To prevent their wrath, which typically expresses itself in the death of children, the shaman hurries to the sanctuary, passes the jaguar sentries, and takes the sacred rattle from its special basket in order to converse with it and assuage the angry supernaturals. Some sanctuaries also contain an especially sacred stone, kept in a sanctified basket, which represents to the Indians the son of either the cardinal god of the north, the east, or the south. When such a spirit is present, the priest-shaman also communicates with it.

Seating himself on his shaman's box or bench, the *wishiratu* lights one of the many long cigars that are kept in the temple hut, holds the rattle in front of him with both hands, and blows smoke into its four mouth slits. The cigars consist of several plugs of a powerful black tobacco within a wrapping from the epidermis of the leafstalk of the manaca palm. It is by smoking a number of such cigars that Warao shamans attain the ecstatic trances that other South American Indians induce with such hallucinogenic preparations as *yopo* and *ebena* snuff (made variously from the *Anadenanthera peregrina* and *Virola* trees), *yage* (*Banisteriopsis caapi*), and others. In time, the interior of the "head" of the Warao rattle is filled with tobacco smoke and begins to "awaken." The shaman shakes it three times up and down and then

Fɪɢ. 5.2.

Healing with the sacred rattle. (Photo courtesy Peter T. Furst)

starts to rotate it horizontally. By now the rattle is fully awake and ready to serve as a medium of communication between the shaman and the gods. The shaman asks which of them it was that appeared in his dream, implores them to remain tranquil as he and his people will continue to feed them adequately, and assures them that there is no need to become upset and remind the people of their duty by killing their children.

After this monologue has been rendered in a long chant to the accompaniment of the rattle, the shaman proceeds to feed tobacco smoke—their proper nourishment—to the gods and their families and to the ancestral shamans who reside with the gods, until they express themselves as completely satisfied.

THE SACRED CENTER AND THE *AXIS MUNDI*

Next to the sacred spirit-stone which only a few Warao communities possess, it is the Calabash of Ruffled Feathers that is the vital focus of Warao shamanism. Where there is no sacred stone, the sanctity of the rattle is second to none. Whoever offends this vital instrument of communication with the supernatural is guilty of a monumental sacrilege, because, as mentioned, such an act places not only his own life but that of the whole community in the gravest danger. Bereft of its sacred rattle, the society would be isolated from the vital supernatural sphere, while the offended crystals would conjure up a cataclysmic epidemic that would surely demand the lives of many, both young and old.

It is for this reason that the shaman keeps his rattle properly protected in a basket, either in the temple hut, on a platform in the eastern corner of his house, or under a makeshift roof of leaves in the forest. But wherever the rattle "sleeps," the crown of its head must always point to the east, with one pair of mouths facing up. In this way the community lives, works, and plays in complete confidence within the protective power of their rattle as the sacred center of the universe and the hub of the *axis mundi,* even when it is not activated by the shaman.

In fact, both old narratives and present beliefs about the fate of shamans after death make the concept of the rattle as *axis mundi* quite explicit. In ancient times, according to myth, a Warao shaman ascended to the zenith by means of his sacred rattle and became the God of the

Fig. 5.3.
The sanctuary where the sacred rattles are kept.
(Photo Johannes Wilbert)

Fig. 5.4.
Winikina priest-shaman with the Calabash of Ruffled Feathers.
(Photo courtesy Sociedad La Salle de Ciencias Naturales, Caracas)

Center of the World. From his celestial abode an invisible path leads straight down to earth. It is this vertical path, symbolized by the staff of the rattle, which Warao shamans frequent on their ecstatic tobacco-trance journeys to the upperworld.

When a *wishiratu* dies, his soul merges with the quartz crystal spirits inside the rattle and ascends to the center of the celestial dome in the form of light. On this final journey up the world axis, he carries nothing but a lighted cigar and his sacred rattle, which he holds vertically in front of him. From the zenith he travels like a shooting star, comet, or lightning bolt to the house of his particular patron deity, who resides either in the north, the east, or the south. Thus the sacred Rattle of Ruffled Feathers, held ritually like an *axis mundi* or world tree in an upright position by the ascending priest-shaman, marks the very center and axis of the cosmology and ideational universe of the Warao. In this way it serves as guarantor of both the physical and the metaphysical equilibrium, with its ancestral way of life and its traditional belief system still relatively intact.

Chapter Six

The House of the Swallow-Tailed Kite

HISTORICAL ANTECEDENTS

To the Western world the Warao Indians have been known as the inhabitants of the Orinoco Delta since the early decades of discovery. According to their own traditional history, however, the Warao date back to a remote era on the Orinoco plains, six or seven thousand years ago, when the island of Trinidad was still connected with the mainland. Judging from their overall culture, this claim of antiquity of occupation does seem justified. The Warao appear to be survivors of an ancient, once more widespread littoral tradition of South America.

As their self-denomination, Warao, meaning "Boat People," indicates, navigation has always formed an integral part of their coastal life-style. Specializing in the exploitation of hydrosere resources through foraging and palm-sago recovery, the Warao relied, until the middle of the twentieth century, on overseas trade to supplement their enchorial commodities. Their social organization, featuring uxorilocal polygynous bands and endogamous subtribes as the largest social aggregates, appears to be of old standing and consistent with the littoral tradition. Given so much cultural continuity in their technological and socioeconomic systems, it is not surprising to find that Warao ideology, so deeply rooted in the history and the nature of their homeland, is most likely the product of generations of autochthonous thought and the wisdom accumulated through contact with Caribbean and Amazonian partners.

Survival of the Warao as a tribal society along the exposed Caribbean seaboard and at the estuary of a major river was endangered throughout their long history by a series of critical imperilments. Among the most stressful was the invasion of their habitat, some four thousand years ago, by expansionist tribes that descended the Orinoco in search of arable floodplains. As the Warao retreated into the tidal swamplands, however, territorial encroachment turned out to be only the lesser symptom of the crisis. A far more serious threat to their existence derived from the presence among the invaders of the "Red Faces" who cannibalized the men among their enemies and carried off the women and children either to swell their own society or to be sold into slavery. The trauma sustained at the hands of so devastating an adversary over hundreds and possibly thousands of years reverberates ruefully through Warao oral lore, and the high status conceded reproductive women in this society is commensurate with their demographic importance over men.

Beginning with the Columbian voyages, Warao survival became threatened by still another formidable enemy in the guise of Old World pestilential disease (Wilbert 1983). Immigrants from Europe, Africa, Asia, and Indonesia came to populate the islands and the areas surrounding the Orinoco Delta, where Warao traders contracted infectious disease that they carried back to their homes. Indigenous populations everywhere along the lower Orinoco were decimated by repeated pandemics of various kinds (Morey 1979). Also from the Warao we know of fulminating outbreaks that destroyed entire bands and of instances when two-thirds of the child population of certain local groups fell victim to a single epidemic attack. The awesome power of such hitherto unknown evil so convinced the Indians of the supernatural origin of pestilence that they came to envision the various diseases as pathogenic arrows in the hands of their directional gods. Similarly, the baneful phenomenon of cannibalism, so otherworldly to the Warao, was associated with werejaguars and the grim lord of the underworld. With cannibals and abductors of women, pestilence, and oppressive gods lurking above and about them, the world of the Warao turned into a landscape of dread. No wonder so many of their myths and rituals reveal a preoccupation with fertility and fecundity and the concept of survival through sexual procreation. In fact, one of the major types of Warao shamanism, *bahana*, concentrates specifically on human reproduction and its attendant physiological, psychological, and social concerns.[1]

---

[1] The bulk of information on *bahana* shamanism has been collected intermittently since 1954 on numerous field trips. I concentrated my research on the Winikina-Warao of the central delta where my principal informant, Sr. Antonio Lorenzano, happens to be a *bahanarotu*.

The Origin Myth of *Bahana*

The Warao possess a rich corpus of oral literature (Wilbert 1970). They distinguish between three different genres of narrative: *dehe nobo*, or "old stories"; *anamonina*, or stories of "metamorphosis"; and shamanic lore. Stories in the first two genres, which are secular in nature, are narrated whenever it is opportune to do so. Shamanic lore, a genre pertaining to ritual, is spoken or chanted by religious practitioners during public ceremonies and shamanic initiations. Shamanic lore, therefore, is not as thoroughly in the public domain as the other two genres; rather, it forms part of the esoteric repertoire of the religious elite. Pertaining to the latter category, the origin myth of *bahana* is presented by a master shaman to a group of (preferably four) candidates in the seclusion of an initiation hut. What qualifies the narrative as a myth is its recounting of the dramatic events surrounding the origin of *bahana* shamanism by employing natural symbols and otherworldly objects and occurrences to convey the sacred message of *bahana* truth (see Cohen 1969, 337). In the process, Warao symbolism is revealed as a native art of thinking in images (Coomaraswamy 1935); and it is my intention to lead the reader through the seemingly bizarre and chaotic mythic imagery to an appreciation of the order established by the artistically creative myth-making mind of these Indians. The myth has three parts: the creation of the birthplace of *bahana*, the quest for

I have also studied with Manuel, the *bahanarotu* of the Arawabisi subtribe, who is known as a famous *daunonarima* (highest ranking *bahanarotu*). Additional information pertaining to the animals of the *bahana* complex has been collected over the past ten years by my Warao field assistant, Sr. Cesáreo Soto. He employed eleven informants originating from almost as many different settlements dispersed throughout the intermediate delta. At the time of recording, the informants were estimated to be between thirty-five and eighty years of age. The data collected by C. Soto were recorded in the Warao language; my own data, in Waraoan and Spanish.

I am very grateful to my colleagues Dr. Philip L. Newman and Dr. Gerardo Reichel-Dolmatoff for their helpful suggestions and constructive criticism, and to Dr. Alan Dundes for his manifold advice concerning the form and the content of this chapter. Dr. Floyd Lounsbury of Yale University discussed with me at length the application of the principles of similarity-contiguity to the analysis of myth. His insightful and generous assistance is especially acknowledged. Dr. Peter Rivière of Oxford University had several helpful conversations with me regarding the methodological implications of the model. Mr. Dany Chalfen was my research assistant for the project. A grant from the Ahmanson Foundation covered research expenses.

bahana power, and the origin of *bahana* shamanism. Rendered here in summary form, the myth details a sequence of eleven episodes.[2]

A. *Creation of the Birthplace of* Bahana

1. At the foot of the eastern world tree-mountain there is a hollow that contained two eggs. From the hollow emerged a youth, the son of the avian God of Origin. Upon leaving the cave the youth adopted the form of a swallow-tailed kite,[3] spread his wings, and pronounced his name, Mawari.[4] With his left wing he held a bow and two quivering arrows; with his right wing he shook a rattle. The plumes of his body rang out the new song of *bahana*.

2. Through the power of thought Mawari created an egg-shaped house northeast of the zenith. Made of tobacco smoke this "Cosmic Egg" looks like a cloud. The house is attached to the earth by rows of red and yellow flowers on the left side and two rows of blue and green flowers on the right side. Inside, the house is divided into upper and lower compartments. On the upper floor six rooms are arranged in a circle along the wall of the house. The doors of the four eastern rooms are black, red, yellow, and blue. Separated by an entrance, the rooms at the two extreme western ends of this open circle are white. A rectangular white-draped table stands in the middle of the floor. It is a game board with four square fields whose colors correspond to those of the eastern rooms. On each of the fields is a calabash cup containing a quartz pyramid (black field), a ball of white hair (red field), oval quartz pebbles (yellow field), and a puff of white tobacco smoke.

3. Mawari has three major and three minor avian companions with

---

[2] A shaman's personal account of the *bahana* appears in chapter four, but here it is necessary to give a brief summary of that account and to add further details to facilitate clarity and comprehension. Although closely following the original account, the wording here is my own.

[3] Known in Venezuela as *gavilán tijereta*: scissor-tailed kite (Waraoan: *hukonomana* or *hukono kahamana*).

[4] Hearing Mawari's name pronounced for the first time by a Warao shaman came as a surprise to me, inasmuch as the name is associated with Carib-speaking Indians. For the Waiwai, for instance, Mawari is the Creator (Fock 1963, 35–36). A discussion here of the related ethnohistorical question is not necessary; suffice it to say that the Warao have been a mobile seafaring nation for thousands of years and probably have assimilated cultural traits not only from the South American mainland, but also from Mesoamerica and the Caribbean as well.

whom he meets, but they do not live together.[5] To occupy his house Mawari invited four couples of insects: the black bees came to live in the black room, the wasps, in the red room, the termites, in the yellow room, and the blue bees, in the blue room. Teaching them the chant of *bahana*, Mawari ranked his new companions below him by assigning Black Bee the role of a chief and Wasp that of a constable; Termite and Blue Bee became the workers. A serpent carrying four colored plumes (white, yellow, blue, and green) on its head occupied the lower compartment of the house. All the inhabitants of the birthplace of *bahana* were changed into tobacco smoke.

4. Mawari placed his bow and arrows on the table and invited his insect companions to approach the game board and play a game of *bahana*. As they danced their way through their companions' fields, the game concluded each time with one of the dancers returning to his home base first. Then the serpent rose through a hole in the middle of the floor and erected itself high over the game board and the players. On the tip of its forked tongue it presented a glowing ball of white tobacco smoke while its plumes chimed a musical note like a bell. Afterward, the insects and the serpent retired to their quarters until the game began anew.

B. *Quest of* Bahana *Power*

5. After the ovoid house of tobacco smoke had been created, a human couple with unformed minds appeared at the center of the earth disk. Their four-year-old son, who unlike his parents was intelligent, reasoned that because the underworld was in the west there ought to be another place in the east. He fasted for four days, fell asleep, and, with the surging heat of a virgin fire that his father had lit beneath his hammock, his spirit ascended along the central world axis to the zenith. The voice of an invisible psychopomp guided him to the colorfully adorned bridge of tobacco smoke. Encouraged by his invisible guide, the boy walked across it and reached the portal of the oval House of Smoke.

---

[5] The three major avian companions of the Warao Creator-Bird are the brown pelican, *yoroa* (*Pelecanus occidentalis*); the laughing gull, *nabakabara* (*Larus atricilla*); and the toucan, *hari* or *hebu hari* (*Ramphastos tucanos*). The three minor companions are the wren, *bikaroana* (*Troglodytidae*); the greater ani, *keribitabu* (*Crotophaga major*); and the silver-beaked tanager, *sonson* (*Ramphocelus carbo*). My thanks to Dr. Thomas R. Howell of UCLA for his help in identifying shamanic birds.

6. The youth heard beautiful music and chanting coming from inside the house. As he was "pure and free of women," Mawari bade him enter and, in the presence of the four insect-companions, queried him as to which one of the items on the game table he wished to possess. Looking at the bow and arrows, the crystal, the hair, the pebbles, and the puff of tobacco smoke, the boy demanded all of them, and for that decision Mawari judged him to be wise. Desirous of learning also the song of *bahana*, the youth was presented to the serpent from beneath the floor, who, with the colorful feathers chiming on its head, erected itself above the boy. When the plumed serpent produced the glowing ball on the tip of its tongue, the youth was filled with intuitive understanding of the ways of *bahana*.

7. Returning from his initiatory journey the boy woke up. For four days he remained in a deathlike trance and refused to ingest anything but tobacco. Ten couples of each of the four insect people and their children appeared around his house, and the youth married a beautiful bee girl. On the fifth day he began to radiate a halo, and four dark spots appeared in the palms of his hands and at the base of each of his fingers. From there, through the length of each arm, opened a lumen that reached the four insect spirits lodged in his breast: Elder Brother Black Bee and Younger Brother Wasp had settled on his right side, Elder Brother Termite and Younger Brother Blue Bee, on his left. The spirit children were feeble and the youth kept nourishing them with tobacco smoke by smoking tubes filled with four wads of tobacco, one for each of the insects. He also abstained from sleeping with his wife until he was four-times-four years old; otherwise the power of *bahana* would have left him.

8. The time then arrived for the young shaman's four insect-"sons" to be introduced to their mother, which the young shaman did by inserting only the head of his penis into his bee-wife's vagina. The insect sons saw their mother and liked her. Also, the mother saw her four white-smoke sons in a dream and found them pleasing. On succeeding occasions the *bahanarotu* penetrated his wife further and deeper; they became the first *bahana* family, and the insect people living around them returned to the House of Smoke in the zenith. The rising smoke from the cigar of the *bahana* shaman maintained a path of communication between the center of the earth disk and the middle of the sky vault above.

9. Upon the death of his parents the *bahana* shaman and his wife began to fast, and after eight days of incessant smoking the two ascended to the House of Smoke. When the bee-woman entered, Mawari suffered a seizure in her presence. She transformed herself into a frigate bird, rustled her wings, and, blowing over his rigid body, soothed Mawari with her beak and her feathers. The Supreme *Bahana* recovered and invited the frigate to stay in his house as the Mother of Seizures.

C. Origin of Bahana *Shamanism*

10. As time went by many people appeared on earth, and the young shaman wanted them to have *bahana* power. He rolled two projectiles, Blue Bee's puff of smoke and Termite's quartz pebbles, into a cigar and aimed them at the breast of a young man whom he had chosen to receive the spirits. Smoke was to function on his right side as the elder brother and Pebbles as the younger on his left. The young man fell over from the impact of the spirits' arrival. They entered his body, but when the youth displayed his *bahana* weapons and rattle his people vanished, turned into River Crab people, and became the first Masters of Earth.

11. Finally the Warao began to populate the center of the earth. Again the *bahana* shaman shot the same two kinds of projectiles into a young man's breast. He sustained the impact and learned about the bridge and the House of Smoke in the sky. Up there he also learned how to preserve his spirit sons and how to use them. Even though nowadays *bahana* power on earth is not as potent as it might have been if the primordial shamans had been strong enough to be inhabited by four instead of only two insect-companions, it has, nevertheless, continued to exist among the Warao to the present day.

BAHANA IMAGERY

The introductory episode of the *bahana* myth presents two symbolically vigorous images: the World Pillar and the Heraldic Raptor.

THE WORLD PILLAR

According to their cosmology, the Warao imagine the world ocean surrounding the terrestrial disk to be bounded by a horizonal mountain range (fig. 6.1). Towering high above earth and sea is a bell-shaped celestial vault which at the cardinal, intercardinal, and solstitial points rests on gigantic world pillars. These sky braces, in turn, are pictured as enormous petrified tree stumps whose flat tops and cavernous interiors serve as portentous abodes for supernaturals and ancestral spirits. The moss covering the base of the eastern world tree-mountain unfolds as impenetrably dense forest and hides the hollow that contains the two eggs of the sun god.

According to modern geography the eastern world tree-mountain and birthplace of *bahana* would have to rise from the Atlantic Ocean; the prototype of the columnar tree exists, however, beyond the southern border of Waraoland in the form of the central Guianan *tepui. Tepuis* are flat-topped table mountains of red sandstone and conglomerates that jut out of the peneplain to altitudes of eight thousand feet. Sheer-cliffed

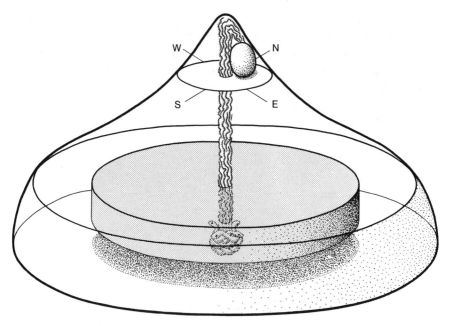

FIG. 6.1.

Diagram of Warao cosmology. The earth's disk is surrounded by water and penetrated by the *axis mundi*. A four-headed earth-monster is wound around the foot of the axis. The house of the swallow-tailed kite is attached to the top of the world axis by means of a bridge of ropes of tobacco smoke. (Drawing courtesy W. Patrick Finnerty)

and scarred with vertical folds and gullies, these truncated mountains appear exactly as described in Warao mythology. They are surrounded by dense piedmont vegetation, their rugged tops are almost daily shrouded in clouds, and an endogenous flora and fauna, unknown below, contributes to their numinous otherworldliness. Traditional history says that Warao shamans of old ventured into the vicinity of the southern cosmic mountain to seek the god's protection. It also seems likely that the image of the sky-bearing world pillar of Warao cosmology is directly or indirectly inspired by the natural model of the *tepui*.

THE HERALDIC RAPTOR

The Heraldic Raptor of the introductory episode is a bird-demiurge in the guise of the swallow-tailed kite (*Elanoides forficatus*). Epiphany of the God of Origin, he represents the plenipotent sun of the zenith and acts with creative force to establish the new order of *bahana* shamanism. As in the Peruvian *montaña*, parts of Amazonia, and Guiana, the swallow-tailed kite is a shamanic tutelary spirit of highest rank (Matthäi 1977, 106–7), and its appearance in the myth as a creator of decisive powers evokes self-evident confirmation in those familiar with the bird and its ways.

The swallow-tailed kite is a medium-sized bird with long and backward-pointing wings and a long and deeply forked tail. Its head, underparts, and wing linings are white like the sun at noon, and its beak, back, wings, and tail are black. It has red-brown eyes, light blue feet, and yellowish talons; its interscapular region is a glossy green or purplish.[6]

The Warao see in the swallow-tailed kite a model for the persistent archer on the hunt. The bird "represents the ultimate perfection of graceful and sustained flight. . . . Its only rival would be the Frigate bird" (Brown and Amadon 1968, 220–30). The kite, which feeds on the wing, seldom alights. Patiently circling high above the land, it quarters the ground for lizards, frogs, tree snakes, birds' nests, and hives of Hymenoptera before swooping down on its target with lightning

---

[6] The kite's colors (black, red, yellow, green, and blue), albeit in different sets, are repeated in the flowers, the rooms, the gambling table, and the plumes on the serpent as the Creator-Bird's signature.

speed. Devastating pirate that it is, the kite tears out entire birds' nests in flight, demolishes them, and feeds on eggs and brood.

THE PRIMORDIAL ARCHER

The Heraldic Raptor is depicted in the myth as the primordial archer and rattler whose paraphernalia are emblematic of the kite's high-altitude stalking and its ability to strike. As for the Primordial Archer, he is believed to be capable of hurling unerring projectiles. For that reason his agent, the *bahana* shaman, is also referred to as a *hata-buarotu* (archer).

The kite's reputation as an archer derives from its nesting behavior. During the mating season, with spectacular aerial acrobatics, the swallow-tailed kite builds its aerie at the top of green trees. While in flight he breaks off dead twigs for nesting material; those that are too large or otherwise unsuitable are dropped from the sky to the ground.

Bahana shamans, considering these sticks to be the arrows of the Primordial Archer, claim to engage the bird in shooting duels. It is said that after the shaman tosses a light arrow of temiche petiole into the air, the kite intercepts the missile in midair (in sea-gull fashion) and then returns it to his challenger below. Whoever, bird or man, fails to catch the arrow forfeits his life, dying a sudden death.

The bow and arrow have a distinctly male connotation in Warao mentality. Women are reluctant to touch the weapon so as not to render the bowstring flaccid and the arrow aimless. Young girls refrain from manipulating a bow and arrow for fear that they may irritate their clitorides and make them grow large. But in the hands of the hunter, especially in those of the solar archer, the bow and arrow connotes generative prowess as expressed by the verb *hatakitani*, which has two meanings: "to shoot with bow and arrow" and "to copulate."

The swallow-tailed kite strikes its prey, such as bees, wasps, and flying termites, not with its beak but with a sudden thrust of one claw or the other. Similarly, the shaman dispatches his magic arrow through an opening in the palm of each hand. In his projectile shooting capacity the *bahana* shaman is also known as *mohokarotu*, "he who discharges through the hand."

Other missiles associated with the Primordial Archer and his shaman are quartz pebbles. For instance, parents call their children inside when they see the kite circling overhead; the bird is said to carry a pebble in its beak which it shoots at children playing, and especially at those eating in the open. Similarly, top-ranking *bahana* shamans are capable of launching their quartz pellets accompanied by an effigy of their avian master. A shaman of this elevated status is referred to as *daunonarima*, "Father of the Wooden Mannequin."

The effigy is a 12-centimeter-high and 2-centimeter-thick sculpture in the round, fashioned either in the stylized form of the kite's head and neck or in a naturalistic rendering of an adolescent boy. The anthropomorphic figure wears a neckband to which two parrot feathers (*Pionus* sp.) are attached as wings (Wilbert 1975, 67–78; Wilbert 1979). When activated by the tobacco smoke-blowing shaman, the mannequin becomes as frenziedly aggressive as the swallow-tailed kite it represents or as the estrous *Pionus* parrot. The shaman sends it forth to annihilate the entire child population of a band. It takes "to the wing," closely following behind three quartz pebbles that fly in a triangular formation, emulating the kite. Hovering over the village with the sound of a strong wind, the preying foursome selects its victims, swoops down, and kills the children one by one. Even adults succumb to the siege, which often lasts for days; just as the kite may devastate a nest of birds, so may its effigy lay waste a settlement in the fashion of epidemics that ravage Waraoland.

The Warao listener to the myth also associates the kite's bow and arrow with the "new song" of *bahana* shamanism. Recall that the journeying novice, upon approaching the oval house in the sky, became fascinated by the music making inside the house where the Creator-Bird played his musical bow. In a similar fashion the Warao hunter uses his bow and arrow as a lure to attract his prey. Holding the bow with his left hand, his left arm outstretched horizontally and pointing away from him, he takes the free end of the bow between his teeth while his right hand taps the string with an arrow to produce a series of twanging sounds. When the animal is within shooting range, the hunter quickly converts the musical bow into a deadly weapon and lets the arrow fly. As will later become clear, this dual function of the bow and arrow as a stalking and striking device makes it a highly appropriate metaphor of the nature of the swallow-tailed kite and of the Heraldic Raptor's order of *bahana*.

Finally, it merits pointing out that within the shamanic context of the myth the kite's bow and arrow becomes a symbol of magical flight and transcendence. Replacing the shamanic drum of other regions, it attracts a sorcerer's pathogens like game. But it also prepares, through music and dance, the trance experience of the shaman's arrowlike flight across the celestial bridge, prefigured in the bow, to the sky-house of *bahana*.

THE PRIMORDIAL RATTLER

Turning now to the image of the Primordial Rattler, it is important to point out that his is a dancing rattle (*habi sanuka*) and not the large ritual rattle (*hebu mataro*) used by other Warao shamans in a different context. Like the bow and arrow, the rattle is a composite symbol of intercourse consisting, as it does, of a phallic axis and a uterine calabash. This notion finds linguistic expression in the word for calabash, *mataru* or *mataruka* (hymen), which refers to a virgin womb that is deflowered by a *mataruka aiwatu*, "someone who pierces a calabash."

The natural model of the kite's rattle is an ovoid termitary or apiary built around the branch of a tree; its rustling interior teems with termites' known reproductive power (figs. 6.2, 6.3). Warao dancers shake the small rattles of the Heraldic Kite during the Dance of the Little Rattle, which features rites to bring fertility to humans and animals. Animal pantomimes are presented by means of steps, postures, and the little rattles, until finally enormous straw images are produced: a vulva (by men) and a phallus (by women). In the ensuing melee the effigies, borne by members of the opposite sex, are shredded and destroyed.

During the ritual of the kite's rattle the affinal kin ties between spouses become suspended and replaced by ritual bonds known as *mamuse*. Husbands agree to exchange wives. Upon payment of a substantial price, called *horo amoara* (skin payment), partners are free to engage in dancing and sex. *Mamuse* relationships are considered honorable and are believed to exercise a fortifying influence on the woman's offspring.

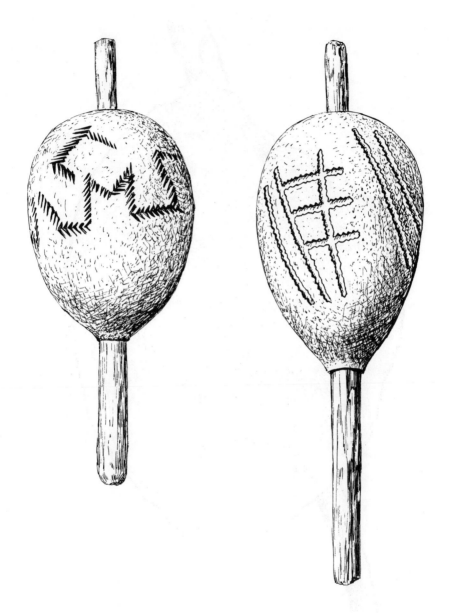

FIG. 6.2

The little rattle of *bahana* ritual (*habi sanuka*) made of a tree calabash (*Cresentia cujete*). The rattle's head is decorated with incised design patterns. (Drawing courtesy Helga Adibi)

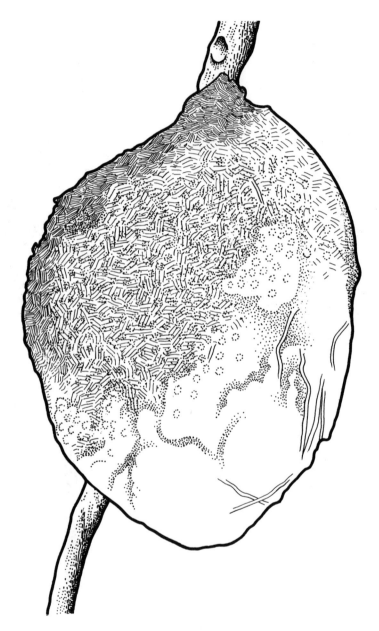

FIG. 6.3.
The termitary mounted on the branch of a tree, resembling a little rattle.
(Drawing courtesy W. Patrick Finnerty)

THE COSMIC EGG

The next three episodes (2–4) of the myth present the image of the Cosmic Egg, created by the Heraldic Raptor through the power of thought (fig. 6.4). Endowed with a proper rhythm of continual generation, the Cosmic Egg represents a central metaphor of the *bahana* paradigm.

The peculiarity of the flowers alongside the celestial bridge between the zenith and the egg is that they consist only of the stems and the florescences of tobacco plants. The harvested leaves are understood to have contributed the construction material, in the form of tobacco smoke, for the Cosmic Egg and its inventory and to have served as the spiritual food of the occupants. Although varied in form, all actors and accessories in the scenario are uniformly made of tobacco smoke, with their telluric realism in narcotic suspension. Thus, although they do not do so in the *bahana* context, potentially the flowers produce the nectareal food (i.e., sex; see below) for the apian companions of the kite in exchange for pollination. This interrelationship is not lost on the Warao who, by employing the verb form *tokoyokitani* of the noun *tokoyo* (flower), metaphorize it to connote "blossoming" in the sense of an estrous female exhibiting chromatic and odoriferous attractants (Barral 1979, 430). Thus the flowers along the celestial bridge are a vignette of the *bahana* paradigm, imitating the essential (food) and formal (sex) characteristics of flower symbolism.

Before commenting on the social model of the kite's community, I want first to indicate that the architectural prototypes of the Cosmic Egg are the nest of the honey wasp (*Brachygastra lecheguana* Latreille) and the testis. The Warao refer to the wasp as *ono* (testis) because of the shape of its nest and its extraordinary fertility. More than fifteen thousand individuals may inhabit a single nest; and when the nest is destroyed the wasps will rebuild it repeatedly as long as some of its base remains intact (Schwarz 1929, 424). If it had a *bahana* game, say the Indians, the *ono* wasp would enjoy the same status as the swallow-tailed kite.

Built of gray paper, the ovoid nest (measuring 60 cm x 45 cm) of the honey wasp resembles the House of Tobacco Smoke in form and color. The testis, also oval in shape, is gray-white in color. Inside and along the distal wall of the genital gland are a number of chambers separated by septa which are like the combs that honey wasps fasten

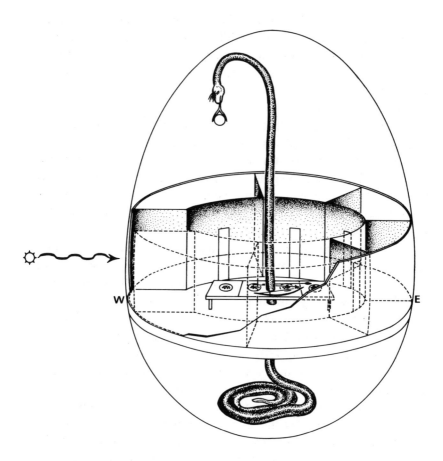

Fig. 6.4.

Cross section of the House of the Swallow-Tailed Kite showing two-story
layout. From the lower story a plumed serpent with a luminous ball on the
tip of her tongue penetrates the floor of the upper story and rises above the
table of the *bahana* game. Notice the division of the *mesa* into four fields,
each with its marker. The arrows are distinguished from one another by the
difference in their points. A ring of six quarters inhabited by insect-spirits
surrounds an inner room. The room north of the entrance is inhabited by the
primordial shaman and his bee-wife. The room south of the entrance is occupied by the Creator-Bird and his (frigate) companion. (Drawing courtesy
Noel Diaz)

to the inside of their nest but which are not, like those of other wasps, arranged in parallel tiers. The nest does not have a central brood chamber with a single queen as do the nests of the other Hymenoptera and the termite of the *bahana* set of insects. Instead, within the honey wasp's hive several reproductive individuals are at work on different combs, just as there are several insect actors in the rooms of the Cosmic Egg (fig. 6.5). It is precisely this absence of a central space of generation that excludes the model of the wasp's nest from *bahana* status, but it is in the existence of such a space that the Cosmic Egg and the testis coincide. The architectural and anatomical layout of both house and gland features a number of peripheral rooms and lobules that interact in a space of convergence. Even the bundle of convoluted ducts which leads away from the hilar side of the testis resembles the rope-bridge that connects the Cosmic Egg with the zenith and the central world axis.

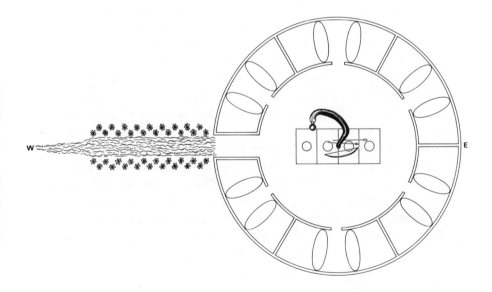

FIG. 6.5.
Floor Plan of the House of the Swallow-Tailed Kite with inner (ceremonial) game room, its table, and a serpent, and an outer circle of living quarters. The bridge of ropes of tobacco smoke is shown, as are the lines of tobacco flowers on both sides. (Drawing courtesy Noel Diaz)

The image of the coresident animal cohorts in the sky-house arouses a measure of consternation in the native listener. In the first place, there is the animosity that exists between insects and humans. The black bee, *hoi* (*Trigona hyalinata branneri* Cockerell), and the wasp, *tomonoho simo* (*Stelopolybia fulvofasciata* DeGeer), in question are fiercely aggressive creatures.[7] The former, although stingless, bites the scalp and twists the hair of those who dare to disturb it. Worse still, black bees of this kind crawl into facial orifices and torture the victim with scores of painful bites. The wasp, in turn, is apt to attack a human passerby even at a considerable distance from its nest; as few as three of its stings are said to cause a fever. The termite, *ahi simo* (*Nasuti-termes corniger* Motschulsky), displays the same stamina as does the wasp in the face of overpowering odds; it returns to the site even after its nest has been completely razed. Termites, which also invade houses, are reputed to be child snatchers.

The second reason for the Warao listener's uneasiness about insects in the sky-house is his connecting each of them with an insect family that mirrors the human family and its interpersonal relationships. This complex model is best illustrated by referring to Blue Bee.

Blue Bee, *asebe* (*Trigona capitata* F. Smith), with the kite's white mark in the center of its face, is the master of the Cosmic Egg. He keeps two nonsororal wives, *aroida*, "long neck" (*Melipona scutellaris lateralis* [Erichson]), and *atekoro*, "cowife," or *kurakasi*, "engorged vagina" (*Melipona puncticollis ogilviei* Schwarz). *Asebe*'s father-in-law is *arahi sanuka* (*Trigona melanocera* Schwarz), as his name indicates, and his daughter, *daihene*, "yellow back" (*Trigona paupera* [Provan-cher]), is wooed by the bachelor *simowata*, "honey penis" (*Lestrimelitta limao* F. Smith), who also goes by the name of *dariamo*, "warrior."

The adult Warao listener knows about the frailty of such family relationships and about the tensions that build up between a son-in-law and his parents-in-law, between a husband and his wives, and between a wife and her cowife; but he also knows about the fears of the wooing bachelor who, upon marriage, faces uxorilocal residence

---

[7] Hymenoptera identification by Dr. Roy R. Snelling (Natural History Museum, Los Angeles County) is based on my collection. Snelling's assistance is gratefully acknowledged. Termite identification by Dr. Kumar Krishna (American Museum of Natural History, New York). The color of mythological insects does not always correspond to the color of the natural prototype.

and bride service for the lifetime of his spouse. To the Warao the image of nest solidarity vaunted by the myth masks a cohering but severely stressed net of family relationships which, in the face of many odds, persevere only under the kite's protection. How poor the odds of survival are may be seen in the example of the bachelor wooer *simowata*. He is the robber bee, who is apt to rape the nest of his *Trigona* parents-in-law, *asebe*, by forcing them out of their home and by taking their food and their offspring. In addition, the fears that govern interfamily relationships within the band are exemplified by Black Bee, who counts among his kin *kohora*, "the musty one" (*Trigona fuscipennis* Friese), an enemy of Termite whose nest he invades to occupy it in forced symbiosis. Finally, the snake in the lower compartment of the Cosmic Egg contributes its share to the volatile atmosphere within the *bahana* house by being modeled after a species of blind snake (*Leptotyphlops* sp.), which bores its way into the bulbous arboreal termitary to feast on the brood and to deposit its egg inside a temperature-controlled environment. In other words, given a chance, the various animals and their kin of the Cosmic Egg tear into one another, invade one another's houses, and cannibalize one another's offspring. The swallow-tailed kite destroys the nests of birds and bees and wasps; the black bee, *kohora*, enters the termite's nest, the robber bee usurps the hives of Blue Bee, and the blind snake breaks into the termitary.

In short, the image of peaceful coexistence of such unlikely companions as the swallow-tailed kite, the insects, and the snake in the Cosmic Egg is foreboding, not only because of the animosity between the insects and man but also because of the piratical nature of the kite's cohorts, and especially because the inmates of the Cosmic Egg relate to one another as members in an ecological food chain rather than as friends. The bees eat the nectar and the pollen of the flowers; the wasp feeds on the brood of the bees and the termites; the snake eats the brood of the termites and wasps; and the kite, at the top of the pyramid, eats the bees' and wasps' honey and eggs as well as the flying insects and the snake. In fact, Warao imagination could scarcely have assembled a more varied set of natural models to create so highly charged an image of latent antagonism. To the Warao listener, any peaceful coexistence among the members of the Cosmic Egg community must depend on the magic power of the Heraldic Raptor.

THE CELESTIAL GAMBLERS AND TOBACCO

The image of the Celestial Gamblers makes it clear that, by assembling the motley group of occupants in the sky-house, the kite pursued a purpose other than mere coexistence. Aware of their piratical dispositions and the conflict inherent in their mutual dependence, he called them to the gambling table to perform the "dance" of survival in the way they know best. Not surprisingly, then, the rules of play in the *bahana* game are truly second nature to its players.

The name of the game is *bahana akotubu*, which means *bahana* "game" or "dance," but it also means "to take excessive sexual liberties" with someone else's wife. Accordingly, the objective of the game is invasion of the checkered house of their fellow "dancers" according to the chances dictated by the kite's arrow dice.[8] The players deposit in the foreign houses their calabashes with seminal content like larvae in a comb. At the end of each game the plumed serpent erects itself like a central house post, and its power fills the winner with renewing life energy. The secret of the Heraldic Kite's success in gaining the cooperation of the antagonistic gamblers is hidden in the plant that he created. The swallow-tailed kite is the Spirit of Tobacco, and tobacco is the sine qua non of *bahana*. The word *bahana* connotes "to smoke" or "to suck." And the *bahanarotu* is the shaman who sucks smoke through hyperventilation from two-foot-long cigars.

From the point of view of its insect occupants, the House of Tobacco Smoke presents a constant image of death. Nicotine, the principal active ingredient in tobacco, is the most potent insecticide in nature; the Warao are well aware of its deadly effect on bees, wasps, and termites and of its soothing influence on the mind of their shaman. Thus, the wisdom of the Creator-Bird in choosing tobacco smoke for the construction of his sky-house lies in his knowledge of its effect on insects. The tobacco alkaloid is his secret magic power that overcomes the innate animosity of his house guests.

From the point of view of the *bahana* shaman, tobacco is also an image of transcendental life. The kind of tobacco used by the shaman is *Nicotiana rustica*, which has powerful psychotropic properties

---

[8] Apparently, having been played mentally by shamans, the exact rules of the game are now lost.

(Wilbert 1987). Saturated and engulfed in tobacco smoke, the Celestial Gamblers experience the illumination of a tobacco trance in whose flash the telluric conditions of their animal nature are transcended. The image of the ophidian master of ceremonies who marks the rhythm of the game is a sign of hope that the inexorable conditions of mundane life may be sublimated by the gambling odds of the kite's game of chance.

The "Quest of *Bahana* Power" and the "Origin of *Bahana* Shamanism" sections of the myth describe a shamanic celestial journey and the acquisition of *bahana* power as a result of the creative dream of a child during which he received the knowledge as a gift. The meaning of the episodal imagery is less culture-specific and its symbolism more generally accessible.

THE WORLD AXIS

In the mystic center of the universe a four-year-old child, the product of two semiconscious protohumans, awakens to his riddle-solving destiny. The virgin fire in whose heat he ascends to the zenith must be produced by men only with the aid of a fire drill. The Warao see this procedure as a simile of the sex act, and women feel inhibited to use it. Through the heat of the fire the youth achieves his ecstatic state and ascends the world axis. The base of this *axis mundi* rests on the bottom of the underworld, below the floating earth disk, and penetrates the earth at its center to rise to the apex of the sky. At the nadir the Warao picture the world axis entwined in the coils of an enormous four-headed serpent with deer horns on its heads. The heads of this all-seeing monster point to the four quarters of heaven, and the coils of its body support the buoyant earth. Thus the image of the three-tiered Warao cosmos produces the common cosmological schema of a solar bird at the top of the central world tree-pillar and a snake at its roots.

Connecting nadir and zenith, the world axis serves as a pathway of communication between humans and the supernaturals who frequent the sacred space above, below, and around it. Initiated men and women travel the *axis mundi* upward to the zenith, and from there go on to destinations at the cardinal and intercardinal points, where their respective patron deities reside. Similarly, the gods descend along the world axis to visit earth. And the world snake, at its base, can leave the netherworld and wind its way up to manifest itself by projecting its torso through the central earth hole or by emerging fully in the shape of a woman sitting astride a fallen tree.

The Warao do not think of the world axis as a solid column; rather, they see it as a bundle of conduits, each one specific to its destination. For instance, one of these lines (before it was destroyed) was an artery that carried human blood from the earth to the land of the setting sun, there to nourish the cannibalistic god of the west and his retinue. Other channels are jets of heat or curls of ascending tobacco smoke. Thus the world axis of the Warao universe represents a dynamic bundle of pathways, one of which leads to the anchor point of the rope-bridge that conducts *bahana* shamans from the top of the sky to the House of Tobacco Smoke.

THE MOTHER OF HONEY

Overcoming his earthboundness through the heat of a fire and his need for food by smoking tobacco, the as yet reproductively inactive youth is acceptable to the kite and his associates as one of their kind. He is capable of receiving the kite's gifts and of nurturing in his breast the gestating offspring of the four insects. Only upon reaching spermatogenesis at the age of sixteen does he have intercourse with his bee-wife, introducing her gradually to the practices of "human" reproduction.

The young *bahana* shaman's wife is a daughter of Blue Bee (*aroida*). She is the Mother of Honey who releases man from the bonds of hunger and sex. Her sweetness is referred to as *diaba*, and experiencing it is *diabaia* (orgasm). Etymologically, therefore, eating honey and nectar connotes copulation.

In actual life this meaning is explainable by the high levulose content of stingless-bee honey, which has an intense and exquisite sweetness. "A delight more piercing than any normally afforded by taste or smell breaks down boundaries of sensibility, and blurs the registers, so much so that the eater of the honey wonders whether he is savoring a delicacy or burning with the fire of love" (Lévi-Strauss 1966, 52). The marriage of the first *bahana* shaman to a bee-girl and other Warao myths take note of this quality of honey (Wilbert 1970, 175–77). And so does a nubile girl in making an unequivocal overture to a man by passing the tip of her tongue across her lower lip while sipping honey. According to several of my male informants, men are attracted to the taste of honey with the same passion they feel in longing for the "sweetness" of a young girl.

Honey is considered a food, like tobacco, rather than a drink. In fact, in preagricultural times, when the Warao lived largely on fish and honey, they were aware of the long-lasting satisfaction they enjoyed after eating a meal of these staples. As one of my informants said, "We would breakfast on fish, insect brood, and honey and go all day without getting hungry again. Sometimes we even turned in at night without feeling hungry enough to eat. Honey was the blood of the Warao." There is no reason to doubt the veracity of this statement, for a meal of fish, insect larvae, and honey would be rich in proteins and high in carbohydrates.

Another aspect of honey consumption by the Warao is worthy of mention in connection with *bahana* imagery. Honey is consumed in its raw state only by the shamans and, through extension, by the gods. Commoners ingest it diluted with water or, during the ritual of the Little Rattles, fermented as mead. The Warao are on record as having collected hundreds of liters of honey at a time when the shaman dispatched the families to prepare an offering of propitiation for the supernaturals. On these occasions macerated honey would ferment, so that the gift of the Mother of Honey contributed, besides natural food, the levulose and alcohol needed to foster the congeniality conducive to procreation, just as the gift of her shaman husband contributed, besides spiritual food, the nicotine to enhance friendship and spiritual well-being.

In a later episode (9), the bee-wife of the first shaman, upon entering the Cosmic Egg, changed into the form of a frigate bird and cured the Heraldic Kite of a seizure he suffered in her presence.

The wife of a *bahana* shaman is invariably recognized as a *bahana* shaman in her own right who identifies with the Mother of Honey in her guise as the magnificent female frigate (*Fregata magnificens*). With its forked tail and especially its white breast, this otherwise black bird resembles the swallow-tailed kite in flight. I have already referred to the similarity of the kite and the frigate in flight. Just like the kite, frigates are relentless pirates. Rather than foraging on their own, they prefer to rob other seabirds, such as boobies, grabbing and shaking them with their long beaks until the victims regurgitate their catch. Before the falling fish reach the surface of the water, the frigate swoops down and pilfers them.

Another characteristic frigates share with swallow-tailed kites is their aerial acrobatics and fighting. Using sticks to build their nests, frigates either pick them up from the ground or purloin them from the kite's or from other birds' nests. Several of these birds may be observed in flight fighting with one another over the possession of a stick, letting it drop on one occasion and catching it in midair on another. As with the kite, *bahana* shamans see in these sticks magical arrows that the shamanic bird shoots at them. The stakes are the same in the game of chance, and frigates may even come down to catch the "arrow" a shaman hurls back at them.

Of additional analogical significance is the frigate's mating behavior. The male bird sits on the nest and inflates its gular sac into an enormous scarlet balloon the size of a rattle. It spreads its wings and throws back its head to call attention to its strutting body. Attracted by the display, the female descends and engages in body contact, touching the male's wings, neck, and gular pouch. Such behavior eventually leads to mating, which, in turn, releases the male bird from its seizurelike state. Hence the name "Mother of Seizure" bestowed by the Heraldic Kite on the bee-wife/frigate bird when she cured him in the Cosmic Egg.

Frigates are enthusiastic rattlers. Sitting on their nests, which they must constantly defend from encroaching neighbors, they use their beaks to produce a clattering noise that can be heard from afar. Again, the symbolic interrelationship of the rattle (in the form of a long beak and inflated gular balloon) and reproduction is alluded to in this startling analogy. The Warao call a bird's dewlap or gular sac (or a man's larynx) *habi*, as in *habi sanuka*, "Little Rattle" of *bahana*.

One other detail remains to be mentioned. It has already been suggested that Mawari, the swallow-tailed kite, found a most compatible counterpart in the female frigate when he invited her to share his room, which is south of the entrance to the House of Smoke, and to become the first female *bahanarotu*.

THE SHAMANIC HEALERS

The last two episodes of the myth (10 and 11) describe the origin of *bahana* shamanism and explain why the modern shaman is less powerful than the first *bahana*: he has only two insect tutelary spirits in his breast and carries only the two younger brothers (Termite and Blue Bee) of the two fraternal pairs in the Cosmic Egg.

The male shaman cures by extracting pathogenic "insects" that were sent to invade a patient's body by a malevolent colleague of his. The wounds caused by such attacks are especially apparent in females, and although the shaman attends to both sexes he nevertheless treats in particular women with menstrual problems, vaginal bleeding, and protracted deliveries, or, in other words, gynecological problems that, although lingering, often take care of themselves. Consequently, healers of such disorders have a high rate of success. The shaman, by consulting the two tutelary spirits in his breast, finds out whether, in the game the Celestial Gamblers play over the patient (the "stake" of the round), one of these spirits (Termite or Blue Bee) has won or whether one of the two more powerful spirits that remained in the Cosmic Egg (Black Bee and Wasp) has been victorious. In the latter event there is nothing a shaman can do. If one of the tutelary spirits wins the gamble, the shaman sends the winner from his breast through the lumen in his arm and the hole in the palm of his hand to effect the cure and, possibly, to claim the patient's body in a kind of peonage, called *ateho wabia*, "selling of the body."

A patient suffering from a protracted ailment is frequently unable to pay the shaman's fee. Payments formerly were made in tobacco which a woman obtained in exchange for her products, such as hammocks and baskets. Because tobacco does not grow in the Orinoco Delta, its acquisition is costly and women must work hard to obtain it. Furthermore, it is indispensable for Warao shamanism because its smoke is the staple food for the practitioner's supernatural patrons. And if a patient is unable to pay for repeated seances, she or he has no choice but to offer her or his body as remuneration. This relationship between shaman and patient often lasts for the latter's lifetime, and, although a shaman has several male *neburatu* clients of this kind, he also invariably has a number of females. Significantly, however, such "earned bodies" are considered "sons" and "daughters" of the shaman, who, therefore may not have sexual relations with the women. They address him as "father" and he calls them "daughter" and treats them as such.

To illustrate the control the "selling of the body" institution gives a *bahana* shaman over reproductively active females in a local group, bear in mind that the average uxorilocal and endogamous Warao band consists of thirteen women, twelve men, and twenty-five children. For example, a *bahanarotu* of my acquaintance has two wives and four married daughters. A seventh woman, the wife of his son, lives virilocally owing to adoption. In addition, the shaman has acquired four women, who belong to other bands of the same subtribe, as ritual daughters through his practice as a healer. This *bahanarotu* then, has stewardship over eleven women: six in-laws, one stepdaughter, and four ritual daughters. Altogether their number is almost the equivalent of a full contingent of adult females in any one band.

The *bahana* shaman has certain "paternal" obligations to his ritual daughters, but he also exercises fatherly rights over them. For example, when visiting their respective villages he may inquire into the comportment of their husbands as providers. He has the right to reprimand the men or to withdraw the women if complaints of continual neglect are not adequately redressed. He may also take revenge on a neighboring *bahanarotu* should one of the women entrusted to him die suddenly, that is, suffer a typical *bahana* death. Ideally, every one of his affinal and ritual sons-in-law renders bride service for the lifetime of his spouse, so that *bahana* shamans, because of prevailing residence rules and ritual kinship, may build self-sufficient, maximally secure, and well-managed settlements with optimal conditions for individual and group survival.

A female *bahana* shaman may also enjoy a high success rate with patients suffering from seizures, although she cures fewer such patients than her husband does. The source of her healing power lies in the pharmacological cause (i.e., nicotine poisoning) of the type of seizure in question. As noted earlier in this chapter, nicotine is the most toxic insecticide found in nature. In addition, nicotine is also one of the most toxic natural substances for humans, producing tremors as symptoms of low-level poisoning and convulsions and death from medium to high levels of poisoning.

Seizures among the Warao caused by tobacco consumption afflict men more than women because they ingest massive doses of nicotine for ritual purposes. The sudden onset of tobacco seizures explains why *bahana* sicknesses, such as exotic epidemic diseases, are characterized by the abruptness of "falling ill" without any previous symptoms. The Warao word for seizure, *sinaka,* is derived from *sinakakitani* (to drop to the ground); and the patient, *sinakabaka*, feels oppressed and shaken by Huru, the earthquake spirit.

Furthermore, the pharmacological basis of a nicotine seizure places its origin in the tobacco-saturated environment of the Cosmic Egg and explains why the primordial female shaman's first patient was the Supreme Spirit of Tobacco himself. Then, as she does in modern times, she cured by leaning over the patient to prevent a more violent catathymic crisis; she may stroke the man's body and blow over it. Meanwhile the nicotine seizure runs its natural course and the spasms subside in replication of the cure effected in the Cosmic Egg and in accordance with the mating behavior the female frigate adopts in response to the strutting display of her partner. As nicotine metabolism in humans is fast, female *bahana* shamans enjoy a high degree of success as curers, although the relatively brief therapy and recuperation period of the patient does not call for his "selling of the body" to her.

THE *BAHANA* PARADIGM

In light of the preceding discussion I am perhaps justified in suggesting that *bahana* imagery bespeaks the intense preoccupation of the Warao with the concerns of personal (sex) and societal (food) survival. *Bahana* symbolism begs the hypothesis that its pervasive imagery of fertility and fecundity signifies the cooperative-competitive tensions inherent in sexuality and attendant cultural behavior. No doubt psychoanalytic theory of myth could profitably be engaged to analyze the emotional conflict and its resolution within the *bahana* complex. The application of structural theory to resolve the intellectual contradictions inherent in the myth should also be promising. My purpose here, however, is to examine by means of the principles of similarity and contiguity the hypothesized pansexual dimensions of the myth so as to derive the meaning of its key symbolism (see Lounsbury 1959; Ortner 1973).

The paradigm of the *bahana* origin myth includes the phallic, conjunctive, and uterine imagery of eleven episodal frames and three—telluric, cultural, and cosmic (or metaphysical)—types of form (table 6.1). In general, the imagery of episodal frames includes what is overtly presented in the myth and what is covertly associated with it in Warao thought. Taking the first episode of the myth as an example (table 6.2), the conjunctive column contains two telluric images: (1) the *tepui* mountain and a cave (containing two eggs) as phallic and uterine attributes, respectively; (2) the vertically soaring flight patterns of the nesting swallow-tailed kite, with the nesting sticks and the nest itself serving as phallic and uterine attributes, respectively.

Also, the conjunctive column of the cultural form contains two images: (1) the rattle, with staff (and seeds) as phallic and the calabash as uterine attributes; (2) the braced hunting or musical bow, with the arch of the bow as female and the taut bowstring and the arrow as male attributes. (The similarity between the imagery of the vertical and rotating movements of the rattle in use and the image of the kite's flight patterns is perhaps particularly noteworthy.)

The conjunctive column of the cosmic form also contains two images: (1) the *axis mundi* with its simile, the World Pillar, as male and the bell-shaped cosmic vault and circular cosmic planes as female attributes; (2) the Heraldic Raptor brandishing his arrows as phallic and his rattle as uterine attributes. On the cosmic level the telluric cave turns into the image of the cave of emergence.

The telluric, cultural, and cosmic forms of the first episodal frame, though not identical, are semantically similar in varying degrees of closeness. The fit depends, in part, on the sophistication of the listener with regard to his or her naturalistic and cultural knowledge and, in part, on whether comparisons of similarity are made in immediate relative context or in total context. Thus, as bundles of connotative meanings, the *tepui* mountain construes in a manner similar to that of the *axis mundi* and the axis of the rattle in immediate relative context, and so does the Heraldic Raptor with the flight pattern, the rattle, and the bows and arrows. The relationship between the *tepui* and the kite is construed within the total form class of the myth because of their common androgynous nature. Although loose fits of this kind may seem too imprecise for scientific discourse, the notion of similarity relates intrinsically to overlapping of less than complete resemblances rather than to idiosyncrasy. At the same time, as the notion of similarity introduces statistical considerations of aggregates and particles, it permits general statements about what is more important and what is less important in form comparisons. And it is by recognition of the validity of tendencies rather than by entirely pervasive generalities that correlates and key symbols in mythic thought systems are derived.

TABLE 6.1
FORMS OF SIMILARITY AND FRAMES OF CONTIGUITY

Form	Phallic	Conjunctive	Uterine	Phallic	Conjunctive	Uterine
Telluric	Component	Image	Component	Component	Image	Component
Cultural	Component	Image	Component	Component	Image	Component
Cosmic	Component	Image	Component	Component	Image	Component
		1. Frame			2. Frame	

TABLE 6.2
SUBSTITUTION CLASS OF FIRST EPISODAL FRAME
AXIS MUNDI AND HERALDIC RAPTOR

Form	Phallic	Conjunctive	Uterine
Telluric	*Tepui* mountain	*Tepui* mountain and cave containing eggs	Hollow mountain cave
	Swallow-tailed kite	Fulminating vertical and soaring flight	Nest
	Nesting sticks	Flight of mating season	Nest
Cultural	Rattle staff	Rattle; vertical and rotating movement	Calabash
	Taut bowstring	Braced bow; musical bow	Arch of bow
	Arrow	Bow and arrow	Arch of bow
Cosmic	World Pillar	*Axis mundi* piercing cosmic planes with coiled serpent at base	Bell-shaped cosmic vault; circular cosmic planes
	Heraldic Archer	Heraldic Raptor with bow and arrow and rattle	Heraldic Rattler Cave of emergence

The tendency of the conjunctive images and attributes contained in the episodal frames is toward signification of the necessity for coexistence for the sake of survival through harmonious sexual relations and the joint procurement of food. The redundancy of images demonstrates the potential, in myth, for multiple representations of the same theme or message. This characteristic permits the forms of a given context to substitute for one another and to construe with their frame in a similar manner to constitute a substitution class.

Phallic imagery is associated with male humans (like elder and younger brothers, grooms, husbands, fathers, and shamans), with erect snakes, and with male birds and insects. It also relates to fire, heat, the sun (solar bird), flight (tobacco trance, plumed serpent), and the upperworld. Masculinity, which is rigid (like nesting sticks, fire drill, arrow, rattle staff, flower stems, quartz pyramid, bowstring, bridge rope, rectangular game table, cigar), is expressed in such phallic images as the World Pillar with a hollow of eggs, the world axis with the Cosmic Egg, the erect serpent with a glowing ball of smoke, and the hollow shaman's arms each attached to a lung and inhabited by a pair of younger and elder brothers. The summarizing symbol that compounds the imagery of fertility is the world axis with its scrotal appendage of the Cosmic Egg. In its concrete form, the symbol recurs in the feathered arrow and particularly in the stick-rattle, consisting of a 2-meter-long staff with a string of seed husks wound around its upper end. During ritual dances officiating shamans carry the stick-rattle like a verger or a crosier.

Uterine imagery is associated with female human beings (such as brides, wives, mothers, and shamans), with coiled-up snakes, and with female birds and insects. It also relates to the family quarters and the underworld. Femaleness is round-featured (bow, arch) and is expressed in vaginal images (flowers, perforated world disks, the bell-shaped cosmic vault), in pregnant images (bulbous and hollow hives, termitaries, calabashes, and the Cosmic Egg), and in specifically uterine images such as rooms, cups, and nests. The summarizing symbol that synthesizes the imagery of fecundity is the calabash of the ritual rattle.

Conjunctive imagery unites these male and female components in such major images as the world tree axis piercing cosmic planes, the Heraldic Raptor brandishing his paraphernalia, the bridge to the otherworld, the Cosmic Egg, the Divine Gamblers, and the sky journey of the ecstatic shaman. These images combine the summarizing symbols of the male stick-rattle and the female calabash into the key symbol of *bahana*; the ceremonial rattle.

With four exceptions, the episodal frames are completely filled with telluric, cultural, and cosmic forms so that, generally speaking, the frames have a tripartite distribution (table 6.3). The contents of the frames show considerable overlap from one row to another in form distributions, and the totality of frames constitutes the frame class or mode of *bahana* imagery. This statement does not imply, however, that the forms have the same distribution; they are unique in every contextual instance. But parts of the distribution of a particular form may appear also in the distribution of some other form. As to be expected in myth, rather than systematic absolute correspondence with every form fitting into every frame, there are only approximations in kind which reveal the contextual tendencies of the myth. An example is the multiple occurrence of quartz pyramid, oval pebbles, hair, and tobacco smoke in telluric frames 2, 4, and 6 as phallic attributes of the conjunctive form of the gambling table with uterine calabash cups as counter pieces. In association with these three frames, the seminal character of the four kinds of contents remains partly concealed, suggested only by their form and color. In frames 10 and 11, however, where they occur in modified contexts, they are lifted, so to speak, out of their uterine cups, placed into a shaman's phallic cigar, and shot into a novice's lungs.

The major tendency of form distribution within the *bahana* myth is a series of androgynous images appearing in a diachronic continuum from macrocosmic to microcosmic models. More specifically, the episodal frames provide three different environments for the images, displaying them in the transcendental context of the cosmos, the social context of the house, and the personal context of the human body (table 6.4).

Thus the frame class of the *bahana* myth is characterized by a three-tiered general model. (1) There is the cosmos with its sea serpent of the underworld, its earth disk with a village of insect tribes around the shaman's house, and the top of the world with the Cosmic Egg and a bell-shaped cosmic vault. (2) The house model has two images: (a) the lower compartment of the Cosmic Egg houses a blind snake and has a round floor with family quarters around a gambling table, and the bell-shaped upper compartment has a glowing ball in the serpent's mouth;

TABLE 6.3
EPISODAL FRAMES OF THE *BAHANA* MYTH AND DISTRIBUTION OF FORMS

		1. World Pillar and Heraldic Kite		2. Cosmic Egg		
	P*	C	U	P	C	U
Te	Tepuí mountain	Tepuí mountain and cave containing eggs	Hollow mountain and cave	Flower stems, quartz pyramid, oval pebbles, hair, tobacco smoke	Stems and florescence	Flower
	Swallow-tailed kite	Fulminating vertical and soaring flight	Nest		Calabash cups with white content	Calabash cups
	Nesting sticks	Flight of mating season	Nest	Ropes of bridge	Youth on bridge	Arch of bridge
Cu	Rattle staff	Rattle; vertical and rotating movements	Calabash	Checkerboard with white pieces	Calabash cups with white content on game table	Calabash cups as pieces
	Taut bow string	Braced bow; musical bow	Arch of bow			
	Arrow	Bow and arrow	Arch of bow			
Co	World Pillar	Axis mundi piercing cosmic planes with coiled serpent at base	Bell-shaped cosmic vault; circular cosmic planes	Upper level of Cosmic Egg	Floor level with central orifice; rectangular game table in circular room	Lower level; round floor with central orifice
	Heraldic Archer	Heraldic Raptor with bow and arrow and rattle	Heraldic Rattler Cave of emergence			

3. Occupation of Cosmic Egg (cont.)

	P*	C	U
Te	Chiefs and workers	Insect families	Family quarters in the round
Cu	Plumed erect serpent with ball of wisdom	Female serpent coiled in lower compartment	Cup-shaped lower compartment
Co			

4. Divine Gamblers (cont.)

	P	C	U
Te	Insect husbands at gambling table	Insect families	Insect wives in family quarters
Cu			
Co	Plumed erect serpent with ball of wisdom	Penetration of floor and oval house by serpent	Cosmic Egg; round floor with central orifice

5. Shamanic Flight

	P	C	U
Te	Fire	Fire on hearth	Round hearth
Cu	Fire drill / Father of youth	Fire drilling / Son	Fire board / Mother of youth
Co	World axis / Rising youth	World axis penetrating cosmic tiers / Novice on celestial bridge and in bell-shaped cosmic vault	Bell-shaped cosmic vault / Bell-shaped top of the world

6. Mystic Enlightenment

	P	C	U
Te	Quartz pyramid, oval pebbles, hair, tobbaco smoke	Calabash cups with white content	Calabash cups
Co	Novice ascending / Plumed erect serpent	Novice in Cosmic Egg / Penetration of floor and oval house by serpent	Cosmic Egg / Cosmic Egg; round floor with central orifice

*P = Phallic C = Conjunctive U = Uterine Te = Telluric Cu = Cultural Co = Cosmic

7. Shamanic Transformation

	P*	C	U
Te	Shaman's arms attached to lungs		
Cu	Husband-Shaman	Marriage	Wife-Shaman
Co	Radiant Shaman	Youth on celestial bridge	Bee-wife

8. Shamanic Union

	P	C	U
Te	Man	Copulation	Woman
Cu	Husband	Intercourse	Wife
Co	World axis	World axis in zenith	Bell-shaped cosmic vault

9. Mother of Seizures and Honey

	P	C	U
Te	Swallow-tailed kite	Mating flight	Frigate
Cu	Male seizure patient	Female shaman joins male patient	Female shaman
Co	Solar creator	Cohabitation of Heraldic Raptor and Mother of Honey	Mother of Seizures and Honey

10. Initiation

	P	C	U
Te	Shamanic cigar with quartz pyramid, oval pebbles, hair, tobacco smoke		
Cu	Shaman	Initiation	Novice
Co	Projectile-shooting shaman in sky	Projectiles penetrating breast of novice	Body cavity of novice

11. Origin of Bahana Shamanism

	P*	C	U
Te	Shamanic cigar with quartz pyramid, oval pebbles, hair, tobacco smoke		
Cu	Shaman	Initiation	Novice
Co	Projectile-shooting shaman in sky	Projectiles penetrating breast of novice	Body cavity of novice
	Ropes of celestial bridge	Youth on bridge bordered by flowers	Arch of bridge
	Spirit sons	Spirit sons in breast of shaman	Body cavity of shaman; Cosmic Egg

*P = Phallic C = Conjunctive U = Uterine Te = Telluric Cu = Cultural Co = Cosmic

TABLE 6.4
EPISODAL FRAMES AND CONTEXT MODELS

Episodal Frame	Context Model
1. World and Heraldic Raptor	Cosmos
2. Cosmic Egg	Cosmos
3. Occupation of Cosmic Egg	House
4. Divine Gamblers	House
5. Shamanic flight	House, cosmos
6. Mystic enlightenment	House
7. Shamanic transformation	House
8. Shamanic union	Body
9. Mother of seizures and honey	House
10. Initiation	Body
11. Origin of *bahana* shamanism	Body

(b) the traditional Warao-style stilt dwelling, built over the water and inhabited by the anaconda, has a floor with family quarters, and its roof is a bell-shaped (traditional) or pyramidal (modern) vault of rafters. (3) The anatomical model of the human body features the abdominal region with intestines and reproductive organs, separated by the diaphragm from the thoracic region with lungs and heart and a bell-shaped rib cage, and the head.

The three regions of the human body are regarded as the seats of four different kinds of self (Osborn 1969). The lower abdominal region is occupied by *obonobu* (potential self). It endows a person with special capabilities and talents and the ability to ponder and to reflect. The designation of the self is related to *obonobuai* (to love, to desire) and is associated with the reproductive potential of the lower body. The thoracic region, occupied by *kobe* (emotional self), produces feelings of guilt, fear, and anxiety as well as those of remorse and shame. The primary meaning of *kobe* is "heart," and it is through the action of this four-cameral organ that the individual acquires the property of "strong blood" or "weak blood." The emotional self determines whether an individual will realize his or her potential: mismatched sexual partners cannot procreate; only couples with strong bloods can.

The head is the seat of *obohona* (personality self). It is the source of inspiration, knowledge, consciousness, and willpower. The personality self pertains to the supernatural world, where it survives after death and hence is immortal.

The fourth self of a human being is *mehokohi* (likeness self), located in the thorax. Still, as the shadow image of a person it reflects the entire body.

By projecting the properties of the abdominal, thoracic, and cerebral personal selves into the three-tiered house, the Cosmic Egg, and the universe, it becomes apparent that *bahana* and its underlying homology of "human body-house-cosmos" (as one of humankind's most archaic thoughts) relates to the problem of self-realization within the physical, cultural, and metaphysical conditions of life. Its key symbol, the rattle, is also three-tiered, featuring a leg (handle), a body (calabash), and a head (upper part of the calabash and distal end of the axis). In other words, the rattle is the collocative expression of the *bahana* myth's substitution-distribution matrix, which amalgamates the meanings of a plurality of forms and frames into the singularity of a key symbol.

Chapter Seven

Warao Cosmology and
Yekuana Roundhouse Symbolism

WARAO COSMOLOGY

To the Warao the earth is a disk that floats in the middle of the world sea. Accordingly, they refer to the earth as *hobahi*, "that which is surrounded by water" (fig. 6.1). From below and along the sides the earth disk is smooth, but its surface is jagged like the skyline of the forested islands of the Orinoco Delta (see map 1.3). The crust of the earth is splintered by a network of waterways into small and large pieces of land that form the deltaic archipelago. From the circular edge of the earth, called *hobahi akari*, "where the earth breaks off," one can see across the broad ring of the ocean that extends to the horizon, or *aitona*, at the end of the world.[1]

Submerged in the ocean and encircling the earth is a serpent whose extreme ends approach each other, *uroboros* fashion, east of the disk. This sea monster is *hahuba* (Snake of Being), whose body contains the amorphous luminous essence of all life forms on earth and whose breathing regulates the rhythm of the tides. The world ocean and the submerged part of the earth are contained in a cylindrical abyss bordered by a circular range of mountains. At the center of this subaquatic realm and below the earth lives the Goddess of the Nadir in the form of a gigantic serpent with four heads, each with deer horns and each pointing in a cardinal direction.

At the cardinal and solstice corners, world mountains in the shape of giant petrified tree trunks rise from the ocean to brace a bell-shaped

---

[1] Data on Warao cosmology pertain to the Winikina subtribe of the Warao.

firmament. Through this transparent glasslike shell the celestial world with its mountainous land, its ocean, and its towering heaven is visible (Barral 1979, 326). The level of the depression around the upper third of the firmament is determined by the maximal altitude of the solstitial suns. Here the Warao envision a plain parallel to the ground plane of the earth and the ocean, but with a smaller diameter. The zenith marks the *kabo meho,* "bosom of heaven," as the shamans call it, where the cosmic vault rests on the tip of the three-pronged world axis which penetrates the earth disk at its center below.

Like the ocean around and beneath the earth, other regions of the Warao universe are also populated by supernaturals. Gods, referred to as *kanobo* (*kanobotuma* pl.), "Grandfathers," "Ancient Ones," reside on the cardinal world mountains. The realm of the Butterfly-God

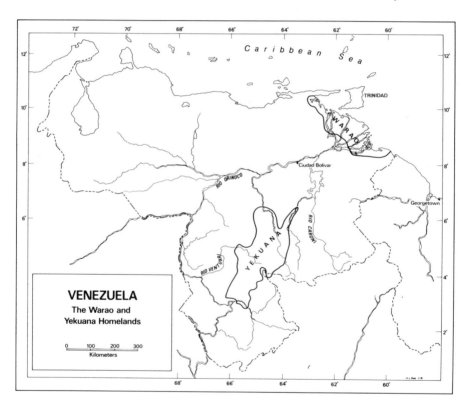

MAP 7.1.
The Warao and Yekuana Homelands

(*Calligo* sp.) sweeps across the northern section of the ocean, between sunrise and sunset of the summer solstice. The Toad-God occupies the southern quarter of the world between the points of rising and setting of the winter sun. The remaining eastern and western realms are the domains of the avian God of Origin and the Scarlet Macaw (*Ara chloroptera*), respectively. The intercardinal mountains are also inhabited—those of the summer solstice by vegetative gods and those of the winter solstice by the Mother of the Forest and Animals.

At the zenith lives a lesser god, a former shaman, who ascended in quasi-historical times. From there radiates a network of paths across the celestial canopy which the gods travel on their way up the firmament and down the central axle to earth. Also, the Goddess of the Nadir, coiled around the foot of the world axis, communicates with the earth by ascending the lower end of the axle. Shamans, in turn, frequent these roads on their journeys to the otherworld. In fact, it is believed that there is heavy trafficking between heaven and earth, humans providing food for the gods and the gods bestowing health and life on humans.

Northeast of the world axis and on the plain near the top of the sky, Warao cosmology pictures a large cosmic egg, a creation of the bird-spirit, Mawari (fig. 6.1). It originated with him at the dawn of time before humankind's appearance. Mawari took the form of a swallow-tailed kite (*Elanoides forficatus*), brandished rattle and bow and arrow as his personal paraphernalia, and created the egg from solidified tobacco smoke through the power of his thought.

The Cosmic Egg is a two-story house (fig. 6.4). The lower floor is occupied by a snake (*Leptotyphlops* sp.) with four colored plumes on her head—white, yellow, blue, and green. The upper floor is arranged as a central space encircled by the living quarters of four pairs of insects,[2] an ancestral shaman and his wife,[3] and the Creator-Bird himself. When not resting or chanting in their hammocks, the male residents congregate in the middle room around a board on which the insects play a game that ensures the perpetuation of humankind on earth. Each time a game ends, the Plumed Serpent emerges from the lower story through the central hole in the floor of the upper compart-

---

[2] For identification of the four insect companions of Mawari, see chapter 6.

[3] The primordial shaman's wife is the frigate bird, *horomaore* (*Fregata magnificens*).

ment, raises its body, and produces a luminous ball on the tip of its tongue. Leading from the western portal of the house is a suspension bridge made of ropes of tobacco smoke which connects the egg with the zenith and the world axis.

THE YEKUANA ROUNDHOUSE

The Yekuana (Makiritare) Indians of southern Venezuela inhabit the headwater regions of the Orinoco River and several of its southern tributaries between 2°50′ and 6°30′ north latitude and between longitude 63°30′ and 66°10′ west (see map 7.1). Close scrutiny of the architectural detail and the symbolism of their communal roundhouse reveals correspondences between that structure and Warao cosmology which seem to be symptomatic of a conceptual relationship between the two tribes (figs. 7.1 and 7.2).[4]

The interior of the Yekuana roundhouse (*ättä*) has two concentric walls: an inner one around the central post provides a space (*annaka*) with a diameter half the total length of the central pole (fig. 7.3); the outer wall, which delineates a ringlike space (*äsa*) encircling the inner wall, has a diameter of double the length of the internally visible central post. Thus, if the protruding upper end of the central pole is subtracted, the house is as wide as it is high. The inner room, largely restricted to men, is a ceremonial space where the shaman officiates, sitting at the foot of the central post, where ritual is conducted, where the bachelors sleep at night, and where men congregate for work and conversation during the day. The outer room is subdivided into family apartments (fig. 7.4). Both inner and outer walls are made of wattle, wattle and daub, or (especially the inner wall and those separating the family quarters) of slabs of tree bark. They are at least two meters high (the inner wall may be as high as six meters), and they follow the circular

---

[4] I am grateful to Dr. David M. Guss for several informative discussions on this topic which have aided me in recognizing the correspondences between the Warao and Yekuana cosmologies and roundhouse architecture. Ethnological data pertaining to the Yekuana round-house and cosmology are derived mainly from Barandiarán's excellent studies (1962; 1966). Additional data were taken from personal field notes obtained during an expedition through Yekuana territory on the upper Ventuari (April 15–May 5, 1958) when I had the opportunity to stay in one roundhouse and witness construction work on another.

FIG. 7.1.
Yekuana roundhouse on a riverbank. (Photo courtesy Barbara Brändli)

FIG. 7.2.
Close-up of a Yekuana roundhouse. (Photo courtesy Ata Kondo)

outlines demarcated by twelve equidistant upright poles at thirty degree
intervals along the periphery of each wall.

The uprights in the outer wall are half the size of those in the inner
wall and a fourth of the total length of the center post. A rectangular
frame of tie beams, three meters above the ground and oriented in an
east-west direction, is fastened to four of the internal upright roof
supports (fig. 7.5). An additional cross beam, in a north-south direction,
is placed on top of the frame across its lateral middle near the center
post. This frame provides horizontal support for the structure and
hammock battens for *annaka* residents.

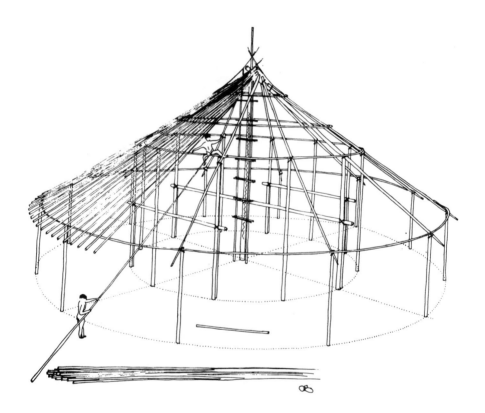

Fig. 7.3.
Architectural detail of Yekuana roundhouse. Outer and inner circles of posts
support roof infrastructure. Four rings of bushrope encircle the roof cone.
Notice zig-zag snake design on central post behind construction scaffolding.
(From Barandiarán 1966; courtesy *Antropológica*)

The conical roof has a lower layer of poles that radiate, like the ribs of an umbrella, from the upper end of the central post toward the outer wall (fig. 7.6). The tips of these poles, however, are not attached to the central mast. Instead they rest closely juxtaposed to one another, on two cross beams that lead from opposite points of the outer wall upward to a point close to the top of the central post, forming the apex of the roof.

To the infrastructure of cross beams and radiating poles are fastened four rings of heavy bushrope: one along the rim of the roof, the second one two-fifths up the width of the cone, the third up three-fifths, and

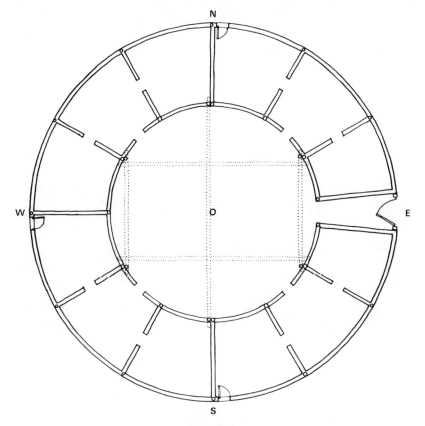

FIG. 7.4.
Architectural detail of Yekuana roundhouse. Concentric ground plan showing inner room reserved for men and ritual use, surrounded by ring of family quarters. Dashed lines indicate rectangular structure of tie beams. (From Barandiarán 1966; courtesy *Antropológica*)

the last ring up another fifth, near the apex (figs. 7.3, 7.6). Resting on these four rings and on the radiating poles is a trellis of saplings and bushrope to which is fastened the actual canopy of thatch, made from two different species of palm.

During construction the central post is decorated, along its entire length, with an undulating or zigzagging snake design. The post, which protrudes more than one meter and which has a flying bird effigy of wood perched on the top, pierces the apex of the roof. Shorter and less prominent are the ends of the two cross beams of the roof's infra-structure, which project like horns (fig. 7.3).

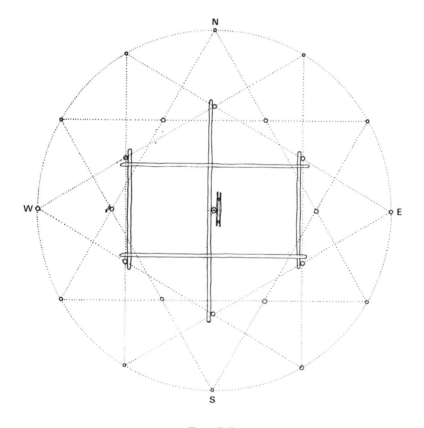

FIG. 7.5.

Architectural detail of Yekuana roundhouse showing position of rectangle of tie beams in relation to central pole and two circles of support posts at thirty-degree intervals. (From Barandiarán 1966; courtesy *Antropológica*)

On one side of the roof, about two-thirds of the way up, a trapezoidal opening (1.5 m wide and 1 m high) is left in the canopy (figs. 7.7a, 7.7b). This aperture is opened and closed by means of a trap window in the roof which is laterally hinged and operated by pulling on a rawhide line (fig. 7.8). When closed, the window forms part of the roof with its upper edge braced against the inner roof and its lower edge overlapping the thatch.

From the main door in the outer wall a corridor leads directly into the inner room. Several window openings and secondary doors providing access to and light for the family apartments are positioned

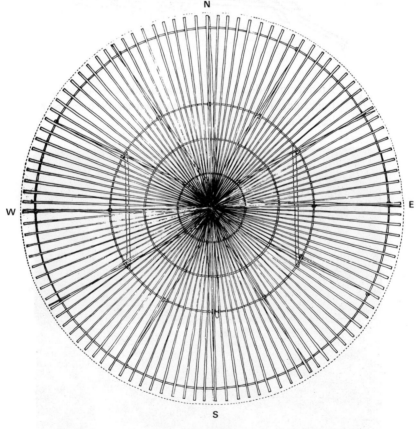

FIG. 7.6.

Architectural detail of Yekuana roundhouse showing top of infrastructure of roof cone. (From Barandiarán 1966; courtesy *Antropológica*)

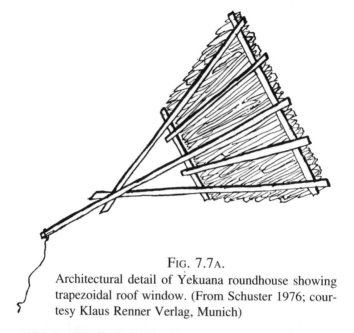

FIG. 7.7A.
Architectural detail of Yekuana roundhouse showing trapezoidal roof window. (From Schuster 1976; courtesy Klaus Renner Verlag, Munich)

FIG. 7.7B.
Interior view of open roof window. (Photo courtesy Walter Coppens)

at irregular intervals in the house wall. In a few roundhouses four major doors in the cardinal directions lead, by way of separate corridors, to the inner room (Schuster 1976, 55, 164).

ROUNDHOUSE SYMBOLISM

According to Yekuana belief, the first communal roundhouse was built by Ättäwanadi at a site where it can still be seen in the form of Kushamakari Mountain. The divine architect of this primordial house was one of several avatars of the Supreme Being, Wanadi (the sun).

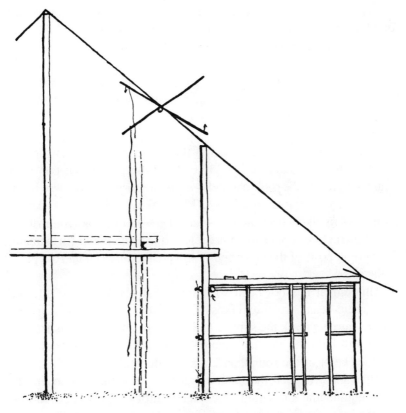

FIG. 7.8.

Architectural detail of Yekuana roundhouse showing relative position of roof window. (From Schuster 1976; courtesy Klaus Renner Verlag, Munich)

The name Ättäwanadi indicates that he was the Wanadi of the first roundhouse (*ättä*), which he constructed according to the blueprint of his own house (situated east of the zenith), and of that of the universe, the house of Wanadi. Every Yekuana roundhouse is an exact replica of Wanadi's invisible house. Its architectural detail is modeled after the celestial sphere and certain landmarks of its mythical geography. The bird sculpture crowning the central pole is the culture hero's signature; Ättäwanadi doubles as the crimson-crested woodpecker (*Campephilus melanoleucos*).

In constructing the first roundhouse, Ättäwanadi began by planting the main post (*anyaduudu*) in the middle of the earth, thereby not only centering the structure but also providing it with a contact between heaven and earth. The inner room of the house, with its wall surrounding the central post, encompasses the sea (*dama*), and the outer ring of family apartments represents the land (*nono*). The center post, as a world axis, reaches deep into the netherworld, a realm of darkness, with subaquatic and subterranean regions. The netherworld is inhabited by condemned souls, by certain spirits, and by giant ophidian earth monsters whose supreme master is a plumed serpent adorned with a rainbow of colorful feathers.

Next, the Creator-Bird oriented the house according to the four world corners. Emulating the Milky Way, he placed the two cross beams supporting the roof in a north-south direction. Today these beams are still known as *adämniädotádi* (Milky Way). The conical canopy of the roof is likened to the celestial sphere and the radiating ribs of the infrastructure supporting it are referred to as *hionooni* (firmament). The upright posts of the outer house wall are the *shidichääne*, or "pillars of the stars."

Although it has not been so described in the literature, the rectangular tie-beam structure represents the solstitial quincunx (figs. 7.4, 7.5). Its corners mark the sunrise and sunset points of the solstices; the center post indicates the meridian position of the sun at the equinoxes, the true center of the roundhouse and the universe.

Ättäwanadi located the main entrance toward the east so that the rising equinoctial sun could enter freely through the walled corridor into the inner room and reach the foot of the central pole. The setting sun, in turn, bursts through the trapezoidal skylight into the interior of the house, illuminating it during the afternoon hours.

CORRESPONDENCES

There is a striking relationship between the imagined shape of the Warao universe and the architectural dimensions of the Yekuana roundhouse. The cylindrical floor of the world ocean and its earth disk in the middle correspond to the doughnut-shaped ground plan of the Yekuana house with its concentric rooms: the inner space relates to the Warao earth disk and the outer ring to the circular sea of Warao cosmology.[5] The Warao *uroboros* snake, a matrix of life, may be likened to the ring of family quarters whose extreme ends, like those of the snake, approach each other in the east.

The celestial sphere of Warao cosmology is architecturally duplicated in the sagging cone of the roof, so that the cylindrical abyss of the netherworld, and the bell-shaped firmament, are mimicked quite closely by the structural outlines of the roundhouse (fig. 7.9).

According to the Warao, the heavens rest on cardinal and inter-cardinal world mountains located along the horizon and having the appearance of gigantic petrified tree stumps. Their doubles in the roundhouse are the twelve upright poles erected at thirty-degree intervals along its periphery.

Instead of the invisible world axis of shamanic conduits to the zenith and beyond, the roundhouse features the central pole which penetrates the apex of the roof cone. The Warao believe their world axis terminates at the zenith in three prongs, each one representing a way station for celestial travelers. Rather than the north-south orientation of the three-pronged Yekuana rooftop, however, the three points of the Warao world axis are aligned in an east-west direction.

---

[5] The Warao adhere to an insular geographical model showing how their land is surrounded by the sea. The Yekuana see the many headwaters of major rivers emanating from the center of their universe and flowing from an imaginary sea to the surrounding earth. The inversion is of little consequence for the present comparison. What matters, instead, is the doughnut-shaped ground plan in both cases.

SYMBOLIC CORRESPONDENCES

In addition to these formal correspondences between the Warao universe and the Yekuana roundhouse, numerous symbolic details suggest a conceptual interrelationship.

Like the Warao universe, the house is oriented according to the cardinal directions. In both the universe and the house, east is the principal direction where the Supreme Being resides. As noted earlier, the Warao call this spirit the God of Origin and relate it to the rising sun. The highest god of the Yekuana is the sun. Additional cardinal spirits of the Yekuana are mentioned by Schuster (1976, 88). Sub-aquatically, at the nadir of both constructs, lives a serpent, four-headed with deer horns for the Warao and feathered for the Yekuana. Both snakes appear to communicate with the world via the *axis mundi*; in the Warao egg-shaped house, the snake is the axis itself.

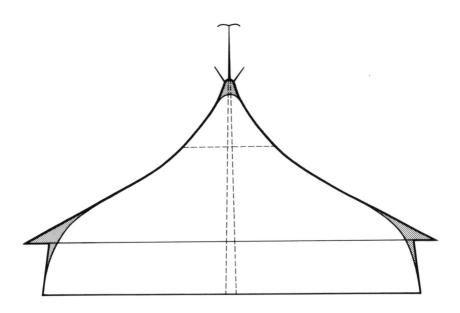

FIG. 7.9.
Bell-shaped universe of the Warao fitted into outline of Yekuana roundhouse.
(Drawing courtesy W. Patrick Finnerty)

The Yekuana identify the conical roof with the firmament which, like the firmament of Warao cosmology, is a hard shell situated under and within a larger house or universe. The Yekuana recognize six to eight superimposed strata, all populated by various spirit beings, anthropomorphic or in animal form (Koch-Grünberg 1923, 378; Barandiarán 1962, 62). The Warao envision one celestial stratum near the top of the bell-shaped firmament, picturing it as a platform (fig. 6.1).

It is noteworthy that the uppermost of the four rings that brace the Yekuana roof is situated at the approximate altitude of the sixth heaven (fig. 7.3). According to Barandiarán (1962, 62, 63), this heaven is of special shamanic significance. It is occupied by three powerful birds whom Ättäwanadi keeps close to his own place at the top of the celestial pyramid and who function as tutelary spirits of shamans.[6]

It will be remembered that Ättäwanadi, the architect of the Yekuana roundhouse, manifests himself as the crimson-crested woodpecker. His residence, in the form of a roundhouse, is believed to be in the highest heaven, which is symbolized by the top of the central pole (Barandiarán 1962, 62), or, according to Arvelo-Jiménez (1974, 162–63), east of the top of the world. Koch-Grünberg (1923, 378) describes this highest and smallest heaven as a globe rather than as a conical roundhouse. It is inhabited by perpetually singing shamans whose chant resembles that of the curing shamans officiating at the foot of the central post.

The Creator-Bird, Mawari, the swallow-tailed kite, also lives at the zenith of the Warao universe. He is the son of the God of Origin and has three major and three minor avian companions.[7] The house he created, northeast of the world axis, is ovoid rather than globular or conical (fig. 6.1), but it does have the same layout as a Yekuana roundhouse (as described below).

The name of the Warao Creator-Bird (Mawari) is Cariban in derivation. It is used to designate supernatural beings in several Carib-speaking societies. For instance, among the Waiwai of southern Guyana Máwari is the Creator (Fock 1963, 35–36). But Mawari's closest kin

---

[6] The three shamanic birds of the sixth heaven of Yekuana cosmology are the great potoo, *müdo* (*Nyctibius grandis*), the Creator's brother; the ferruginous pygmy owl, *höhöttu* (*Glaucidium brasilianum*); and the fork-tailed *nacunda* nighthawk, *tawadi* (*Podager nacunda*) (Civrieux 1980, 175–95).

[7] For the identification of the companions, see chapter 6, fn. 5.

is found among the Akawaio, who know his namesake as the Imawali bird (Butt 1962, 35–40). Here the relationship is not only in name and status but also in species (*Elanoides forficatus*) and in the symbolic character of the bird as well. The bird is closely related to the tobacco spirit to whom, in fact, it often seems to be identical. As such, the bird is associated with shamanism, and the Akawaio refer to it as "Shaman-Bird." The Yekuana employ the name Máwari with a phonemic accent on the first *a* to designate black magic and the death demon. With stress on the second *a* the word refers to ophidian water spirits, members of the entourage of the Plumed Serpent of great shamanic power (Barandiarán 1979, 95). Adapting the Cariban name to their language, the Warao put the accent on the second *a* in Mawari. They use the name to refer not only to the Creator-Bird but also, like the Yekuana, to the immanent power of shamans, which allows them to partake of the status of the God of Origin and of that of Mawari, his son (Barral 1979, 290).

Furthermore, like its Yekuana counterpart, the Warao Creator-Bird is an architect who built his ovoid house on the celestial platform northeast of the zenith. Although the Yekuana roundhouse does not feature a visible platform at this level, it is appropriate here to point out a roundhouse type that does, namely, that of the Cariban Wayana and Aparai Indians of Demarara, French Guiana, and northern Brazil.[8] These Indians construct a beehive roundhouse with a concentric ground plan and a central support pole that pierces the middle of a decorated wooden disk (*maluwana*) fastened a short distance below the rooftop (fig. 7.10). According to available measurements, the so-called sun disk is 78 centimeters in diameter and 5 centimeters thick (Cruls 1958, 288). Like a ceiling, it closes off the uppermost space under the roof. Vivid polychrome designs (red, blue, and white on black) decorate the underside of the disk. Besides prominent double-headed caterpillars (Butt, pers. comm.), anthropomorphic and zoomorphic creatures, such as turtles, frogs, birds, and anteaters, as well as other four-legged animals, are in evidence. Nothing is known about the symbolism involved, but it certainly represents an architectural model of the

---

[8] I am grateful to Dr. Peter Rivière, Oxford University, for having drawn my attention to this fact and to Dr. Audrey Butt-Colson, also of Oxford, for supplying a black-and-white photograph of a Wayana central pole disk from the Pitt Rivers Museum, Oxford University. References to the Wayana disk include Crevaux (1883), Darbois (1953; 1956, 14, pl. 7), and Cruls (1958, 286–89, pl. 38).

FIG. 7.10. Decorated roof disk of Wayana roundhouse. (Courtesy Pitt Rivers Museum)

imaginary disk of the Warao universe and that of the upper celestial stratum of the Yekuana house and heaven.

Nevertheless, a closer look at the structural detail of the egg-shaped house of Mawari reveals additional parallels to the Yekuana round-house. Mawari's house was shown to be in the same general location as Wanadi's personal roundhouse, at the zenith or east of the top of the firmament. Furthermore, Wanadi's house is the prototype of the roundhouse that he erected on earth, and both are modeled after Wanadi's house, the universe.

Mawari's house is an ovoid two-story building made of solidified tobacco smoke (fig. 6.4). The stories are separated by a floor across the lower third of the upright standing structure. There is no central post, but a plumed snake that lives in the lower compartment erects itself periodically and rises vertically through the hole in the ceiling.

This ceiling is the floor of the upper story of the house. Its layout distinguishes between an inner round space and a concentric outer room (fig. 6.5). The latter space is designed as a ring of six living quarters separated from one another by walls. The central room is a ceremonial space where ritual is performed. Four adjacent rooms are occupied by four couples of insect-spirits, collectively referred to as the Creator-Bird's *amawari*. The apartment at one extreme of the circular suite is occupied by the ancestral shaman and his wife; the room at the other end, by Mawari himself. The ends of the circular apartments approach each other on the west side, toward the center of the bell-shaped universe, but they do not meet. Instead, they leave a corridor that leads. from the central room to the only door of the house, which is oriented in a southwesterly direction. A rope-bridge of tobacco smoke spans the celestial abyss and connects the threshold of Mawari's house with the top of the *axis mundi*. Novice shamans who approach the house on their initiatory journey hear its occupants' chanting, which sounds like that of curing shamans.

Mawari has designed the house as a replica of the two eggs that appeared, in primordial times, at the foot of the eastern world mountain. In doing so, he provided a place for the insect-spirits to play a game that determines the fate of life on earth. The board on which the game is played is a rectangular *mesa* divided into two sets of two fields and occupied by two sets of brothers. Located in the middle of the central room of Mawari's house, it is reminiscent of the rectangular structure of tie beams in the Yekuana house, where, as is explained below, the sun plays a game of seasonal fertility.

THE ROOF WINDOW AND THE SUN

One further correspondence between Warao cosmology and the Yekuana house—that which concerns the roof window—is somewhat more covert and speculative. As the roof window has been observed in Yekuana houses in all major areas of tribal distribution, it undoubtedly represents a standard architectural feature of this house type. Koch-Grünberg (1923, 323), the first to report its presence, interpreted the roof window in terms of cultural borrowing from Europeans. Schuster (1976, 58) concurred and, following Koch-Grünberg, based his argument on the Yekuana designation for the window, *mentána* (sp. *ventana*). Barandiarán (1966, 18), on the other hand, refuted this thesis, indicating that the roof window is mentioned in traditional (unpublished) oral literature of the Yekuana, where it is related to the actions of Wanadi, the divine architect.

There is also some disagreement concerning the location of the roof window. Koch-Grünberg (1923, 323), Gheerbrant (1954, 295), Grelier (1956, 95), and Civrieux (1959, 123) omit reference to its directional orientation altogether. The other authors, except for Arvelo-Jiménez (1971, 191), who places it in the east, observed the window on the west side of the roof. Of those, Barandiarán changed his original opinion from northwest (1966, 17) to west (1979, 200), a position coinciding with Coppens's (1981) observation. Schuster (1976, 57, 58), Guss (pers. comm.), and (less assuredly) Heinen (pers. comm.) indicated a southwesterly location.

All authors tend to agree on the two principal functions of the window: to serve as a flue for the entire house and as a skylight for the central room. Barandiarán (1966, 17), who has had many consecutive years of field experience among the Yekuana, vividly describes the prevailing conditions in the roundhouse when the roof window is closed. During the dry season the window is closed at night to keep out vampire bats and evil spirits, but in the wet season the window remains shut practically all the time to keep out the rain. Whenever the window is closed, however, the entire house fills up with as-

FIG. 7.11.
Sunbeam from the roof window penetrating the darkness of the inner room
of a Yekuana roundhouse. (Photo courtesy Barbara Brändli)

phyxiating smoke which, for lack of a flue, filters slowly through the trellis of the roof cone.

As a skylight, the roof window is most effective during the days of the dry season, when it remains open all the time and when the sun pours in "in a great beam as though into the nave of a cathedral" (Gheerbrant 1954, 295). This sunbeam, like a powerful floodlight, bursts into the dark interior of the house with a circumference somewhat larger than that of the window (fig. 7.11).

In order to fulfill its functions of conveying smoke and sunlight, the window's directional position may at first seem to be incon-

FIG. 7.12.
Wind direction in Yekuana territory (shown by arrows) throughout the year. (After *Atlas de Venezuela*, 2nd ed., 1979, 195, Cartografía Nacional de Venezuela. Drawing courtesy Noel Diaz)

sequential, but it is not. An important consideration for favoring a western or, better still, a west-southwesterly location of the roof window relates to the direction of the prevailing winds. In Yekuana territory, southwest is the side of the wind shadow (fig. 7.12). As the winds are southeasterly to northwesterly during the rainy season, a southwestern flue would rarely catch the wind and permit free passage of smoke at all times. Furthermore, because the window remains closed during much of the rainy season (April to September) and because the sun is

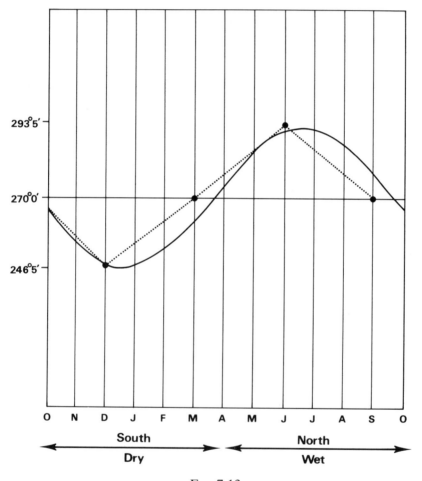

FIG. 7.13.

Annual path of the sun over Yekuana territory calculated by the first day of each month. (Drawing courtesy Noel Diaz)

in the southern sky during the dry season (October to March), the optimal position for the roof window to function as a skylight is the southern half of the roof cone, where it has been observed by several ethnographers in the southwestern quadrant (fig. 7.13).

During the morning hours the Indians rely for light on the rising sun, whose rays enter the inner room through the main entrance and the corridor in the east (fig. 7.14). In the afternoon hours the house is illuminated by the skylight, to which the setting sun of the southern sky has free access. The practice of positioning a house on elevated ground, within a spacious clearing and on a riverbank, may serve the purpose, among others, of securing a minimally obstructed horizon so as to prolong the hours of daylight inside the structure. On the basis of descriptions by Koch-Grünberg (1923, 325–26) and Barandiarán (1966), it would seem that in times past the Yekuana had highly

FIG. 7.14.
Rising sun entering through the main entrance and illuminating inner circular room of Yekuana roundhouse. (Photo courtesy Barbara Brändli)

qualified architects who knew how to situate a house according to solar movements.

Following the divine blueprint, the architects must have known that the optimal location of the approximately 1.25-meters-wide skylight to avoid the wind and to catch a maximum amount of sunlight was roughly west-southwesterly. At three degrees north latitude and close to the site where Ättäwanadi, according to tradition, erected the first roundhouse on Kushamakari Mountain (lat. 3°43′ N, long. 65°45′ W), celestial bodies rise and set almost vertically, and the equinoctial noon sun reaches the meridian at 87 degrees altitude (fig. 7.15).[9] About the time of the autumnal equinox, the setting sun falls obliquely through the window and sends the light beam in the direction of the southeastern corner (fig. 7.16), thereby entering, so to speak, the solstitial rectangle in the house at the sunrise point of the winter solstice (fig. 7.17). The dry season is about to begin.

Moving northward fairly rapidly along the eastern wall of the central room, the light beam focuses on the southern wall of the entrance corridor on or about October 1. By the time of the winter solstice the beam of the setting sun aligns with the central pole and reaches the northeastern corner of the rectangle, which marks the sunrise point of the summer solstice, its chronological opposite. The beam lingers in this northeastern part of the rectangle for more than four months and reaches the northern wall of the entrance corridor by about March 1. From there it spreads relatively quickly across the entrance corridor back to the southeastern corner of the rectangle. As the rainy season is now approaching, the skylight is closed and the beam "turned off." On an occasional sunny afternoon during the rainy season, one can glimpse the sun's position (and ascertain the time of the year) by opening the skylight and observing a weak sun along the southeastern quadrant of the inner room, until it aligns again more perfectly with the window after the autumnal equinox. Thus, during the six months of the dry season, the sunbeam twice scans the width of the eastern solstitial rectangle, once moving northward and then moving southward. The

[9] I am grateful to Dr. Harland W. Epps, UCLA, for his assistance with the astronomical calculations. Dr. E. C. Krupp, director of the Griffith Observatory, Los Angeles, discussed with me the astronomical details in this chapter and helped me with the reproductions of some of the architectural and astronomical illustrations. For this help, and especially for making the planetarium available to assist me in the study of the night sky over Yekuana territory, I am deeply grateful.

movement of the sun within the house could allow a knowledgeable community leader to calculate calendrical time and to schedule events with some precision.

In addition to the horizontal movement of the sunbeam, its vertical motion should also be considered (fig. 7.18). Every sunny day, at about 1400 hours, the light beam comes into the inner room of the house at an acute angle and reaches the foot of the inner wall on the eastern side. The angle increases while the sun is setting, and one can observe an oval disk of light ascend the wall, like the hand of a clock, until it eventually fades away, after 1700 hours, owing to the low altitude of the sun and horizonal obstruction. In a house where the interior wall is as high as the ring of the inner columns, the sunbeam reaches the uppermost corner between wall and roof before it starts gliding up the underside of the canopy. On his drawing of a cylindrical cosmos, Arvelo-Jiménez's (1974, 160) informant placed Wanadi's house or

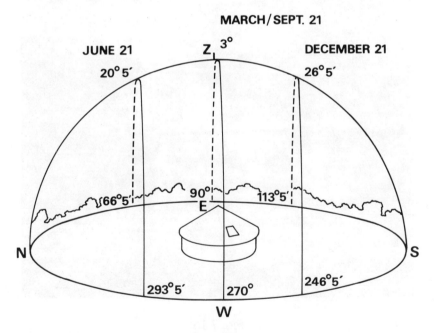

FIG. 7.15.
Noon position of the sun at equinoxes and solstices over Yekuana roundhouse and roof window. (Drawing courtesy Noel Diaz)

village approximately at this juncture. In houses where the interior wall is only as high as the exterior wall, the ascending sunbeam jumps across the wall and against the roof and then it moves upward toward the apex.

For most of the dry season, approximately from November to February, the sunbeam reaches the northeastern corner of the solstitial rectangle inside the house, and the sun disk ascends toward the upper roof, above the summer solstice line. The northeasternmost position of the disk is reached on December 21, when the beam aligns with the central pole and the sunrise corner of the summer solstice. As on so many days of high summer, the sun ascends the central pole, and when the light disk eventually reaches its highest position under the roof, it marks the area where Ättäwanadi (the sun) is at home and where, in the cosmos of the Warao Indians, the oval house of their sunbird, Mawari, is located.

FIG. 7.16.

Weak sunbeam illuminates southeastern corner of decorated internal wall twice a year, following the solstices. (From Schuster 1976; courtesy Klaus Renner Verlag, Munich)

It will be remembered that the Warao hero's house is situated northeast of the zenith and on a plain determined by the meridian positions of the solstitial sun. The sunbeam marking a similar place under the roof of the Yekuana house penetrates the upper smoke-filled cone, making visible the curling patterns of opaque smoke, which look like the bridge of tobacco smoke connecting Mawari's house (sunspot) with the world axis (central pole) in a northeasterly direction. Here, in the inner room of his roundhouse, the solar deity of the Warao and his companions engage in the perpetual game of life, played out on a rectangular *mesa*, just as the solar god Wanadi of the Yekuana plays

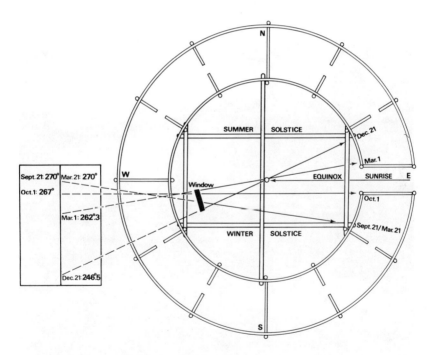

FIG. 7.17.

Ground plan of Yekuana roundhouse showing direction of sunbeam through the open window during the dry season. At equinoctial sunrise light enters straight through the main entrance and reaches the foot of the central post. (Drawing courtesy Noel Diaz)

the game of the seasons on the solstitial quincunx in the ceremonial center of his roundhouse.

Although recorded Yekuana ethnoastronomy remains mute with regard to the sunbeam's symbolism and function as calendar and clock, future fieldwork might produce the needed evidence despite the obvious decline of modern Yekuana architecture. Other South American Indians, like the Kogi of Colombia, make use of a similar sunbeam calendar in their beehive-shaped temples, which feature a hole in the top of the roof apex for this purpose (Reichel-Dolmatoff 1978, 18–19). It would be of particular interest to find out whether there is any relationship between the zoomorphic iconography on the inner wall of the roundhouse and the movement of the sun along this gallery of art. For instance, might the combination of the two represent a zodiac? Could the sunbeam entering upon the different sections of the wall

FIG. 7.18.
Sunbeam moving upward over the interior wall of bark planks marking the time of day. (Photo courtesy Walter Coppens)

indicate the seasonal availability of certain food resources (fig. 7.19)? Was the possible gnomonic function of the protruding center pole and the roof apex recognized (fig. 7.20)? These questions cannot be answered at present. In view of the fact that the animals depicted on the house wall represent mythological star people in Yekuana mythology, however, it might be rewarding to inquire into any relationship the roundhouse and the roof window might have with the day and the night sky.

It seems to be of interest, for example, that at the winter solstice, when the setting sun aligns through the skylight with the center post and the sunrise corner of the summer solstice and when, symbolically, the sunspot marks the place where both the Yekuana and the Warao Creator-Birds are at home, Orion is in opposition to the sun. In other words, the constellation rises in front of the main entrance of the house at the time of sunset and transits at midnight. At two o'clock in the morning the trapezoidal asterism reaches the place on the western sky vault (i.e., the roof of Wanadi's house) where it mimics the trapezoidal skylight of the roundhouse and "illuminates" the sun in its house.

Like the sun in connection with the skylight, so the constellation of Orion is a sign of seasons and weather. In Yekuana country its rising at midnight marks the autumnal equinox and the beginning of summer. At the winter solstice, as pointed out earlier, Orion opposes the sun. Its rising at sunset, transit at midnight, and setting at sunrise mimic the sun and announce the height of the dry season. At the vernal equinox Orion's transiting at sunset and setting at midnight mark the beginning of the wet season at whose peak, the summer solstice, it catches up with the sun and brings it back by rising and setting simultaneously with it. Despite the lack of ethnographic evidence, it is not unreasonable to suggest that the Yekuana, like so many other peoples around the world, have recognized Orion's connection with the sun, the weather, and the seasons, and that they might have related it to the calendar function of the roof window in their roundhouse.

THE ETHNOHISTORICAL QUESTION

The preceding comparison of Warao cosmology and Yekuana roundhouse architecture raises an interesting ethnohistorical question: Given the geographical and cultural distance separating the tribes, how can one account for the communalities observed between the two?

FIG. 7.19.
Close-up of decorations on the interior wall of a modern Yekuana roundhouse.
(Photo courtesy Barbara Brändli)

Apparently, each tribe claims to have inhabited Trinidad at some time. To the Warao, the island forms an integral part of traditional geography, and regular trading connections were maintained with various groups and peoples until the 1940s. If Barandiarán (1979, 142) is to be believed, Trinidad for the Yekuana is a province that was conquered by one of their culture heroes. He subsequently ceded it to other Cariban tribes in exchange for iron tools and merchandise.[10] No one can tell whether and how long ago the alleged conquest of Trinidad by the Yekuana hero occurred. His departure dates from the time when iron became the intensely sought-after El Dorado of the Indians.

In historical times, and after the foundation of Angostura (Ciudad Bolívar) in 1764, the Yekuana established contact with the Spanish on the Orinoco (see map 7.1). At that time the Yekuana had only recently, in 1744, experienced their first encounter with Europeans. The people of Ankosturaña (Angostura) were incorporated into Yekuana mythol–ogy as the good children, Iaranavi, of their creator Wanadi, who provided them with the heavenly gifts of iron and cloth. To shorten the 1,600-kilometer-long trade route along the Orinoco, the Yekuana established an overland connection, fluvial in part and partly along a forest trail, which cut the distance in half. From Esmeralda on the upper Orinoco it led northward to Angostura on the lower Orinoco. Beginning in 1764, large-scale trade relations by way of this overland route established the presence of the Yekuana among the citizens of this struggling Spanish settlement. Trading continued until 1776, when the Indians abandoned and partly destroyed the trade route to escape the increasing oppression of their European partners.

The Ankosturaña episode of Yekuana trade relations coincided roughly with the tenure (1766–1776) of Don Manuel Centurión Guerrero as governor of Guayana. Breaking with the *reducciones* tradition of mission-ruled Indian settlements, this flamboyant autocrat ordered the abandonment of several villages near Angostura and incorporated their predominantly indigenous populations into the nascent town. In addition, and as a measure designed to boost the population of this urban center, in 1768 Centurión, intent on resettling the Warao at Angostura by force, dispatched raiding parties into the

---

[10] Dr. David Guss has pointed out to me that, rather than to the Island of Trinidad, Yekuana tradition might refer to a certain interfluvial island in the Uraricoera River, called Traenida.

FIG. 7.20.
Aerial view of Yekuana roundhouse during afternoon hours
showing open roof window and shadow of roof apex and of top
end of central pole. (Photo courtesy Barbara Brändli)

Orinoco Delta and regions to the west (Archivo General de Indias, Leg. 20, fol. 3, V:1779). Altogether he seems to have expatriated no less than 1,170 Warao and to have settled them in five neighborhoods (Orocopiche, Maruanta, Buenavista, Borbón, and Carolina) around the town (Lodares 1930, 241). Here they lived in close association with Spanish and Indian settlers and may have established contact with Yekuana traders from the upper Orinoco. Also, the Warao mention Angostura as one of the earlier mainland trading posts they frequented to obtain iron tools and other goods generally unavailable in the delta but indispensable to their shamans (i.e., tobacco, quartz crystals, and *caraña*). It is precisely these latter items that Yekuana traders carried in their baggage.

Cariban Indians believed that smoking Yekuana tobacco, which was traded throughout Guiana as "tiger tobacco," endowed their shamans with power over the jaguar spirit. The Warao, on the other hand, identify the Carib with the jaguar and explain that by smoking tobacco their enemies are able to transform themselves into this feared beast (Alvarado 1945, 57; Barral 1960, 257–59; Butt-Colson 1973, 47; Coppens 1971, 36; Grelier 1954, 127).

Various kinds of spirit stones and quartz pebbles were obtained from Yekuana traders because they were believed to contain Imawali, the Forest Spirit, and could be shamanically dispatched as pathogenic agents. His namesake, Mawari, of the Warao, is also "sent" in such a capacity. As a wooden mannequin and accompanied by three quartz pebbles, the spirit-bird's *amawari* (companions), the pathogenic foursome, is believed to represent a devastating force (Butt-Colson 1973, 45, 57; Wilbert 1979, 296). *Caraña* of the Orinoco (*Protium heptaphyllum*) is a resin burned by the Warao shaman as incense in the sanctuary and rolled in his cigar for fragrance and as an agent of transformation.

It is difficult to ascertain whether the Warao ever obtained the goods they needed directly from the Yekuana traders at Angostura or elsewhere. We do know that groups from both tribes frequented the town for trading purposes and that, if they ever engaged in barter, the Yekuana carried desiderata of high value to the Warao which were associated with Mawari-related cosmology and shamanism.

Around the turn of the nineteenth century, and subsequent to their disillusionment with the Spaniards of Angostura, the Yekuana established intensive trade relations with other Europeans. This time they discovered the Dutch of Demarara in distant Georgetown (Amenadiña) at the mouth of the Essequibo (Barandiarán 1979, 43, map of trade routes), where ships arriving from across the sea brought the cargo of Wanadi in even greater abundance than at Ankosturaña. This new contact with Europeans lasted throughout the nineteenth century and continued into the recent past (Butt-Colson 1973, 10; Guss 1981, 29–34).

The Warao settlers of Angostura escaped from the town after the province of Guayana was recaptured by the patriotic forces in the War of Independence (Lodares 1930, 2:11, 241, 254; Humbert 1976, 270; Carrocera 1979, 84). In an attempt to leave the Spaniards and their turbulent warfare behind, the "refugee Warao" fled to Demarara and placed themselves under the protection of the Dutch. They settled along the coast between the mouth of the Orinoco and the Barima, near Arawak and Carib Indians at the mouth of the Essequibo, and beyond Georgetown on the lower Corontijn and Nickerie rivers (see Nimuendajú's map in Gillin 1948, 800). The Warao so increased the Indian population of that colony that by 1840 they numbered 3,150 of the 7,250 Indians in the colony (see frontispiece map in Menezes 1979). There has since been considerable contact among the so-called Spanish Warao in Guiana, the Carib and Arawak tribes around them, and their kin in the Orinoco Delta. But whether an exchange of concepts relating to the Yekuana roundhouse and Warao cosmology actually resulted from such trade contacts remains, of course, uncertain. All the available evidence shows is that these widely separated populations entered one another's zones of influence in historical and possibly prehistoric times around the delta, near Angostura and in Dutch-British Guiana, and that opportunities for cultural exchange may have presented themselves on these occasions.

SQUARING THE CIRCLE

It remains to be pointed out that the solstitial square in a circular cosmic plain is a concept familiar to the Warao and that, like the Yekuana, they relate it to their houses. Modern Warao Indians live in rectangular saddle-roofed stilt houses, but elder tribesmen remember a more traditional house type they refer to as *bakoakobo*, "round shelter," or *onobako*, "testicle (-shaped) shelter." It consisted of a horizontal rectangular frame (2.5 m x 2.0 m) of manaca palm stems (*Euterpe oleracea*) resting on four posts (1.75 m x 2 m) of the same wood. The frame was braced by two diagonal tie beams.

The name of the shelter was derived from the peculiar shape of its roof, which consisted of a large number of giant leaves (10 m x 2 m) of the temiche palm (*Manicaria saccifera*) whose sturdy rachises were stuck close to each other into the ground around the supporting infrastructure of the shelter. The broadly overlapping leaves were bent toward the center of the shelter and tied down with bushrope. The rectangular pole structure of the traditional round shelter is said to have been oriented in an east-west direction, and its upper corners were believed to be inhabited by a number of solstitial lords.

The same belief continues to be associated with the modern rectangular stilt house. Oriented, at least ideally, in the same direction, the horizontal northern header beam of the roof is thought to parallel the course of the summer sun, the one on the south side that of the winter sun, and the ridgepole that of the equinoctial suns. In other words, the roof of the modern Warao house relates to the solstitial rectangle within the circular ground plan of the cosmos (and, one should add, the *mesa* relates to the circular floor plan of the House of Tobacco Smoke) as the rectangular tie-beam structure relates to the circular ground plan of the Yekuana roundhouse.

Nevertheless, despite all the correspondences between Warao and Yekuana cosmologies, the blueprints of both reveal so much originality that it is difficult to account for similarities by pointing to sporadic and relatively recent trade relations. For instance, apparently unrelated to Yekuana beliefs is the emphasis in Warao cosmology on a horizontal distribution of supernatural beings along the edge (*aitona*) of the cosmic plane. In contrast, the Yekuana cosmos is vertically populated by supernaturals who inhabit a series of superimposed tiers.

As indicated earlier, the Warao believe the solstitial areas of their world to be inhabited by several fertility gods. More specifically, along the summer solstice the Indians place the Lord of the Sacred Trumpet. His wind pollinates the primordial moriche palms with which he shares the sunrise region. The abundance of moriche fruit and sago throughout the year depends on his benevolence. At the sunset point of the same solstice resides the Lord of Ritual and Dance, who offers survival through propitiation of the directional gods. Along the winter solstice lives the Mother of the Forest and Animals who provides the abundance of sylvan resources. And, finally, the equinoctial suns pertain to the God of Origin in the east and the Land of Death in the west. During the dedication ceremony of a new house, the priest-shaman propitiates these spirits of fertility by sprinkling libations into the four corners of the roof and along its three major horizontal beams.

The correspondences and the differences between Warao and Yekuana cosmological beliefs thus point to a larger cultural tradition of which these tribal ones are simply two surviving examples. Coastal and seafaring peoples like the Warao have probably inhabited the northeastern corner of South America for more than 6,000 years. Beginning at about 4,000 B.P., they were joined in this region by Arawakan and later by Cariban tribes, and together they forged a distinct Amazonian subculture. Continental, but also insular and possibly circum-Caribbean, elements were amalgamated over time, giving rise to local cultural variants with a common denominator.

In view of the obviously profound nature of the ideological characteristics of this common cultural denominator, diffusionist arguments of donor and donee cultures seem to acquire a tinge of triviality. More significant, it seems to me, is the fact that in both tribal cosmologies the squaring-of-the-circle archetype is clearly recognizable as the organizing principle of personal and societal identity. And through this "archetype of wholeness," as Jung (1959, 388) called it, both cosmologies provide an Amazonian response to the universal question of how to reduce the chaotic forces that threaten telluric survival to the generative unity of the celestial round.

Chapter Eight

The Lords of Rain

One of the biggest surprises of my career as an ethnographer was to find the Warao in possession of an elaborate system of weather shamanism. I had often heard the tribal rainmaker sing his magic chants or had seen him blow against upcoming storms, but I had assumed those functions to be the extent of Warao weather magic. It was not until the rainy season of 1975 that I learned otherwise.

The Warao Indians inhabit the extensive swamplands of the Orinoco Delta on the east coast of Venezuela. Not only is their world, *hobahi*, "surrounded by water," but it is also crisscrossed by a dense network of drainage rivers, saturated by tides and groundwater, and flooded annually by the Orinoco River. Furthermore, Waraoland, situated between eight and ten degrees north latitude, is subjected to the winter solstice humidity of the northeast trades as well as to the Amazonian monsoonlike rains that follow the spring equinox. From May to October rains are heavy to torrential; even during the so-called dry season there are often rainy days. With so much water from above and below, why would the Warao bother with shamanic rainmakers? One would suppose that rainmakers and rain gods are ordinarily found among peoples living in arid regions, or among agriculturalists for whom a reliable pattern of precipitation is a sine qua non of survival. In such regions food and drink depend on rain and on the manipulation of the supernatural masters of the precious commodity. But in the Orinoco Delta these conditions do not exist; there is a superabundance of water and the Warao, traditionally a nonagricultural people, do not need rain to fertilize fields. Consequently, the explanation for the presence of weather shamanism among the Indians has to be other than a conventional one.

The Warao population is roughly 20,000. With the exception of a common language, however, there is little cohesion among the tribe's members. Far more important for the individual's daily needs is the local group or band, averaging fifty persons—thirteen women, twelve men, and twenty-five children. A remarkable achievement for a society at this level of cultural development is the availability of an array of professional careers from which each adult may choose a challenging and meaningful pursuit. Among the posts open to men are shamanic craftsman, ritual musician, and priest-, dark-, and light-shamans; those open to women include shamanic artisan, herbalist, and priest- and white-shamanesses. Rainmaking is thus only one of a number of career opportunities. What distinguishes the careerist individual from others is that he or she acquires, in the process of enculturative learning, not only technical and mental skills, socioeconomic stability, and recognition, but also the benefit of supernatural patronage. Warao careerists live and labor *sub specie aeternitatis*, motivated by the usual mundane interests of personal advancement while keeping an eye on eternity. Warao rainmakers today do not enjoy the same power as do other shamans or shamanic artisans, a result, I believe, of an acculturative process during which the tribal life-style has been changed and weather shamanism deemphasized.

The Warao refer to their weather shaman as *naharima*, "father of rain," and there is usually one in every local group. Rainmakers tend to be elderly persons, and, although most of them are men, I have also become acquainted with a "mother of rain" (*naharani*).

To become a rainmaker, a person seeks out an accomplished practitioner to whom he can apprentice himself. Nowadays, women do not undergo formal training but learn from their husbands by observation. Young people are not eligible, ostensibly because they are apt to abuse their power in youthful irresponsibility. In addition to being at the proper age, the novice must have sufficient money or goods to compensate the teacher for his efforts. The apprenticeship period lasts three to four days. I have known rain shamans who had engaged as many as six teachers successively for fear that none might be in full command of the wisdom of his office; and I know of yet another case where an aspiring novice traveled to the very end of Waraoland to find a competent master teacher.

An important difference among rainmakers, or among efforts to become one, is that one may acquire the art of rainmaking by "listening," as the Warao would say, or by "dreaming." Some rainmakers learned their trade through informal education only, whereas others also underwent a shamanic initiation which brought them face to face with the Lords of Rain. Although I do not have supporting evidence, it is likely that in the past all rainmakers were trance-initiated and that today's "secular" practitioners are symptomatic of a deculturative process.

For the study period, master and apprentice retire to an isolated place to practice the chants and transmit and learn the skills of the profession. At the end of the instruction the confident student applies his newly acquired power by calling or repelling a thunderstorm. To call a storm the rainmaker addresses the rain gods in traditional incantations. Done properly, a chant is expected to bring prompt results. To ward off a storm, the rainmaker rubs the palms of his hands together and, while holding them close to his lips, blows forcefully between them. After a few seconds he flings his arms skyward and waves his hands toward the approaching storm, shouting

> Rainbow, Rainbow
> That is enough
> Listen to me
> It is enough
> Hear my words
> Let the rain go by.

For a trance-initiated weather shaman, the period of skill-training is followed by an initiation ritual. During his apprenticeship the novice has refrained from eating and drinking, while smoking tobacco heavily in the form of two-foot-long cigars. *Nicotiana rustica*, a high-nicotine species of tobacco, is preferred for this purpose and, like other Warao shamans, rainmakers rely on its potency for hallucinatory experiences. In his emaciated state the novice soon falls into a trance, to meet Kanamuno, the black giant. This demon of colossal proportions approaches the novice with wide-open mouth, lifts him up, and swallows him. Without being crushed or hurt the initiate experiences his passing through the giant's body as a long journey, which ends with his ejection, as an old man, from the buttocks of the devourer. In his new form and in the land of the Lords of Rain, the novice meets the deities, is recognized by them, and is endowed with the power of saying their names. Some rainmakers have visited the rain gods without experiencing the ordeal of transformation; but those who have done so claim to possess the power of a patron god in their breasts—the trademark of true Warao professionalism.

Kanamuno, the black transformation giant, has a female companion, Tarita, suggesting that, at least in the past, rainmaker initiations for women also took place. In any event, isolation during initiation is sought, not only to achieve close concentration but also to prevent any unexpected noise from awakening the novice during his narcotic sleep (while still inside the devourer). If he does wake up he may become disoriented, fall ill, and die.

The Warao recognize eight Lords of Rain (fig. 8.1), whose generic designation is *kabo arotutum.* They reside on eight world mountains

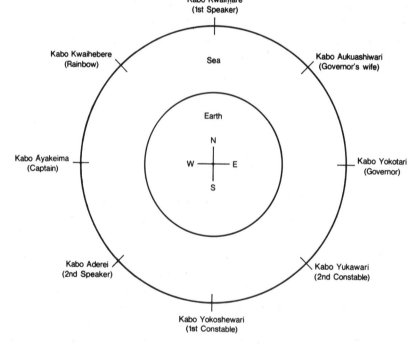

THE LORDS OF RAIN

Fig. 8.1.
The Lords of Rain. (Drawing courtesy Noel Diaz)

at the cardinal and intercardinal points around the horizonal edge of the universe. According to their geocentric worldview, the Warao picture the earth as a disk surrounded by the sea. The world mountains along the circular outer edge of the sea support the cosmic vault. The rain gods live in mansions on top of these sky-bearing mountains. The doors of their houses face the center of the universe. During the rainy season, when the doors are wide open, the rain gods sit on benches in the doorways, looking toward the world. The doors are closed for the rest of the year.

Both the mansion and the personal appearance of a rain god have an air of opulence about them which the Warao tend to associate with wealthy Venezuelans. Indeed, the Indians do not envision the rain gods as Warao but as Criollos, with the peculiar difference that the lords have large flaring heads. During the rainy season the gods wear black and during the dry season they don white tunics. They wear sandals and spectacles and smoke elbow pipes. In their hands the rain gods carry large walking staffs that produce lightning. Their voices roll like thunder through the cloud-draped skies, while rain exudes from their bodies.

Of the eight Lords of Rain seven are male and one is female. Among themselves they form a stratified elite that parallels the political hierarchy of the subtribe. Table 8.1 lists the rain deities according to seniority and to their location in the world. I believe that the order in which the rain gods are ranked and placed along the horizon is deliberate rather than random inasmuch as the power vested in each lord corresponds and appears to be relative to the frequency and velocity of winds along the delta littoral and the Gulf of Paria. Many more meteorological data, specifically for the Orinoco Delta, are needed to substantiate this claim.

The political titles of the lords in tables 8.1 and 8.2 are the English translations of their Waraoan equivalents, most of which, in turn, come from Spanish. The Warao refer to the governor as *kobenahoro*, to the governor's wife as *kobenahoro atida*, to the captain as *kabitana*, to the constable as *fisicali* (from "fiscal"), and to the speaker as *dibatu*. The titles are used as terms of reference rather than address. The rain shaman calls the lords by singing, using their personal names. The chant included below was sung by a Warao, whose patron rain god is Kabo Kwaihebere of the northwesterly world mountain. Uttering the name of his patron rain god is taboo; in addressing him a person uses the title Hubanashiko, "Rainbow," because during his initiation he had adopted this rain god's name and is "embarrassed" now to use it publicly. Translating the appellations of the Lords of Rain is fraught with difficulties because they rarely represent words or word combinations employed in common parlance. In fact, one of my informants, who had spent a year among the Pemon Indians of southern Venezuela, suggested even Cariban provenance in certain instances.

Nonetheless, the etymology of personal names of the rain lords suggests meaningful connotations which, not surprisingly, appear to be associated with weather phenomena. It makes sense, for instance, that "Thunderers" would be associated with the southern trade winds,

TABLE 8.1

RANKS AND LOCATIONS OF THE WARAO LORDS OF RAIN

	Name	Rank	Location
1.	Kabo Yokotari	Governor	East
2.	Kabo Aukuashiwari	Governor's wife	Northeast
3.	Kabo Ayakeima	Captain	West
4.	Kabo Yokoshewari	First constable	South
5.	Kabo Yukawari	Second constable	Southeast
6.	Kabo Kwaimare	First speaker	North
7.	Kabo Aderei	Second speaker	Southwest
8.	Kabo Kwaihebere	Rainbow	Northwest

TABLE 8.2

RELATIONSHIP OF RAIN LORDS AND WIND CONDITIONS

		Wind		
Rank	Location	Frequency (percent)	Direction	Average velocity (kph)
Governor	E	20	Easterly	5
Governor's wife	NE	11	Northeasterly	5
Captain	W	7	Westerly	3
Second constable	SE	5	Southeasterly	3
First constable	S	3	Southerly	3
First speaker	N	3	Northerly	3
Rainbow	NW	3	Northwesterly	2
Second speaker	SW	1	Southwesterly	1

Source: *Atlas de Venezuela* 1979, 195. Meteorological data corresponding to Güiria, Sucre.

which carry humidity around the winter solstice, and with intertropical southern and southeasterly winds, which bring the spring equinoctial storms with resplendent lightning.

As explained above, communication with the rain gods is possible only during the rainy season. Once they have retired into their houses, the rain gods no longer attend to the shaman's wishes, nor do they react to his protective spells or to his incantations to provoke a storm.

Incantations may be directed by a rainmaker to any one of the eight lords. Included below are the Warao text and my translation into English of a chant, recorded in August 1975 with the assistance of Jaime Zapata, senior rain shaman of the Winikina subtribe. This chant is addressed to Yokotari, the supreme Lord of Rain residing in the east.

WEATHER SHAMAN'S CHANT TO YOKOTARI

I

Ihi kabo arotu ihi
ihi weyo a buaranoko
arotu
ihi tata arotu
otuida arotu
hi [wai] karamuna
nanoarate ine.

You are the lord of heaven
you rule where the sun comes
aflame
you are the lord of yonder
lord of remoteness
I shall pronounce and
repeat your name.

Hi karamuna
hi wai ka- karamuna
hi wai ka- karamuna
nanoarate
hi wai karamuna
nanoarate ine.

I shall raise it
your name I shall raise
your name I shall raise
and repeat
your name I shall raise
and repeat again.

Otuida arotu
ma nobo diawara
ma nobo diawara
hi karamuna
manobo diawara ihi
kabo arotu ihi
kabo arotu
otuida arotu:
YOKOTARI.

Lord of remoteness
my grandfather god
my grandfather god
I call upon you
my grandfather god
you are the lord of heaven
lord of heaven
lord of remoteness:
YOKOTARI.

II

Karamunai	You trembled
hi karamunai	you trembled
hi karamunai	you trembled
hi karamunai	you trembled
nanoarate ine	I shall repeat your name
hi kanamane	so you will rise
hi kanamane	you will rise
hi kanamane.	you will rise.
Hi natorobo aida	Your mighty staff
orebekware	preceding
orebekware	ahead of you
kabo sisi a witu	right on the road of heaven
orebekane	ahead of you
hi urunaka tane	will not weigh you down
hi urunaka tane	will not weigh you down
neriwakate	so you be content
neriwakate ine	and I be content
hi urunaka tane	it will not weigh you down
neriwakane.	being comfortable.
Neriwakane	Being agreeable
hi anatoro aida	your mighty staff
memo sabane	pass me by
memo sabane	pass me by
hiyakakune	to the *cuajo* tree
doko mare	with its wind-blown leaves
nisinatahine	there you plant it and
hi abate ine.	I shall leave you.

III

Hi nasaribuna tane	With your voice like
domu turu tuyuna	the *tigana* bird's
tuyuna ware	the snake-necked *tigana*
taisi a yekoita	with its cry
ahi hatekore	its piercing cry
mu yaritanu	become enraged
mu yaritanu	become enraged
hi tehori	your body
mu yaritanu	become infuriated
mu yaritanu.	become infuriated.

Ori kanamanu	Arise
hi kanamane	to your full height
hi kobukane	stand up
hi kobukane	stand up
kabo sisia	on the road of heaven
hi kobukanewitu ine	stand straight [I say]
hi kobukane	stand up
hi kobukane	stand up
hi kobukane	stand up
kabo sisia.	on the road of heaven.

IV

Kabasimo hi tehori	Your body like a fiery wasp
hi te abane	brace your body
mu yari tanu	become enraged
ma nobo diawara ma nobo	my grandfather god my grandfather
ma nobo diawara	my grandfather god
ma nobo kabo arotu	my grandfather lord of heaven
kabo arotu diawara.	lord of heaven.

Kabo meho kasaba yana	Now then at the bosom of heaven
kasaba yana toate ine	there then shall I place
ma weraribuyawitu	my tongue's own words
ma nasaribuyawitu	my very words
kabo arotu	lord of heaven
isa ine nanoarane.	wherewith I repeat your name.

| Ne mu yaritanu | Eh! Become infuriated! |
| mu yaritanu. | Become infuriated! |

| Miana | Dim-visioned, |
| diana. | that is all. |

♩ = ca. 104 m.m.

I - hi ka-bo a-ro-tu i-hi // i-hi we-yo a bu-a-ra-no-ko a-ro-tu i-hi

ta-ta a-ro-tu // o-tu-i-da a-ro-tu hi ka-ra-mu-na na-no-a-ra-te i-ne

Hi ka-ra-mu-na hi wai ka-ka-ra-mu-na // hi wai ka-ka-ra-mu-na

na-no-a-ra-te hi wai ka-ra-mu-na na-no-a-ra-te i-ne // O-tu-i-da

a-ro-tu ma no-bo di-a-wa-ra // ma no-bo di-a-wa-ra hi ka-ra-mu-na

ma no-bo di-a-wa-ra i-hi // ka-bo a-ro-tu i-hi // ka-bo a-ro-tu

o-tu-i-da a-ro-tu: YO-KO-TA-RI Ka-ra-mu-nai // Hi ka-ra-mu-nai

hi ka-ra-mu-nai hi ka-ra-mu-nai na-no-a-ra-te i-ne // hi ka-na-ma-ne

hi ka-na-ma-ne hi ka-na-ma-ne Hi na-to-ro-bo a-i-da o-re-be-kwa-re //

o-re-be-kwa-re ka-bo si-si a wi-tu o-re-be-ka-ne hi u-ru-na-ka ta-ne //

hi u-ru-na-ka ta-ne ne-ri-wa-ka-te ne-ri-wa-ka-te i-ne // hi u-ru-na-ka

ta-ne ne-ri-wa-ka-ne // Ne-ri-wa-ka-ne hi a-na-to-ro a-i-da me-mo

Rendering Warao religious chant in a form intelligible to the outsider is handicapped by a series of complicating factors, one of which is the accelerated speed of performance. The above example, for instance, took only one minute and fifty seconds to record. The voice of the speaker is low-pitched and articulation is difficult to understand. Under normal circumstances, chants of this kind are often performed quite audibly in the quietude of predawn hours, but just as frequently they are whispered by the rainmaker, intelligible only to the immediate bystander.[1]

A second complicating factor is uncommon language employed in ritual chanting; the use of the word *diawara* in everyday language, for instance, is discouraged by religious practitioners and so is rarely heard. A word like *weyo* is employed only by shamans, whereas the common person would say *hokohi* to designate the sun. But rather than dwelling on the formal details of Warao chants, I comment instead on the content in order to facilitate the understanding of the text.

The first part of the chant (I) is an evocation proclaiming the station of the lord in question, his place of origin, and his name. To have the power of *kabo* shamanism means to be able to envision or to "scan" the body of a rain god while addressing him. The rainmaker's familiarity with the god's corporal features derives from the experience of his initiatory journey when he transformed to become his elder, his classificatory father.

More important, *kabo* power entails the capability of pronouncing the rain lord's name. This ability is the true power of knowledge, knowledge of the essence of the deity as it is bound up in his secret name. The power of grasping and of naming the rain gods turns the weather shaman into the formidable person that he is, the *naharima*, "Father," "Master of the Lord of Rain."

When the weather shaman utters his name the rain god must listen. Thus, the second part of the chant (II) shows the deity arising from

[1] I transcribed the text of the "Weather Shaman's Chant to Yokotari" from a cassette recording. Translation was aided by field notes and by commentaries made by two Indians: Antonio Lorenzano and Cesáreo Soto. Dr. Dale Olsen kindly provided the musical transcription from a copy of the field recording. Transcription entailed slowing the music down from 7.5 ips to 3.75 ips. Several text corrections made by Olsen in the process of musical transcription are gratefully acknowledged. I should like to thank Dr. Floyd Lounsbury and Dr. Gerardo Reichel-Dolmatoff for their helpful comments on this chapter.

his stool. He is encouraged to walk toward the zenith and to use his walking staff, step by step, until he can thrust it into a *cuajo* tree (*Virola surinamensis*). Hit by the staff of lightning, the tree falls and, so it is believed, produces a rainbow as evidence of the rain shaman's success in raising the god.

Encouraged, the rainmaker changes his suggestions to the deity to commands in part three of the chant (III). So that his body will exude copious rainfall, the shaman admonishes him to become irritated by the penetrating, high-pitched double whistle of the sun bittern (*Eurypyga helias*), whose spread wings, incidentally, display a "sunburst" effect that turns the bird into a fitting symbol of a rain lord who resides "where the sun comes aflame." Furthermore, the god is provoked by the image of the fiercely aggressive and noxious wasp (*tomonoho simo*, *Stenopolybia fulvofasciata* DeGeer). The weather shaman performs all these duties by directing his words to the heart of the cloud heaven where, as expressed in part four of the chant (IV), they echo and reecho to keep the rain god in a state of rage.

Strangely enough, the Warao incantations to the Lords of Rain do not resemble humble supplications to obtain a gift of fertilizing rain from benevolent deities. Instead, Warao rain lords are provoked to unleash a deluge of rattling thunderstorms and to drench the world with cataclysmic downpours. Thus we return to the question of the significance of Warao weather shamanism.

When asked directly, the Warao do not understand the question; the rain lords have no *anamonina*, they say, no transformational genesis. They do not have a previous form and are without beginning. Consequently, rain shamans have existed since the beginning of humankind and need no further explanation. Observing the role of the rain shaman over time, however, does offer some clues that help explain the phenomenon. Why does he make it rain? As punishment, is the stereotypical answer, punishment for the greed of his fellowmen.

As elderly persons, rainmakers belong to the nonproductive sector of society, and herein seems to lie the real reason why the young and energetic are excluded from the profession. Elderly weather shamans beg for food, goods, and favors, and they are not to be sent away empty-handed or humiliated. They ask for a share of the hunting bag, of the catch of fish, or of other staples. They ask that something be brought back for them from trading expeditions. They ask for shelter in provisional camps and, generally speaking, for consideration. If the requests are rejected, the offenders will pay by being scared and doused by thunderstorms. Even in response to annoyance suffered because of an insect sting or an accidental injury, the weather shaman will retire to his hammock and sing or whisper for rain. Rainmakers thus receive a great deal of attention and are treated with much respect.

At first this explanation of Warao weather shamanism may impress the Western reader as exceedingly facile and the seeming opportunism of the person as disappointing and degrading. When viewed from the perspective of the senior men and women of the tribe, however, rain shamanism becomes a most effective institution. Care for the aged is accepted by the Warao as a social obligation of the entire group. Even at the food-foraging level this sharing of responsibility makes the system of old-age care work.

The severity of punishment meted out by the rainmaker is also easily underestimated by the outside observer. Can scaring the people by thunder and lightning or pouring water over them really lessen their selfishness and induce them to share resources? To be considered first in this respect is the truly awesome spectacle of a tropical thunderstorm, especially when one has to endure it with the simple means of a primitive technology. The discomfort and sheer misery of having to sit out one storm after another in a boat on the river, under a branch, or in a palm-thatched house without walls are indescribable, particularly when one is faced with the prospect of weeks and months of such circumstances.

Furthermore, the small fires of wet firewood do little to alleviate the cold weather brought by cold wind and rain. Diseases begin to take their toll. Bronchitis, common colds, and coughs all take a turn for the worse, as do rheumatic diseases and asthma, especially if cooling temperatures are accompanied by strong northerly winds. Discomfort and illness of these kinds are no harmless bogeys in a swamp, but serious forms of punishment allegedly brought about by the intervention of the weather shaman.

One further aspect needs consideration in this connection. Before the recent introduction of agriculture, the Warao exploited sago of the moriche palm (*Mauritia flexuosa*) as their staple. The availability of this starch within the trunks of moriche stems fluctuates according to the pattern of precipitation throughout the year. But it is precisely during the period of heavy rains, between May and the beginning of August, that the sago starch becomes very scarce and the food economy is seriously strained. Inclement weather, disease, and hunger conspire effectively against the general welfare of the Indians and make the weak among them vulnerable to death. Seen in this context, the rainmaker assumes a most important position in the group; he is the one who can divert a storm from his people's territory, but he can also conjure up the fear-inspiring specter of a rainy season in its grimmest form. These are, I believe, the essential reasons that the Warao bother with weather shamanism: it provides for their elderly, it engenders congenial social behavior, and it offers the hope of survival in an environment essentially hostile to humans.

Thus far I have not come across any other South American Indian tribe with a similarly developed system of weather shamanism. Of course, outside the subcontinent one's attention is readily drawn to the *tlaloc* Lords of Rain in the pantheon of the Aztec.

The ethnohistorical question as to the provenance of weather shamanism among the Warao is initially posed by the Indians themselves, who consider the rain gods, like the Criollos, to be foreigners. Compatible with this belief are the titles of the Lords of Rain which, with the exception of *dibatu* (speaker) and *hubanashiko* (rainbow), represent administrative and military ranks of Spanish derivation. As such they parallel the titles and the ranking of modern political leaders of bands and subtribes, among whom the Warao, at the instigation of Criollos and missionaries, distinguish between a *kobenahoro* (governor) of a subtribe, and less important officials such as a *kabitana* (captain), a *fisicali* (constable), a *dibatu aida*, and a *dibatu sanuka* (first and second speakers) of a local band. Following the same etymological reasoning one might even derive the generic name *kabo* of the rain gods from Spanish *cabo* (corporal), although this official is of low rank and such a derivation would require a reinterpretation of significance.

I do not believe, however, that explaining the origin and hierarchical order of the Warao Lords of Rain is quite so simple. Although there can be no doubt that linguistically the elite terminology is largely Spanish derived, I suggest that the ranks the terms denote are not. Instead, the titles seem to substitute a set of more traditional ones which used to designate an autochthonous elite of "strong men" (*aidamo*), patriarchs (*araobo*), local headmen (*arahi*), and speakers (*dibatu*) on the one hand from the commoners and workers (*nebu*) on the other. Membership in these social strata is not by birth or for the lifetime of the individual. Rather, as in a cargo system, there exists an upward mobility within the ranks from worker to strong man through which every ambitious and socially successful male individual can aspire to ascend. This set of Warao titles and their corresponding ranks probably predate the Conquest, and, but for their "modern" colonial titles, the Warao Lords of Rain may have nothing in common with Spanish tradition. The white skin color imputed to the rain gods is characteristic of all supernaturals of the highest order in the Warao pantheon. Also, their attire, while apparently Criollo, does include several aboriginal elements such as the sandals, the staff, and the goggles, all of which point toward the advanced cultures of South America and Mesoamerica. Since Mesoamerican parallels to features of Warao culture have been uncovered in other contexts, the possibility of a relationship of the Warao Lords of Rain with those of Mesoamerica should not be dismissed without thorough examination.

Chapter Nine

Compelling the Clouds

CLIMATIC CONDITIONS OF THE ORINOCO DELTA

The Orinoco Delta lies well within the tropics: its annual mean temperature reaches a high of 26°C, its diurnal temperature range is above the yearly average, and its annual temperature range is less than 5°C. The mean annual rainfall for the western delta (Pedernales, Araguaito) is 1,500 to 2,000 millimeters; for the central and eastern sectors (Winikina, Curiapo) it ranges between 2,000 and 3,000 millimeters.

Four Seasons

Accordingly, seasons in the Orinoco Delta are determined, not by variations in annual temperature, but by the amount of rainfall. An alternating pattern of dry and wet weather is conditioned primarily by the meandering, northward and southward, of the equatorial trough. Its absence over the delta causes a dry season; its presence produces a wet season. Following the sun, the equatorial trough passes over the delta twice in a single year: the first time on its sweep northward toward the Caribbean, the second time on its way southward toward Amazonia. Thus, the delta is subject to a wet climate characterized by four seasons, two of equinoctial dry weather and two of solstitial rains.

Wind Regimes

Waraoland is governed by four major wind regimes: sea and land breezes, trade winds, local winds, and whirlwinds.
Sea and land breezes.—As the Warao favor a 60-kilometer-wide strip of coastal land for settlement and exploitation, most of the deltaic

territory they occupy is subject to the influence of the small-scale convection system of both sea breeze and land breeze. This tug-of-war across the shoreline is driven by an alternating pattern of terrestrial and maritime heat radiation. Thus the breezes take turns in fanning the littoral region of the delta, the onshore sea breeze blowing by day and the offshore land breeze by night.

Trade winds.—Ranging across the subtropics and the tropics, the trade winds are of planetary scale. Governed by vertical overturning loops of circulation (Hadley) cells between the equator and thirty degrees north latitude and thirty degrees south latitude, respectively, the northern trades dominate the delta during dry seasons and the southern trades prevail during wet seasons. Owing to the rotation of the earth, the trade winds acquire a steady easterly component.

Local winds.—Strong local winds, known in Venezuela as *Barinés*, are generated by pressure differences during the primary rainy season around the summer solstice between the excessively hot llanos and the cold regions of the Andes in western Venezuela. Converted into large expanses of low pressure, the llanos experience the influx of cold air from the Andean high pressure area. Over the inundated llanos the local winds absorb humidity and then bring rain in the form of violent thunderstorms to the lower Orinoco and its delta.

Whirlwinds.—Although the Orinoco Delta is not situated directly in the path of Atlantic hurricanes, it nevertheless lies on the southern periphery of the hurricane maturation grounds. Thus, at least from the sidelines, the Warao experience the roaring force of a windstorm, torrential rain, and ocean surges. Sometimes whirlwinds in the form of tornadoes materialize on the fringes of a hurricane, but the Warao more frequently encounter waterspouts less violent than tornadoes but equally awe-inspiring.

PRECIPITATION

In the Orinoco Delta precipitation takes various forms. The usual distinction is between gentle and strong rains, with distinct subtypes in each class. Dew, drizzle, and soft rain are variants of gentle rains, whereas rainstorms, thunderstorms, and hurricanes are forms of strong precipitation.

WARAO WEATHER LORE

It is my purpose here to examine the climatic conditions of the Orinoco Delta from a Warao point of view.[1] Traditionally, Warao weather specialists have mythologically and ritually transformed these conditions into models of normative socioeconomic behavior. The models point to critical components of a complex famine syndrome and to a diversified strategy of coping with seasonal hunger and recurrent starvation.

WIND MYTHOLOGY

Sea and land breezes were the first winds to move the trees. The silent forest, after it had been created by Sea Turtle, stood entirely motionless, and plant life had no procreative power. Then, one day, a multitude of laughing, singing, and shouting animals invaded the delta. Oka, the nine-banded armadillo (*Dasypus novemcinctus*), was the powerful headman of the newcomers. After inquiring among the local animals as to the identity of their leader, he was taken to Huru, the earthquake. The two giants agreed to engage in a fight over supremacy. Using convex curved rectangular combat shields of juxtaposed moriche stalks as weapons, each champion pushed and shoved from behind his shield, attempting to displace his opponent. To and fro went the duel, each champion alternately advancing and retreating. While the thumping of their colliding shields resounded in the air, it became evident that neither of the two rivals was able to push his opponent off the field and thus end the conflict. But their forceful alternating movements and their hard breathing stirred the atmosphere, thereby creating the shifting regime of sea and land breezes. Armadillo became the master of the water people. Earthquake lay down underground to rest.

In Warao mythology the trade winds are a pair of powerful storm birds. Hia, the ruler of the northern trades, who manifests himself in the form of the green-backed heron (*Butorides striatus*), is regarded as the original Father of Wind. He governs the intense primary dry

---

[1] Cultural information pertains mainly to the Hoanarao (Winikina, Mariusa, Arawabisi) subtribes of the Warao. As described in this chapter, weather lore is closely related to a nonagricultural, palm-starch recovery economy of the Warao. The adoption of swidden agriculture has undermined the institution of weather shamanism, which seems to have suffered a decline in recent decades among the diverse subtribal groups of the Warao.

season in the months around the vernal equinox and the less intense, secondary dry season around the autumnal equinox.

Warao weather lore identifies the heron as a culture hero of singular importance. He is a powerful *wishiratu* shaman and the creator of the moriche palm (*Mauritia flexuosa*). His close friend is Kasisi, the rufous crab hawk (*Buteogallus aequinoctialis*), who, in turn, is a *bahana* shaman. Urged by the hawk, the heron created the moriche palm by planting a seed and making it germinate and grow with miraculous speed. Because trees and plants derive their nourishment from the wind, the heron, as Father of Wind, found it easy to accelerate the growth of the palm. Eventually the two friends conducted the first moriche sago ritual, the heron providing the sago, the hawk contributing the crabs. Later in time, moriche sago became the staple food of the Warao. And because sago and crab were served as the fare at the heron's first banquet, they have acquired a sacramental quality.

Ruler of the southern trade winds is Tuyuna, the sun bittern (*Eurypyga helias*), known in Venezuela as *tigana*. Associated with the intense primary and the less intense secondary rainy seasons around the southern and northern solstices, respectively, the sun bittern is a conveyer of strong rains and tropical thunderstorms. No wonder, then, that in Warao lore he is considered a thunderbird, not in this world but in the netherworld. To the inhabitants of the lower world, his deep trills sound like thunderclaps and crackling discharges of lightning. And, whereas to human eyes this thunderer appears in the form of a bird, in the world below he is manifested as a four-headed horned serpent coiled around the foot of the world axis. When Huru (Earthquake), resting inside the earth's disk, moves his body, only certain parts of the land tremble. But when Tuyuna, in the form of a master snake, moves, the center post of the cosmic vault becomes unsettled and sends shock waves from the nadir throughout all the regions of the universe.

Beginning in May, the westerly local winds carry muffled thundering from the distant llanos to the delta. The western rain lord has arisen from his bench and has begun to demonstrate his overpowering rage. Between May and August, he intermittently invades Waraoland with tempests of uncommon violence. The thundering of his footsteps heralds the end of the low-river period (September to March) and the beginning of the high-river period (April to August), when the delta is flooded by the runoff waters of the vast Orinoco Basin. Consisting, as we shall see, of only sweat and urine of the southern and western rain lords, these floodwaters are polluted and carry disease to which many Warao are doomed to succumb.

Whirlwinds are manifestations of the storm-spirit Kaunasa. He assaults the delta with hurricane strength or, more commonly, in the form of a tornado or a waterspout. His body resembles a giant serpent and his head is enormously wide. On his way across the sea, over land, or along a river course, he picks up boats, houses, people, and animals and swallows them whole. The suddenness with which Kaunasa can appear as a tornado or a waterspout gives him a particularly ghostly quality. In Warao mythology the two forms of this weather denizen enter into a contest to determine which one is better able to appear without warning and to cause the most damage.

RAIN MYTHOLOGY

Dew, drizzle, and soft rain are manifestations of the cloud people when they materialize as drifting mist, as veils of spray in the forest canopy, or as swishing droplets falling on the river, the swamp, and the sodden soil. Sometimes from behind the curtain of moisture, beautiful cloud-girls, laughing seductively and enticing young men, suddenly appear. Soon after the embrace, however, the human lover finds that he has acquired the watery nature of the cloud-girl's body. He turns into a water person himself, perspiring heavily and incessantly until he dies of exposure in the cold of the night (Lavandero 1982, 56–58).

Soft showers, which fall when the sun is shining, are often accompanied by rainbows. Like other weather lords, the rainbow has a body of serpentine shape. Married to the daughter of the Mother of the Forest, he lives uxorilocally along the southern solstice. But occasionally, when he becomes homesick and is distressed by separation from his kinfolk, he bends over across the firmament to slake his thirst in the clear rivers of his homeland along the northern solstice. Fully saturated, he relieves himself over the earth in showers of urinary rain.

On occasion, Rainbow appears in the sky accompanied by his wife (i.e., forming a double rainbow). Showers that fall in such instances consist of the tears of the rainbow-woman and those of her mother and sisters. They are overcome by grief because somewhere on earth one of their kinswomen, a red cedar (*Colophyllum lucidum* Benth.), was killed so that she could be fashioned into a dugout canoe. Distraught, the celestial women bemoan the death of their kin and accuse human-kind of the crime. Rain showers of tears may also fall when a human being dies. The lament of his or her kinswomen is sometimes so mournful that the tears of the bereaved may cause the sky to weep.

Unlike the intermittent rains of the cloud-people, rainbows, and mourning women, rains brought on by the *hoarotu* sorcerer's alligator power may fall for days on end. The alligator is the otherworldly double of the sorcerer. With the rising flood of the rainy season it travels over land and prowls about for victims. The reptile's teeth and its hissing bring on continuous precipitation which, like the sorcerer's malevolent chant, is considered harmful and evil.

Although intermittent rains may fall throughout the year, stormy rains are typical of the rainy seasons. They precipitate as a consequence of the weather shaman's sorcery and originate with the Lords of Rain. The Warao recognize eight lords, who reside on an equal number of mountains at the cardinal and intercardinal points along the horizonal edge of the universe. The rain gods live on the tops of these sky-bearing mountains in mansions whose doors and windows face the center of the earth. During the dry seasons the doors remain shut, but during the rainy seasons they are wide open, and the resident lords sit on benches in the doorways looking toward the earth. In the dry seasons the gods wear long white tunics, which they exchange for black ones during the rainy seasons. Their eyes are framed by spectacles, their mouths hold large elbow tobacco pipes, and their feet are protected by sandals. They wear black wide-rimmed hats, and each god clutches in his right hand a sturdy walking staff with which to steady his gait.

At the onset of the long rainy season, and after an extended period of seclusion in the preceding dry season, the Lords of Rain need to urinate. They push open the doors of their houses to relieve themselves. The southern gods in particular become very restless, and their urinating causes the rivers of the Orinoco Basin to overflow and flood the land.

The rain gods form a hierarchical assembly of one female and seven male supernatural beings. Their rankings seem to be determined by directional frequency and average velocity of wind conditions in the delta (see chapter 8).

WEATHER SHAMANISM

The power to invoke the rain gods and, in so doing, unleash heavy rains and coiling storms is invested in the weather shaman. Only elderly men and, rarely, elderly women may become rain shamans, for fear that younger people might misuse the accompanying power. In their evocational chants weather shamans proclaim the placement and station of the lords and eventually pronounce their names. Such announcement is believed to make the lords rise, become increasingly more infuriated as the chant spurs them on, and stride, singly or in groups, with pounding heels toward the center of the celestial plaza below the top of the cosmic vault. In walking, and while dancing on the plaza, the gods perspire copiously and thus bring on pouring rains. Their stomping thunders throughout the universe, and their staffs explode in violent lightning flashes. Thus, like the sorcerer's (*hoarotu's*) chant and the chanting (hissing) of his alligator double, the chant of the weather shamans is tantamount to a spell of black magic that causes punishing rains to fall.

The weather shaman is invested with the awesome power to control the rain lords during initiation when, in a tobacco trance, the candidate awaits the arrival of Kanamuno, a black giant of colossal size. As the spirit approaches, the giant's serpentine body and widely flaring head come into view. The apparition, drenched in rain, is surrounded by thunder and lightning. He reaches down for the mortal, lifts him up, and puts him into his gaping mouth. Inside the giant's body the novice embarks on a long journey, during which the essential nature of the devourer is revealed to him: Kanamuno is the manifestation of the supreme rain god, who has come to induct him into the ranks of the Lords of Rain. Thundering and lightning reverberate in the "traveler's" body as he realizes that through them he is encountering Tarita (Thunderer), the consort of Kanamuno and a manifestation of the supreme rain lord's female companion. Upon leaving the giant's body (via the rectum), the new shaman has aged at an accelerated pace and rejoins his people as a wise old man, the equal of the rain gods.

POLLUTING RAIN

It should be emphasized at this point that, in Warao thought, precipitation is pathogenic and rain lore is an expression of deep-seated anger and fear. Rather than bestowing life-giving virtues from heaven, rain drowns the world in darkness, spreading death and disease. Precipitation pertains to the dark sky of the rain lords, the sorcerer's twilight of the underworld, and the threatening aspect of alligator-infested floods. It deals with man-eaters, devastating thunderers, and shape-shifters. The rain lords throw tantrums when hearing themselves threatened by the shaman's chant. The treachery of beguiling sirens, the frustration of thwarted lovers, the insecurity of uprooted rainbow-husbands, and the bereavement of women lamenting the death of their loved ones are felt. No wonder, then, that the Indians fear the water that falls from the sky as the urine, sweat, and tears of these embittered protagonists. The Warao, considering such excretory rain harmful, bathe in the river to protect themselves from its pollutional effects.

STAVING OFF FAMINE

At the root of the anxiety generated by the Warao weather lore lies the fear of recurrent famine. In tribal mythology, Hunger is personified as a mysterious loincloth-dragging visitor who thrives on hunger but sickens on food. And indeed, wet seasons do often turn into episodes of seasonal hunger, while famines recur every four to five years (Heinen and Ruddle 1974, 120). During such catastrophic events, sago retrieval suffers local or regional failure, the ritual sago-distribution system collapses, and mortality, especially of children, women, and the elderly, rises sharply owing to starvation and decreasing resistance to associated diseases. Upon closer inspection, in fact, Warao weather lore reveals itself as an accumulation of carry-over experiences of past periods of starvation. It recognizes famine as a syndromic phenomenon and institutionalizes it in the Warao style of life.

PRIMARY CAUSES OF FAMINE

The primary causes of famine in the Orinoco Delta are unfavorable weather and the concomitant decline in sago intake. Warao famines are naturally triggered and conditioned by the prevailing weather regime of the Orinoco Basin. The hydraulic pattern of precipitation and floods is strongly seasonal and varies from year to year. Western (*Barinés*) storms and the approach of the tropical trough in May trigger the blossoming of the moriche palm. Simultaneously, sago production in the palm stem is impeded either by continuous regional rainfall—lasting ten or more hours—or by local, sporadic, and fast-moving downpours (Heinen and Ruddle 1974, 124). Prolonged rains may produce a widespread shortage of sago and cause famine throughout the region. Short downpours may provoke random starvation in smaller areas. As most of the precipitation in the delta comes in brief storms, localized starvation occurs more often than regional famine. Experience has taught the Warao that to mitigate starvation and to forestall famine they need surplus production of sago during the favorable primary dry season (around the vernal equinox), and that they must store surplus sago for distribution during the following primary wet season (around the summer solstice).

Thus, encoded in the mythology about Hia, ruler of the northern trade winds, is the knowledge that during the months of his rule the moriche palm—whose creator he is—carries sago in its stem. Especially during the first months of the calendar year, the northern trade winds are reputed to transport the sago from the northeastern world mountain across the sea into the delta. During this season of plenty, the Warao extract more stem starch than required for their daily sustenance. Prestige ranking of households based on differential giving for the common good spurs optimum production and helps overcome the drudgery of the intensified extraction process. Quotas of surplus starch pledged by household heads are deposited in a barrel-shaped container on the lower level of the sanctuary. Here an estimated 1,500 kilograms of sago may be stored by the constituent local bands of a subtribe—some 250 people strong—for several months preceding and during the primary rainy season. Deferred communal consumption of carefully measured portions is permitted after the starch has been offered to the directional gods (not the rain lords) and has been sanctified by the priest-shaman (*wishiratu*) according to the ritual precepts established by Hia, the Father of Wind. This gift amounts to a propitiation of the directional gods; failure to appease them with a gift of sago results in higher than normal mortality rates of children and the infirm during the rainy season.

SUBSTATES OF FAMINE

The occurrence of excess deaths is the essential characteristic of famine which differentiates this catastrophic phenomenon from crises of seasonal hunger and starvation. Substates of the famine syndrome include, among others, personal symptoms of disease, loss of body weight, malnutrition, and the consumption of emergency foods (Alamgir 1981, 20–21). Throughout the year, weather shamans remind their people that all these symptoms will be aggravated by selfish behavior. They champion a positive attitude toward resource sharing, a personal quality that is deeply ingrained in Warao character. In their attempts to uphold a congenial attitude of sharing as the single most important preventive of hunger and famine, weather shamans threaten to punish egotism by calling on the rains to fall. This warning is usually sufficient to exact compliance with the rule of altruism. If not, weather shamans may be heard arousing the ire of the rain lords with their spells or may refuse to rebuke the clouds. Weather-connected diseases like bronchitis and rheumatism, for instance, or the scourges of infectious disease are the expected consequences of such stubbornness. And, in the guise of influenza, pneumonia, tuberculosis, whooping cough, diarrhea, or gastrointestinal infections, among others, disease takes an excessively high toll among children and famished adults.

The disruption of cultural integrity as a social symptom of famine is repeatedly treated in Warao weather lore and is safeguarded against in traditional behavior. Young husbands who succumb to the yearning of homesickness when thirsting for unpolluted waters expose themselves to the ridicule of the earth-people who admonish them to stop drizzling on them. Young men are warned against the temptation of subtribal exogamy and the fatal consequences of a stranger's embrace. The invasion of the delta by people under Huru (Earthquake) present the disquieting scenario of war, in itself not an uncommon trigger of famine in other parts of the world. Intergroup conflict is still settled among the Warao by imitating the primordial fight between contending bands. Pent-up aggression among hostile parties is released and friendships are renewed. Exogamous bands of this type tend to constitute endogamous subtribes whose members cooperate in the annual production of sago surpluses. The joint labor force of a subtribe guarantees a sufficiently large store of surplus food and offers a better chance to stave off starvation and famine. Tampering with marriage or residence rules, or leaving smoldering intergroup animosity unresolved, threatens subtribal solidarity and the dissolution of family bonds. Such threats are major factors contributing to famine.

Thus, Warao weather lore seems to identify sundry personal and social—environmental, sociocultural, psychological, and health—symptoms of the famine phenomenon. Through oral art, rituals, and shamanic practices the Indians maintain a fund of related experiences and enforce appropriate customs to correct untoward attitudes and behavior. In this fashion, famine management has become institution-alized in Warao culture. It allows for corrective monitoring of constituent symptoms of the famine syndrome on a continuous, small incremental basis and the prompt elimination of the problems before they can escalate into a crisis. But it also permits the mitigation of seasonal hunger and the postponement of catastrophic famine.

Chapter Ten

The Fiddle and the Dancing Jaguar

The violin, *sekesekeima* or simply *sekeseke*,[1] is of nearly universal distribution among the Warao of the Orinoco Delta. To my knowledge, and at least until quite recently, the instrument has failed to find acceptance only among the Hoanarao (Mariusa, Winikina, and Arawabisi) subgroup of the central delta. All other groups have adopted the violin as the typical instrument of the *hohomare* dance. Homesteads near and far are abandoned by their residents who congregate in the house of the host to dance, to sing, and to drink. Anyone passing by a merrymaking village is almost pressed into partaking of the feast. Nobody may leave as long as any *guarabo*[2] remains to be drunk. And, although brawls may sometimes erupt after the intake of too much alcohol, a *hohomare* is ostensibly an occasion when grievances are forgiven and forgotten.

The dance invariably takes place inside a large house. A line of men facing a line of women step back and forth, each dancer holding his or her neighbors around their waists. In the center of the arena stands the fiddler (*maremare*), spurring on the singing men and women with his music. The feast may last for several days and nights depending on how much *guarabo* has been prepared by the host. But long after

---

[1] Barral (1979, 394–95) derives the name *sekeseke* from the verb *sekekitani*, "to rub," "to scrub." It may also signify hiccup. Roth (1924, 463) explains *seke-seke* as an onomatopoeic designation. Although this definition is etymologically satisfactory, it is nevertheless worthwhile to point out that the Warao and the Criollos of Venezuela (Aretz 1967, 181) build the violin of cedar wood, commonly referred to as *saquisaque* (Alvarado 1953, 315). As this term is similar to the name of the violin, there may be a connection between it and the wood used to make the instrument.

[2] From *guarapo*, possibly of African origin, signifying sugarcane juice and, in general, any sweet juice or water whether fermented or not (Alvarado 1953, 187).

the dancers have returned to the routine of daily life, memories of cordial fellowship and the tunes of the indefatigable fiddler linger on in their minds and hearts.

Central to these events is the violin. Other instruments like the *cuatro*, the mandolin, the accordion, and the *picó* ("pick-up" gramophone) have lately been brought in to form an orchestra or to replace the more traditional violin. These substitutes, however, are without roots in Warao culture, and even today many Warao would probably consider a *hohomare* with a good fiddle second to none. In order to explain the basis of such sentiment, it is necessary to tell the story of the violin.

THE ORIGIN OF THE VIOLIN

A long time ago, when Trinidad was still connected with the mainland, there lived in the mountains of that island a black monkey. The monkey was held in high esteem by his fellow animals because he was an expert musician who knew how to entertain them with exquisite music. The monkey used a *sekesekeima*, or violin, which he had invented and made himself; its delicate sounds swept the listeners off their feet in waves of deeply felt emotion. Even the animals were so entranced by the instrument's music that they stood on their hind legs and danced to the beautiful sounds. And the birds, finding the *sekesekeima* music irresistible, spread their wings and staggered about in company with their four-legged fellow creatures.[3]

In the mountains of Trinidad the black monkey owned a huge house. It was so large that it easily accommodated all the animals that came to dance as soon as the monkey began to tune his fiddle. While dancing continued through the night, the *sekesekeima* could be heard all over the world.

This happy state of affairs lasted for many years, until one day the black monkey decided to visit what is now the mainland. He wanted to befriend the animals living there as well as those who inhabited the island. They had never heard the monkey's music, nor did they know how to dance properly. It took him an entire day to get ready for the

---

[3] The power with which the violin entrances the Warao is stressed by Richard Schomburgk (1847–48, 1:1, 118), who says that "the notes of the violin are, however, as irresistible to them as was the magic pipe of the pied piper to the children of Hamelin."

long journey, and the next day he left his house and descended from the mountains, fiddling as he went.

As the monkey was crossing the lowlands that stretched between the island and the mainland, a hurricane erupted in his path. The wind blew so violently that the trees of the forest came crashing down with a noise like thunder. The soil split open, and the waves of the ocean filled the cracks.[4] Undaunted by these frightful events, however, the monkey kept on playing his violin until he reached the mainland. Upon his arrival he tuned his strings anew and, with his music, began to call the animals together to enjoy their first *hohomare*.

The fiddling monkey had not long to wait, for the delta animals soon gathered around him. Even before they realized what was going on, their bodies started to react to the magical sound of the monkey's fine instrument. Standing up on their hind legs, they said: "Let's all dance together, the men in one line and the women in another, opposite the men. Let's embrace our neighbors and be friends."

While they were dancing, the animals kept shouting to the monkey: "How good that you have come to play for us! You must stay forever!" That was fine with the monkey. "Alright," he said, "I will stay, now that we have become such good friends. I am happy that all of you have come to listen and to dance and that nobody has stayed behind. You look like the same kind of animals for whom I used to play in the place where I lived. And so,—on with the dance!"

The monkey, however, was mistaken in thinking that his audience included all the animals, for not everyone had come to the festival. There was one animal in the delta—the jaguar—the monkey had never seen before. The jaguar, resisting the call of the new sounds, was unwilling to accept the other animals as friends. Although the monkey did not miss the jaguar, the other animals were well aware of and deeply troubled by his absence. They waited through one day and even through a second one, but when the jaguar had failed to put in an appearance by nightfall, they decided to send an emissary to him in the morning.

"Look," said the emissary when he reached the jaguar's den, "we have been visited by a black person from the island who plays an instrument that fills our hearts with joy. Music makes us embrace one

---

[4] The memory of the havoc created by the hurricanes harks back to the early stages of the Meso-Indian epoch in Venezuela.

another and dance together like good friends. Why don't you come and join us?" "Whence did this visitor come?" asked the jaguar. "What is his name?" "He came from the island, that much I know. But I have not heard him mention his name. What matters, however, is not his origin or his name, but rather his playing of the violin, whose sounds make us forget all enmity and turn us into friends."

After thinking for a while, the jaguar said: "Now I know; the visitor's name is Naku." And he laughed. "You don't know what you are asking. I could never become friends with Naku, for his meat is the most delicious of all. Go back and tell your visitor that nobody asked him to come, that he does not belong here, and that he should prepare himself to receive my visit. Three days from now, I will come and I will catch him. I will kill him. I will eat him. No meat tastes better than Naku's.

The animals were greatly worried when their emissary returned with the bad news. "Look," they said to the monkey, "you'd better heed our warning. You don't know the jaguar. He is a ferocious beast who devours other animals. He eats all animals but he likes your kind the best." The monkey listened attentively, but seemed to regard the warning as of no concern to him. "Believe us," insisted the animals. "He will finish you off. He is not like the rest of us who live in harmony. The jaguar, although he lives in the same forest we do, rejects our friendship. If he grabs us, we are doomed."

The monkey remained calm despite the animals' stern warning. He just sat there for two days tuning his violin. Then, in the morning of the third day, all the animals heard the jaguar approach. "Aye, poor Naku," they heard him say. "Your last day has arrived. Only a short while from now you will be dead. How sad, for you, poor monkey, that your meat is so good, so delicious." Thus growled the jaguar as he drew near. Then, breaking out of the forest, he stood before the animals, right next to the monkey. "So there you are, Naku." "Where else?" asked the monkey. "Will you not eat me no matter where I go?" "Right you are," replied the jaguar. "You can't cross the water to go back to your island." "As this is to be my last day," said the monkey, "perhaps you will grant me a favor. Let me play a final piece on my violin, here before you and all the others. After that you may kill me if you wish."

As the jaguar had no objections, the monkey quickly raised his bow to the strings and began to play what everybody believed would be his last performance. But how mistaken they all were! The monkey played so well that the jaguar began to squint his eyes. He closed them fully. And then, as though in a trance, he lifted himself up on his hind legs, let his head roll all the way back, and began to dance to the magic sounds of the monkey's fiddle. "Aye, Naku, what music is this? Never have I heard such notes before. Go on!" implored the jaguar. "This beautiful music makes me happy. We have all been sad over here, so sad. I did not know you could play such marvelous music." Still dancing, the jaguar approached the monkey and embraced him, saying: "By all means, let's be friends! Let's be brothers! Your music lifts me up and makes me dance with joy." In the embrace of the jaguar the monkey finally had to stop playing. He lowered the violin and kept repeating the words of the jaguar: "Friends! Brothers!"

By this time the other animals had regained their courage. They stepped up to get a closer look at the magic violin that had made a friend even of the jaguar. They saw the instrument's head and neck, the mouth, the tongue, the body, and the back. They observed every little detail and gave the monkey's *sekesekeima* a proper Warao name, *eboma sanuka* (little girl). She was very beautiful, and her strings were made of the finest wire. Soon some of the more skilled craftsmen among the animals rushed into the forest to get cedar wood. They made their own violins. True, theirs did not turn out as well as Naku's; they had to use fibers for strings and the walls of the instrument were rather coarse (fig. 10.1). But there were violins now in the delta, and the animals, as well as the Warao later on, learned to love the beautiful tones of their "little girls" more and more. Nobody stays at home when the violin plays the *hohomare*.

Although this episode turned out well for the Warao, it was not as beneficial for the soul of the violin, for it had remained in Trinidad when the monkey carried the violin's body across to Waraoland. The soul of the violin, leaving the mountains where he used to dwell with his woman, remained on the shores of Trinidad. "What am I going to do," asked the violin's soul, "now that the water separates me from my body? I cannot live here alone, without my woman. I must go after

FIG. 10.1. Playing the violin in a seated position. (Photo courtesy Paul Hooks)

her. He waited for two long weeks before sighting a schooner with its two masts and bulging sails. He jumped on board and was off. The captain and the crew of the ship were, of course, unaware of the presence the invisible passenger. But when the schooner approached the coastline near the village of the monkey and the animals, they heard a strange song: "I am *sekesekeima*, the most excellent one."

Only the animals on the mainland remembered the song; it was the same tune they had heard the violin play when the black monkey had carried her over the water. There was a motley crowd on the ship besides the crew and the captain: men and women and a good many teenage girls. Hearing the song, they all felt it caress them like a balmy breeze, but none of them could see the singer. And then, as soon as the ship had reached the mainland, the singing stopped. How could the people and the animals have known that the soul of the violin had come to be united with his woman?

THE BODY OF THE VIOLIN

The separation of body and soul of mythical personages is a familiar theme in Warao religion. As to the violin, however, the sexual dualism of the soul and the body of the instrument may have to be interpreted in terms of the less subtle difference between the (feminine) form of the instrument and the (masculine) bow.

The Warao designate the components of the violin by using body-parts terminology. To begin with, there is the scroll or the *sekesekeima a kua*, which means "head of the violin." The string holders are called *sekesekeima a kohoko*, the "ears." The fingerboard is identified as *sekesekeima a do*, the "neck." The resonance chamber is called *sekesekeima a teho*, the "body." The strings of moriche fiber or commercial material, *sekesekeima a hutu*, are strung across the bridge, *sekesekeima a wahiriba* (lit., "the raised gunwales of the boat") and are fastened to the *sekesekeima a hotomomu*, the "behind."[5] The music is heard through the sound holes, called *sekesekeima a kaba*, "cut-in mouths," and the sound is produced by a *sekesekeima a hono*, "tongue." More specifically, below the soundboard and a little below the "waist"

---

[5] The violin has four strings which are designated, respectively, as *a hutu arani*, "the mother string," *G*; *ariatuka ariatuka*, "the second one," *D*; *akua ariatuka*, "the second one from the head," *A*; and *akua*, "the head," *E*.

of the violin, the Warao fiddle maker places a wooden block which sticks to the soundboard and the bottom board of the instrument, reinforcing its mid portion. Through the center of the block the fiddle builder drives a sewing needle which vibrates like a tongue when the violin is played. The instrument is made entirely of cedar wood. The bow, *sekesekeima a hataburu*, is a one-meter-long staff strung with fine untwisted moriche fiber, *sekesekeima a hataburu a hutu*. A good homemade Warao violin has a robust sound, especially when the strings are made of commercial material.

Because not every Warao man knows how to play the violin, a virtuoso enjoys considerable prestige. When not in use, the instrument hangs under the roof on the east side of the house. To protect it from cockroaches, termites, and other insects, it is wrapped in a cloth or an old shirt. No one but the owner may touch the violin, and he himself never does so with the smell of fish on his hands. Violation of this taboo causes him to be afflicted with grave illness. As my informant explained, "You see, it is because the violin is kept in our house that there arise certain dangers. Children have to stay away from the violin, and when I leave the house, my wife takes care of it."

DANCING THE *HOHOMARE*

When a man goes to fetch his violin, those who see him call this to the attention of others so that everybody can listen to the playing. It may happen at any time, during the hot part of the day, or toward evening, or at night—in short, at the pleasure of the fiddler. A dance in which everyone takes part, on the contrary, is held on the basis of no such arbitrary whim. It usually starts with the appearance, in a dream, of the house-spirit to the owner of the house. The spirit demands that a *hohomare* be held and that enough *guarabo*—*kasiri* (manioc beer) or *sikara a ho* (sugarcane liquor)—be prepared to fill a trough.

The next day the owner of the house announces: "He wishes to dance, he wants to drink, and he wants to enjoy *guarabo*." This announcement sets into motion a series of activities. Some men go to prepare the drinking trough, while others set up the sugarcane press. The sugarcane must be cut and crushed. If *kasiri* is to be the drink, manioc must be brought in from the field, cassava must be baked, and the fermentation process begun. Once some fifteen or twenty large

FIG. 10.2.
Warao man playing the violin. (Photo courtesy Lucy Millowitsch)

buckets of beverage have been poured into the trough, the spirit of the house sees that the beer is ready. "How much longer?" is the question most frequently asked. "A few more days," answers the owner of the house. "Then the full moon will rise to brighten the night." The house owner also provides oil lamps for the occasion.

Finally the day of the *hohomare* arrives. In the afternoon the house owner visits the *wishiratu* shaman, saying: "I would like you to talk to the spirit of my house. Give him the *guarabo* he wants." The *wishiratu* comes the same afternoon. He sits down in the house and sings to the spirit of the house: "Owner of the house, it is for you." The spirit of the house is quick to answer (through the voice of the shaman): "*Hanoko arotu, hanoko a kobe, ine.* Owner of the house, heart of the house, am I. Would you like to dance?" "Yes," says the shaman. "We would like to dance." "It is time then?" "Yes, it is time." "Alright, you may dance. I am happy and you are happy. You cannot see me, but from my location I can see all of you. I am happy with you. Now let's dance together!"

Then the shaman blows tobacco smoke into the rafters of the roof. He walks over to the trough of *guarabo*, takes a calabash full of the liquor, and swishes the *guarabo* up to the place where the spirit resides, right in the center of the roof. A good shaman knows how to fling the liquor up to the roof for the spirit of the house so that hardly a drop falls to the floor. Four additional calabashes of beer are flung up, one for each corner of the house. "Watch out!" warns the shaman. "The beer is strong. Let us all be friends." "Don't fight," urges the host. "If you fight, people will talk badly of my feast." Next come the elders of the group. They sit to one side, all in a row, and the owner of the feast hands each one of them a calabash of beer.

Finally the fiesta can begin. The fiddler takes his place at the center of the house, the men and woman line up, and everybody begins to dance and to sing (fig. 10.2).

THE SONG OF THE VIOLIN
SEKESEKEIMA A KOITA[6]

Kwanera nera	Kwanera nera,
kwanera nérane	kwanera nérane,
kwanera nérane	kwanera nérane,
kwanera ne.	kwanera ne.
Sekesekeima	Violin,
sekesekeima	violin,
naba autumo kwane	from the middle of the ocean
ka yaronai kwane	you have come to us,
ka yaronai.	you have come to us
Sekesekeima	Violin,
kwa marida	your scrolled head
ma mituru, hai,	I enjoy seeing it, yea.
ma mituru.	I enjoy seeing it.
Dahiatuma	My little sisters,
sekesekeima	the violin,
barokoida kwane	the big schooner,
a hoka kwane	[there] it is inside.
A hutu kwane	The strings,
a koita kwane	their song
ma nokoturu,	I enjoy hearing it,
dahiatuma.	my little sisters.
Sekesekeima	Violin
a hutu kwane	your strings
hima kadera	are made of wire,
hima kadera.	steel strings.
Na, na, na, na. . .	Na, na, na, na. . .

The word *dahiatuma*, "little sisters," makes it clear that the singers of this version of the *sekesekeima* song were women; men use an equivalent but different kin term. And, indeed, women seem to enjoy violin music even more than men. Frequently they can be heard encouraging the fiddler when he gets tired and sits down to rest. "Play the violin, *maremare*! Go on! Play 'the little girl!' "

---

[6] For additional songs of the violin, see Barral (1964, 422–26).

Then the *maremare* once again takes up his violin and plays the songs everybody likes to sing.[7]

Physical exhaustion eventually brings the *hohomare* to an end. The beer trough is empty and everybody is asleep. The fiddler takes the violin, wraps it in a covering, and hangs it from the ridgepole on the east side of the house. When the night breeze blows across the violin and makes the strings hum, the fiddler hears the sentimental air and knows that the soul of the violin is now reunited with his little girl.

NATIONS OF MUSIC

According to the origin story of the violin, the Warao believe the instrument to be of great antiquity, dating back to a remote past, some six or seven thousand years ago when Trinidad was connected to the mainland. This exaggeration is rather curious, because even among post-Columbian instruments the violin is actually a latecomer. Only around the turn of the eighteenth century did it experience a wide distribution in the New World. Its precursor, the viol (*vihuela de arco*), came much earlier, probably by being tucked away among the meager belongings of pioneer missionaries, intent on sweetening the rustic chorus of their fellow friars. The viol was used by Indians at the Franciscan missions in Mexico early in the sixteenth century. So successful were the padres in teaching the Indians how to play this difficult instrument that, in 1561, the First Mexican Council denounced the fact that New World missionaries were retaining too many instrumentalists, including an excess of viol players. And Torquemada (1723) reported, in 1615, that viols were among the first musical instruments manufactured by the Indians (Grenson 1950–51; Stevenson 1968, 169, 170n, 172, 221).

For the South American continent there are dates that match this early documentation for viols in Mexico. Here, besides the missionaries, were free-lance musicians who, before 1553, came from Spain to Peru, where they fanned out across the colony and taught the Indians how to make and play viols (Stevenson 1968, 290–91). In lowland South America, the Jesuits, especially those of Austrian heritage, "attached great importance to music" (Métraux 1949, 649) and furthered the

[7] Barral's (1964, 253–74) collection includes many of the most popular songs.

distribution of the violin, particularly among the Indians of the southern cone and Amazonia.

Fortunately, there is early evidence of the introduction and distribution of the violin among the Carib Indians of eastern Venezuela and the Guianas (Armellada 1980, 206–7). Furthermore, references in Carrocera (1979, 2:20) and Rionegro (1918, 2:180) place the violin in territories adjacent to the Orinoco Delta by the second half of the eighteenth century. Reporting from the missions of Píritu, in the province of Cumaná, Rionegro writes that the Indians played viols and violins at church services:

...they celebrate as solemnly as possible the daily holy sacrifice of the Mass, the processions of the annual round, and all the other ecclesiastic functions the same way they are conducted in the parishes of Spain. The Indians participate on all such occasions, some with their sonorous voices and others by masterfully playing their viols and violins. But in whatever form, they do it with as much virtuosity as devotion.

The presence of the violin on the Orinoco during the second half of the eighteenth century is further confirmed by Padre Gilij's report that Indians in the Jesuit missions near the middle course of the river had the instrument. Gilij's experience with tribes like the Tamanaco, Maipure, Otomac, and others goes back to his tenure among them as missionary, roughly between 1749 and 1768. Still, it is probably true that the violin antedated his arrival among the Indians ("Orinoquenses") and that his mentor, Padre Gumilla, saw the instrument there even in the first half of the eighteenth century. In his testimony, Gilij (1965, 3:64) stated:

It is the natural predisposition of these Indians and Americans generally of being born musicians which prompted the introduction among them of our music. And if I may express my thoughts freely, nothing has ever been brought here from Europe that gives them more pleasure and that they would imitate with greater success. They sing in different voices at all sacred services, and according to the unanimous judgment of those who have heard them perform, they sing well and with devotion.

Just as they learn how to sing well, so do they learn how to play the violin, the harp, and any kind of wind instrument. Instructed and converted thus into a nation of music, it is beyond words to describe the pomp of voices and the sound of the sacred functions which, in turn, help to attract new Indians. . . . We have here a musical people. And this serves no other purpose but to enhance the decorum of the church and to accustom the savages to the reduction.

Even after the Jesuits had left the Orinoco Indians, the situation described by Padre Gilij continued. Father José Cortés de Madariaga, who visited the Macuro mission inhabited by Sáliva in 1811, was surprised to find, after "hearing in the choir of the church the orchestra of the Indians consisting of violins, violoncellos, flutes, guitars, and triangles" (Blanco Azpurúa n.d., 3:291), that the Indians displayed a special gift for music.

Apparently some Indians of Guiana, like the Cariban Yekuana (Cardona, in Aretz 1967, 117) as well as others, including the Warao, never used the violin as a liturgical instrument to embellish church activities. Instead, the Warao adopted it for recreational purposes and for celebrating their own festivals, probably in the early eighteenth century. By that time, at missions and reductions near the Orinoco Delta, Warao groups had come into contact with other Indians. For example, the large groups of Warao which had settled near the mouth of the Guarapiche River met Carib Indians who adopted the violin from Europeans. The first Warao were reduced in 1714, when thirty families agreed to live at the mission of Santa Ana de Sopocuar on the upper Guarapiche River, in the heart of Carib territory. The Capuchins launched a campaign to reduce the rest of the Warao, who until then had been untouched by their influence (Carrocera 1968, 1:283). The several Warao missions established as a result of the campaign lay outside the delta habitat of the Warao and were all in Carib territory.[8] In fact, some of the missions were inhabited by Indians of different ethnic origin. Although by the mid-seventeenth century some Carib were apparently still cannibals, the Warao learned in the missions that, at least with some of their fierce neighbors, a *modus vivendi* could be reached under the protection of the Europeans. It is thus likely that extensive cultural borrowing between Carib and Warao began at that time and that the "primordial" times of the violin legend really mean the first half of the eighteenth century. It was in that period that the

[8] San Juan Bautista de Soro (or San Juan Bautista, or Santa Isabel), 1739; Divina Pastora de Catucuao, 1751; Nuestra Señora del Rosario de Yaguaraparo, 1760. According to Carrocera 1968, 1:373, "during the years of 1783 [–1786] the Capuchin began to establish various settlements of Warao Indians between Morichal Largo and the mouths of the Orinoco."

violin and the components of an agricultural complex, such as cultigens, alcoholic beverages, and possibly the *maremare* itself, found their way via the mission Indians and peripheral western Warao groups into the Orinoco Delta. Furthermore, the *maremare* is particularly characteristic of the Carib of eastern Venezuela, and they use the rattle rather than the violin to accompany their singing.

Like most littoral Indians, the Warao also ventured across the sea in their canoes to the island of Trinidad, where the Jesuits had sister institutions and the Capuchins had built (1795) a mission at Naparima on Trinidad (Carrocera 1968, 1:385). The Warao maintained trade relations with the island Indians and Criollos, and it is likely that the story's black protagonist of the north was better known as the bringer of the violin to the Warao (or, at least to some of them) than to the Carib to the west. I have personally known Warao men who as youngsters had accompanied their elders on trading expeditions to Trinidad. They know the mountain chain and the hill Naparima, a name that means "Father of the Waves" in their language. This mountain in central Trinidad marks the northernmost extension of the Warao disk-shaped earth. And, in reference to the black violinist, it is noteworthy that the Warao are not alone in associating a black hero with the *hohomare* dance. The Carib of the Anzoátegui, in their traditional *maremare*, also sing a song that features a black person (Civrieux n.d., in Acosta Saignes 1961, 128):

> The black man, here is the black man,
> the good Indian talking with sincerity.
> Here I am, a good Indian; I am a good Indian.
> That Criollo, that good friend of ours, that Criollo,
> I have wanted to befriend him for a long time.
> You are a fine gentleman,
> you have been good to us, a fine gentleman.

Here the theme of interracial friendship evokes the intentions of the mythological violinist of the Warao narrative. And, of course, both the black man of the Carib and the black fiddler of the Warao could very well be derived from a common historical tradition.

Of particular interest also is the account by Appun (1961, 388), who, when traveling in the mid-nineteenth century along the southern border of Warao territory in Venezuela, observed a dance by these Indians at Santa Catalina, close to the apex of the delta. The instruments which accompanied them were violins and the rattle. But, as observed by the German naturalist:

These instruments are not made by them but traded with civilized settlements in the vicinity for hammocks, medicines, dried fish, and so on. In size they are about half as big as the violins used in civilized countries and similar to violins one can buy in Germany as toys for children. But they are of a far better quality, more solidly constructed, and not much different in tone from the larger instruments; they are vaulted and equipped with good strings.

Appun (1961, 389) went on to describe the dance itself. Lines of women and children, and behind them lines of men, faced the musician and

moved to the rhythm of the music, jumping alternately one step forward and one step backward so that they remained on the same spot. A dance. . .lasted at least one hour. . . . After a pause during which both men and women drank much *chicha*, a primitive music began once more and another dance commenced.

Schomburgk (1847–48, 1:151), who saw the violin being played by the Warao in Guyana, describes a scene that recalls Gumilla's (1963, 144) beautiful characterization of the Warao. Dancing and singing, writes Schomburgk, "are ordinary occupations of theirs. No more light-hearted and joyful people has ever been known than the Warao." Traveling through Guyana in the first half of the nineteenth century, Schomburgk came across a Warao group whose members enjoyed listening to an old fiddler. He made music by passing the bow, with short and longer strokes, across two strings without modulating the notes by fingering the strings. Schomburgk believed that the fiddler had bought his instrument in the colony and that he usually played after sundown, when old and young made merry and danced with great joy to his music. The patience of the musician is described as nothing short of stoic; he would play his two notes for hours on end, without changing the stern expression on his face and without moving except for his arms. Only when he finally paused to rest did he walk up to the traveler to request a glass of brandy. Without that stimulant, no power on earth could have persuaded him to continue his playing.

Among the Warao of Guyana, Hilhouse (1832, 239) came across a rustic viol whose indigenous features, combined with those of the violin, gave origin to a peculiarly hybrid instrument "manufactured from a short length of a thick bamboo, along which are stretched the three, sometimes four, kuraua-twine (*Bromelia* sp.) strings, attached to pegs and raised from off the underlying convex surface by means of a bridge. Strong kuraua twine also keeps the bow bent" (Roth 1924, 462–63, fig. 239B). So-called self-cord fiddles, obviously made in imitation of the violin, were also widely distributed among other tribes in Guiana: "...the strings (usually three)...are raised over bridges and are cut from, and are still attached to, the bamboo or ite palm [*Mauritia* sp.] stalk forming the body of the instrument..." (Gillin 1948, 854).

To sum up this brief historical survey, the violin proper has had wide distribution throughout Latin America ever since the turn of the eighteenth century. The Warao have adopted the instrument, together with indigenous dances, probably from the Carib Indians surrounding their territory or via trade relations with Indians and non-Indians of Trinidad. Some Warao groups may have been in possession of the violin for 275 years or more; nowadays, it is of near-universal distribution among them.

Another facet of the distributional picture of the violin in Venezuela is that not only the Indians, but also the Criollos, seem to have enjoyed alternating the viol and the later violin with other string instruments which the Spaniards had brought over from the Old World. Among contemporary Criollos of Venezuela the violin is played among "people of Yaracuy, Táchira, Falcón, Portuguesa, Trujillo, Mérida, Anzoátegui, Monagas and Bolívar, where we have often seen it together with the cuatro" (Aretz 1967, 118).

FORAGERS TURNED FARMERS

That the Warao of the central delta have remained outside the distribution area of the violin may be explained in part by the fact that they were among the last subgroups to come under the permanent influence of Europeans, some fifty years ago. Another reason may be that materials required for constructing the instrument are less easily available in the *morichals* these Warao inhabited as sago producers than in the gallery forests on the deltaic islands, which they began to frequent upon adopting agriculture. As suggested earlier, I believe that the violin was adopted simultaneously with elements of an agrarian life-style. But in studying the functional significance of the Warao violin, it is necessary to regress in order to gain perspective on the Warao as swamp foragers.

The majority of the Warao Indians inhabiting the Orinoco Delta continued to forage for food until the beginning of the twentieth century. In 1925, Capuchin missionaries finally succeeded in establishing a permanent foothold in the southwestern delta. Their presence strongly reinforced an earlier trend among the Warao of the eastern delta to adopt agriculture on the basis of taro, a newly introduced cultigen. Agriculture then spread slowly across the region until it had reached the Warao of the central delta by the 1940s. In the process of becoming agriculturalists, the Indians abandoned the swampy *morichals* and moved to levees on the riverbanks, where taro, bitter yuca, potato, *mapuey*, sugarcane, bananas, maize, and other crops could be planted. Gradually, the small nuclear family shelters were replaced by more substantial pile dwellings, large enough to house several nuclear families. Political officers, appointed by the missionaries, replaced in most areas the native band and subtribal leadership. *Gobernadores*, with certain paramount powers over several subtribes, often built structures large enough to house their families and also to provide space for gatherings and dances.[9]

Moriche sago, extracted from the stem of the palm (*Mauritia flexuosa*), was the staple food of the forager Warao. Fish, shellfish, reptiles, birds, occasional game, palm cabbage, honey, and fruits were also important in their diets. To prepare for the annual festival of moriche sago, bands of a subtribe produced hundreds of pounds of stem starch and stored it in a large barrel-shaped container in the temple. This activity engaged most of the able-bodied men and women of the band for several months before the harvest festival was held. The gods were invited by the priest-shaman to the temple, where they offered honey and tobacco and received offerings of sago. The festival was accompanied by long cycles of formal *aruhoho* ("sago dances"), otherwise quite atypical for the Indians of the Guianas. The dances were

---

[9] Lizarralde et al. (1956, 54) depict a large dance hall, and on the accompanying photos (plate opposite p. 65) a large group of adults surrounding the fiddler and frequenting the dancing platform, made of nailed-down boards, can be discerned.

performed specifically for the protection of children and for the assurance of fertility in a general sense.

Two typical beverages, moriche sap and honey water, were consumed on such occasions. Both are highly appreciated by the Warao for their extreme sweetness and their (low) alcoholic content; moriche sap does ferment and honey water is a good basis for mead. Gumilla (1963, 133) says this quality of the moriche sap was known in the first half of the eighteenth century:

They excavate two holes in the stem of the felled palm, one in the young shoot and one at the extreme opposite end of the trunk. There are no cracks through which even a single drop of the liquor, which starts accumulating in the excavations will be lost. . . . Once these cavities, called canoes, have been made, the palm starts exuding a remarkably abundant flow of clear white sap. The daily production is stored in containers that were prepared the night before, and in this manner the Indians continue scooping out the sap for days until the palm's supply is exhausted. For the first two days the collected sap of a palm stem is delicious and sweetish. From then on it acquires a punch, and the delighted Indians inebriate themselves with it for a protracted period of time until it turns to vinegar.

Although the fermented moriche liquor is unquestionably alcoholic, I doubt that heavy intoxication could have resulted from drinking it, even in large quantities. Honey mead may, of course, have been more potent, but I have never seen the Warao intoxicated from drinking it. Nevertheless, both sap and mead were indispensable for the moriche harvest festival, and the large intake of sugar together with whatever alcohol was imbibed did much to heighten the spirits of the dancers. Both beverages were largely seasonal.

The musical instruments used for the ritual *aruhoho* dance were primarily the sacred trumpet (technically a clarinet) and secondarily the drum and basketry rattles. The latter's symbolic relationship to fertility is so universal in South America and elsewhere that here it need only be mentioned in passing.

The adaptation of the forager Warao to an agricultural life-style brought substantial changes to the traditional sago complex. Sago's preexistence, however, made its substitution by an agricultural ritual of basically the same functional significance a considerably easier process. For some time the two rituals may have existed side by side in a given local group, until sago production ceased and the older ritual was finally phased out. This kind of complementary cultural borrowing is relevant to a discussion of the drinking feast, called *hohomare* or *maremare* (happy dance). The beer used at such a function was based on agricultural products, mainly sugarcane and bitter manioc, and the violin rather than the sacred trumpet was the preferred instrument.

Basically, I believe, the *hohomare* functions in the same context and within the same conceptual framework as the sago festival. Both are fertility rituals during which the people offer the first of their staples to the supernaturals. Moriche sago, however, becomes abundant only once a year (during the primary dry season), whereas the newly adopted cultigens ripen in a staggered and multiple fashion which makes occasions for harvest festivals more frequent. Moreover, as Barral (1964, 473) points out:

In Amacuro the Indians distinguish between different kinds of bacchanals or so-called *casiri* dances: natal *casiris*, to celebrate the birth of a child; nuptial *casiris*, to solemnize matrimony; harvest *casiris*, prepared with the first products of the fields, in honor of the *jebu* or spirit; funeral *casiris*, to honor the soul [*mejokoji*] of someone who, upon passing away, left behind a producing field; and *casiris* the priest-shaman instigates when he receives in his dream the order of the spirits to honor them with a bacchanal.

Obviously "fertility" is the common theme that dominates all such occasions for a drinking feast, and the circumstances under which they come about are practically the same as those governing the annual harvest festival of moriche sago.

As explained earlier the *kasiri* drink itself retains the ritual significance of moriche sap and honey mead; not only is it used to "feed" the spirits in the chest of the shaman, but the latter also sprinkles it into the corners of the house and on the walls up to the roof, the symbolic world corners, where the gods of the Warao cosmos reside. Of course, the alcoholic content of *kasiri* is unquestionably higher than that of the palm and honey drinks. No longer are the guests attracted as much by the sweetness and alcoholic prickle of the latter as they are by the strongly intoxicating effect of beer, said to be "as necessary [for the feast] as the wind for sailing" (Barral 1964, 491). Incidentally, the magic of the music of the violin, described as irresistible in the story, is attributable, at least in part, to the coercive effect of alcohol habituation on the dancers. The magic certainly never fails, and it should have given the threatened monkey-fiddler the confidence in his art which he did indeed display. Yet, to insist on the purely hedonistic character of traditional Warao drinking feasts is certainly myopic, just as calling them "social amusements…combined with singing, dancing, and sex play" represents a misleading oversimplification (Gillin 1948, 853). Instead, the so-called drinking spree is to the agricultural Warao the same basic fertility ritual as the moriche sago festival was to the traditional *morichal* foragers. The only significant difference is that the modern dance festival is based on a potent alcoholic intoxicant which can be produced in quantities of hundreds of liters, not once but several times a year. By drinking it, all men and most women become heavily intoxicated, something that formed no part of the original design of the sago-based fertility ritual.

Another important substitution for a component of the sago dancing ritual is the violin. Adopted by the Warao as part of an agricultural complex, it replaces the traditional sacred trumpet, which is so deeply rooted in *morichal* culture that blowing it during a modern feast would be unthinkable. Drum and basketry rattle are less specifically related to the moriche complex and can be orchestrated with the violin. I remember the bursts of laughter which overwhelmed me and my informant when we suggested that a violin be played during a moriche festival: the hilarious response told me that it was impossible to implement such an idea.

At this point it is worthwhile to refer briefly to the house-blessing ceremony (described earlier) in which the shaman propitiates the spirits of the four corners and the roof of the dwelling. The ceremony is reminiscent of similar rituals performed by priests of the Catholic Church to bless ceremonial buildings and ordinary houses. In performing this rite, called *Benedictio Domorum*, the priest sprinkles holy water on important areas of the house, on the inhabitants, and into the four directions of the cross. Although, as suggested earlier, sprinkling on the cardinal points and the zenith makes perfect sense in Warao ideology, the ritual parallel may suggest a Christian origin of the indigenous house-blessing ceremony.

Before we jump to any conclusions, however, we must remember that such ceremonies are by no means restricted to the Warao. They are also used by other South American Indians, like the Mojo of eastern Bolivia whose priest-shamans offer chicha to their gods in drinking houses or temples and in places where dancers, both male and female, drink large quantities of the liquor to propitiate their deities (Steward and Faron 1959, 256–57). It is noteworthy that the drinking houses of the Mojo are intimately associated with the jaguar cult whose ceremonies make the animal a friend of the Indians.

In order to explain why I tend to believe that the *hohomare* is equivalent to the sago ritual and not necessarily a borrowing from Christianity, I must review pertinent cosmological beliefs of the Warao before returning to the symbolism of the jaguar and the violin.

By sprinkling *kasiri* into the four corners of the house and onto the highest part of the saddle roof, the Warao shaman propitiates the supernatural beings residing at the solstitial and equinoctial points of the cosmos. Who are these gods? Do they have any relationship to the symbolic fertility complex of the drinking feasts? In this sense the setting of the *hohomare* is revealing. The shamans and elders who first perform the offering ritual and then preside over the feast place themselves along the long sides of the rectangular dance house, thus marking the imaginary solstitial line(s). In the same pattern, the violinist who positions himself at the center of the house marks the zenith and the sun's path during the equinoxes. It is significant that the northern solstice points of Warao cosmogony are said to be inhabited by supernatural guarantors of sustenance and fertility. The Mother of Sago (Aruarani) is at the midsummer point of sunrise in the northeast; the God of Dance (Oriwakarotu) is at the midsummer point of sunset in the northwest. The northern solstice is identified with the sacred trumpet, whose gigantic mythic prototypes and master spirits reside with the God of Dance. Also located in the same place are the Grandmothers (Natue), patronesses of the moriche palm fiber. If the violin of the *maremare* has replaced the sacred trumpet of the sago feast, the logical cosmic anchorage point of the adopted instrument would be on the northern solstice. As the sacred trumpet assures the insemination of the moriche palm on earth, so, one might suppose, the violin guarantees fertilization of the cultivars in the fields.

Opposite the supernatural fertility beings of the northern solstice, the Mother of the Forest (Dauarani) resides at the southern solstice of the midwinter sun. Just as the Grandmothers of the northern solstice are patronesses of female artisans (hammock makers) and of women in general, the Mother of the Forest of the southern solstice is the patroness of male artisans (boat makers) and of men in general. The division between the sexes is clearly maintained during the dance, when a line of female dancers opposite a line of male dancers moves toward the equinoctial line of the violin and back again.

It is my contention that these dancers simulate simultaneously the movement of the sun during the year and of the moon in a month. Because of a cosmic location and a distinct ritual function the violin might have acquired as a substitute for the sacred trumpet, it has probably inherited a solar connotation. A symbolic meaning of this type may also adhere to the characteristics of the jaguar, who is out to kill the monkey during a dance when the mediating violin keeps the two archenemies apart. Thus Cardona (1952), in describing the *hohomare* of the Warao, says the dancers form "a circle with the violinist taking his position in the center...a strategy designed to impede the fiddler's escape." When he does manage to break free, the chorus is dissolved and the dance in two lines resumes (Acosta Saignes 1961, 124–25). This procedure recalls the original scene of the violin story, depicting the jaguar as the inexorable hunter of the monkey. Thus, it may be significant that the dancers, as described by Barral (1964, 573–83), instead of completely encircling the violinist, approach him in concave and convex semicircles reminiscent of the pattern of a waxing and waning moon.

Other Indians on the Orinoco also have placed the jaguar in a mythical lunar context, an interpretation that becomes especially clear when Acosta Saignes (1961, 121–38) reconstructs the *maremare* celebration as a "dance of the moon and the jaguar":

The dance, called *maéma* by the Otomac, is very formal and worthy of its station. It takes its name from the jaguar from whose attacks an Indian, sitting in the center of the circle, pretends to defend himself. Eight or ten Indians perform the dance, gracefully singing...and tightly pressed against one another. Off and on, when least expected and as though the jaguar had come to carry off the encircled person, other dancers, lances in hand and poised to use them, enter from the four quarters of the circle.

Acosta Saignes (1961, 138) concludes that the *maremare*, "either in the form it is presently danced as part of the folklore of eastern Venezuela or as it survives among various groups of Indians, is simply a relic of an ancient lunar cult of several tribes of the Orinoco."[10]

---

[10] See Rosenblat's (1964, 256–59) description of the lunar identification of the jaguar among the Orinoco Indians.

If indeed the Warao have adopted the ritual from the agriculturalists of central and eastern Venezuela, they have still succeeded in rooting it firmly in their ideational system. Thus it is no wonder that they consider it to be autochthonous, believing that the original dance between the monkey and the jaguar took place *in illo tempore*. In contrast, the possibility of a connection between the *hohomare* of the Warao and the Christian house-blessing ceremony seems less convincing, even improbable.

Concerning the deep-rootedness of the agricultural ritual and the violin, another circumstance merits attention. The simian violinist descended from his mansion on the mountain to bring the violin to the Warao of the delta, but the instrument's soul remained in Trinidad. In the minds of the Warao, the mountain is most likely identical to the Naparima (a Trinidadian toponym) mountain chain and specifically to Naparima Hill on the central west coast of the island. In Warao cosmology this mountain is the abode of the northern earth-god, whose name they pronounce as Nabarima, meaning "Father of the Waters or of Waves." It would not have been the first time in mythological history that the Warao received from this Nabarima a novel kind of music and a social mandate, for the adulterated "mothers" of their culture hero, Haburi, were taken there in a canoe invented by their son. The boat subsequently changed into a serpent-woman and the paddle became a serpent-man. They came back from Nabarima in the form of a red cedar (*Colophyllum* sp., *bisi*) and a white cedar (*Colophyllum* sp., *babe*), respectively, to reside temporarily in the center of the disklike earth. The boat-red cedar-serpent-woman became the first shaman of the Warao and, traveling as a boat-serpent between Trinidad and the mainland, sang, like the soul of the monkey's fiddle on the schooner, a new order of music. She chanted like a priest-shaman whose function it is to placate the gods and, in so doing, to guarantee health, fertility, and longevity to the people in the community. (Incidentally, when referring to the bridge of the violin as *wahiriba*, "the raised gunwales of the boat," the Warao allude to the condition of a trading canoe they used on their voyages to Trinidad.) The mythical paradigm then fittingly represents in Warao thought a preexistent matrix in which the new agrarian ritual, with its specific dance and musical instrument, the violin, was able to thrive as perfectly as in any agricultural ideological context.

A convincing case of complementary cultural borrowing, in which an adopted agricultural fertility ritual replaced a ritual of preagricultural foragers in all its essential components and functions can thus be made. Warao culture, however, was not programmed for the impact of the new ritual beverage, based on agricultural products. This component of the agrarian complex, more than any other, posed a problem of acculturation for which no solution emerged from within the traditional pattern of a nonagricultural society like the Warao.

THE DANCING JAGUAR

Any good Warao storyteller will succeed in eliciting sighs of relief from his audience when, in telling the story of the violin's origin, he relates the incident of the jaguar's being overpowered by the beautiful music and embracing the monkey in a fraternal dance. A close parallel that comes to mind is the story of the Greek poet Orpheus, of whom it is said that whenever he "played his seven-stringed lyre and sang, the animals would forget their pursuits and listen to him. Lions and tigers lost their fierceness when they heard Orpheus sing, and the shy deer and all the creatures of the forest came to him" (Oswalt 1969, 218).

In order to appreciate more fully the Warao concept of the mediating role of the violin and music, we must look beyond the relative intoxicating strengths of ritual beverages and the magic effect of music on a jaguar. The basic antagonism between the violin and the jaguar in Warao tradition has another meaning, more earthbound but still no less transcendental. The climactic intensity of the story is beautifully revealed when the dancing jaguar, in a state of rapture, embraces the monkey-fiddler (his preferred prey), as he exclaims: "Let's be friends! Let's be brothers!" In the mind of a traditional Warao, even more than in the mind of a Western listener, this response clearly demonstrates the ultimate mediating power of the violin; it is a power that achieves the impossible.

This perceptual difference between Warao and Westerner stems from the Warao concept of the jaguar, not as simply a carnivorous beast, but as a cannibalistic Carib Indian in animal guise. For centuries before the Conquest and for some time thereafter, Carib cannibals raided Warao settlements, first to slaughter and eat the Indians and later to capture, enslave, and ultimately sell them to Europeans living in the Guiana colonies. Even today, some Warao may cling to the belief that the Carib can instantly transform themselves into jaguars, even in the presence of Warao (Barral 1960, 257). According to García (1971, 57–58), this concept is "one of the most widespread ideas among them [Warao]; they even have songs that allude to this belief and urge them escape [the cannibals]." Another comment is found in Barral (1964, 161–62):

The contemporary Warao believe that there still exists in our times a tribe of *Jebu*-Indians [spirits] whose members can transform themselves into jaguars. They are called Musimotuma and Mamo-araotuma, "Red-Faces," "People of the Mamo." According to the latter appellation these Indians originated in the region of the Mamo [River], in Guayana [of Venezuela], close to Ciudad Bolívar. . . . The Carib Indians of the Mamo know about this belief and preoccupation of the Warao.

Only slowly, and only after centuries of contact are the Warao learning that some Carib were cannibals and others were not. Nevertheless, the nightmare of being prey to cannibalistic jaguar-people, as the monkey-fiddler was, continues to reverberate ruefully through Warao songs and lullabies. Carib-jaguars also live on in many of their narratives (Barral 1960, 134–36, 251–53; Barral 1964, 312, 390). One of the stories explains that the enmity between jaguars and humans stemmed from a kidnapping incident during a *maremare*. The violin that reached the delta early in the eighteenth century may have become the symbolical agent that terminated the predicament of being neighbors to cannibals, for at about that time cannibalism and trafficking in human lives were abolished in Venezuela and Guiana.

Nowadays, however, the situation is changing, and the unsolved problem of alcohol remains to haunt the survivors. Because of the availability of Western medicines, vaccines, antibiotics, and anthelmintic remedies, infant mortality among the Warao has been drastically reduced. "Now we have the nuns," I was told by a village chief in the delta. "We don't have to placate the gods anymore, because it is the medicine of the missionaries which protects our children, not the annual sago festival." Also, the idea of offering to the gods the firstfruits of various field products loses its appeal as *kasiri* becomes a second-rate alcoholic beverage, inferior to the more powerful rum. Distilled alcohol is completely dissociated from any fertility ritual, whether based on sago or on cultigens. The modern drinking bout, now with a life of its own, shows only a vague resemblance to the harvest festival of the past. The typical instrument, at a present-day drinking party is neither the sacred trumpet of the midsummer solstice nor the violin of the sacred mountain. Replacing them are electronic devices—transistor radios, gramophones, tape players—which have no intrinsic symbolism. Concepts of ritualistic fertility with profound symbolic meaning are giving way to hedonistic precepts of survival, as all the symbols of the cult, the gods, the dance, the beverages, and the musical instruments have lost their generative powers. By 1945 the Orinoco Delta was home to communities of which Turrado Moreno (1945, 233) could write: "As they consider the *maremare* fully and always a secular dance, they do not hesitate to organize one for any reasonable purpose in daytime or at night, for short periods of time and never for an entire day or night, embellishing it with large draughts of *cachiri* and sugarcane liquor with which they satisfy their palates at intervals and at the end of the dance." Today, almost fifty years later, hearing with increasing frequency of such sprees of drinking *kasiri* or straight rum, the ethnologist who has seen the *hohomare* with its fiddler and whose memory reaches even to sago festivals with the sacred trumpet, hopes that the traditional refrain—"The Warao will weep when their fiddler dies" (Barral 1964, 422)—is not an ominous prediction.

Bibliography

Acosta Saignes, Miguel
 1961   *Estudios de etnología antigua de Venezuela.* 2nd ed. Ediciones
         de la Biblioteca, vol. 3. Caracas: Universidad Central de Ven-
         ezuela.
Alamgir, Mohiuddin
 1981   "An Approach towards a Theory of Famine." In John R. K.
         Robson, ed., *Famine, Its Causes, Effects and Management*, pp.
         19–40. New York: Gordon and Breach Science Publishers.
Alvarado, Lisandro
 1945   *Datos etnográficos de Venezuela.* Caracas: Biblioteca Venezo-
         lana de Cultura.
 1953   *Glosario de voces indígenas de Venezuela.* Caracas.
Appun, Karl Ferdinand
 1961   *En los tropicos.* Ediciones de la Biblioteca, vol. 2. Caracas:
         Universidad Central de Venezuela.
Aretz, Isabel
 1967   *Instrumentos musicales de Venezuela.* Colección La Heredad.
         Cumaná: Universidad de Oriente.
Armellada, Cesáreo de
 1980   "Los violines entre los indios Guayanos." *Venezuela Misionera*
         (Caracas) 491:206–7.
Arvelo-Jiménez, Nelly
 1971   *Political Relations in a Tribal Society: A Study of the Ye'cuana
         Indians of Venezuela.* Latin American Studies Program, Disser-
         tation Series. Ithaca: Cornell University.
 1974   *Relaciones políticas en una sociedad tribal: Estudio de los
         ye'cuana, indígenas del amazonas venezolano.* Instituto Indi-
         genista Interamericano, Ediciones Especiales, vol. 68. Mexico
         City.
Atlas de Venezuela
 1979   Ministerio del Ambiente y de los Recursos Naturales Reno-
         vables. Caracas.

Barandiarán, Daniel de
1962   "Shamanismo Yekuana o Makiritare." *Antropológica* (Caracas) 11:61–90.
1966   "El habitado entre los indios Yekuana." *Antropológica* (Caracas) 16:3–95.
1979   *Introducción a la cosmovisión de los indios Ye'kuana-Makiritare.* Caracas: Universidad Católica Andrés Bello, Instituto de Investigaciones Históricas, Centro de Lenguas Indígenas.

Barral, Basilio María de
1960   *Guarao guarata. Lo que cuentan los indios Guaraos.* Caracas.
1964   *Los indios Guaraúnos y su cancionero.* Biblioteca "Missionalia Hispánica," no. 15. Madrid.
1979   *Diccionario Warao-Castellano, Castellano-Warao.* Caracas.

Barthel, Thomas
1966   "Mesoamerikanische Fledermausdämonen." *Tribus* (Stuttgart) 15:101–24.

Bernau, J. H.
1847   *Missionary Labours in British Guiana, with Remarks on the Manners, Customs, and Superstitious Rites of the Aborigines.* London: John Farquhar Shaw.

Blanco-Azpurúa
n.d.   *Colección de documentos para la historia. . .* (Incomplete reference after Alvarado 1953, 440).

Brett, W. H.
1868   *The Indian Tribes of Guiana: Their Condition and Habits.* London: Bell and Daldy.

Brown, Leslie, and Dean Amadon
1968   *Eagles, Hawks and Falcons of the World*, vol. 1. New York: McGraw-Hill.

Butt, Audrey
1962   "Réalité et idéal dans le practique chamanique." *L'Homme* 2(3):5–52.

Butt-Colson, Audrey
1973   "Intertribal Trade in the Guiana Highlands." *Antropológica* (Caracas) 34:1–70.

Cardona, Miguel
1952   *Coreografía del Maremare.* Apuntes mecanográficos del Servicio de Investigaciones Folklóricas. Caracas.

Carrocera, Buenaventura de
1968   *Misión de los Capuchinos en Cumaná.* 3 vols. Biblioteca de la Academia Nacional de la Historia, vols. 88, 89, 90. Caracas.
1979   *Misión de los Capuchinos en Guayana.* 3 vols. Biblioteca de la Academia Nacional de la Historia, vols. 139, 140, 141. Caracas.

Civrieux, Marc de
1959   "Datos antropológicos de los indios Kuna-hana." *Antropológica*
        (Caracas) 8:85–146.
1960   "Leyendas Maquiritares." *Memoria.* Sociedad de Ciencias
        Naturales La Salle (Caracas) 20(56):105–25; 20(57):178–88.
1970   *Watunna: Mitología Makiritare.* Caracas: Monte Avila Editores.
1974   "Religión y magia Kari'ña." *Montalbán* (Caracas) 3:371–471.
1980   *Watunna: An Orinoco Creation Cycle.* Ed. and trans. David M.
        Guss. San Francisco: North Point Press.
n.d.   *Informe inédito sobre los Caribes de Anzoátegui.* Caracas.
Cohen, Percy S.
1969   "Theories of Myth." *Man* (n.s.) 4(1):337–53.
Cohen, Yehudi A.
1971   "The Shaping of Men's Minds: Adaptations to Imperatives of
        Culture." In Murray Wax, Stanley Diamond, and Fred Gearing,
        eds., *Anthropological Perspectives on Education*, pp. 19–50.
        New York: Basic Books.
Coomaraswamy, Ananda K.
1935   *Elements of Buddhist Iconography.* Cambridge: Harvard Uni-
        versity Press.
Coombs, Philip H., and Manzoor Ahmed
1974   *Attacking Rural Poverty: How Nonformal Education Can Help.*
        Baltimore and London: Johns Hopkins University Press.
Coppens, Walter
1971   "Relaciones comerciales de los Yekuana del Caura-Paragua."
        Antropológica (Caracas) 30:28–59.
1981   *Del canalete al motor fuera de borda. Misión en Jiwitiña y otras
        áreas de aculturación en tres pueblos Ye'kuana del Caura-
        Paragua.* Fundación La Salle de Ciencias Naturales, Instituto
        Caribe de Antropología y Sociología, Monografías, no. 28.
        Caracas.
Crevaux, Jules Nicolas
1883   *Voyages dans l'Amérique du Sud.* Paris: Librairie Hachette et
        Cie.
Cruls, Gastao
1958   *Heléia Amazônica: Aspectos da flora, fauna, arqueologia e
        etnografia indígenas.* Rio de Janeiro: José Olympio.
Cruxent, José María, and Irving Rouse
1974   "Early Man in the West Indies." In *New World Archaeology:
        Readings from Scientific American,* pp. 71–81. San Francisco:
        W. H. Freeman.

Darbois, Dominique
    1953   *Indiens d'Amazonie.* Paris.
    1956   *Yanamale: Village of the Amazon.* London: Collins.
Dobrizhoffer, P. Martin
    1822   *An Account of the Abipones, an Equestrian People of Paraguay.*
            Trans. Sara Coleridge, from Latin edition of 1784. 3 vols. Lon-
            don.
Durán, Fray Diego
    1971   *Book of the Gods and Rites and the Ancient Calendar.* Trans.
            Fernando Horcasitas and Doris Heyden. Norman: University of
            Oklahoma Press.
Eliade, Mircea
    1964   *Shamanism: Archaic Techniques of Ecstasy.* Bollingen Series,
            no. 76. New York: Pantheon Books.
Fock, Niels
    1963   *Waiwai: Religion and Society of an Amazonian Tribe.* National-
            museets Skrifter, Etnografisk Raekke, vol. 8. Copenhagen:
            National Museum.
Garcia, Argimiro
    1971   *Cuentos y tradiciones de los indios Guaraúnos.* Caracas:
            Universidad Católica Andrés Bello, Instituto de Investigaciones
            Históricas, Seminario de Lenguas Indígenas.
Gheerbrant, Alain
    1954   *Journey to the Far Amazon.* New York: Simon and Schuster.
Gilij, Felipe Salvador
    1965   *Ensayo de historia americana.* 3 vols. Biblioteca de la Academia
            Nacional de la Historia, vols. 71, 72, 73. Caracas.
Gillin, John
    1936   *The Barama River Caribs.* Papers of the Peabody Museum of
            American Archaeology and Ethnology of Harvard University,
            vol. 14, no. 2. Cambridge, Mass.
    1948   "Tribes of the Guianas." In Julian H. Steward, ed., *Handbook
            of South American Indians* 3:799–860. Bureau of American
            Ethnology Bulletin no. 143. Washington, D.C.: Smithsonian
            Institution.
Girard, Rafael
    1969   *Die ewigen Mayas: Zivilisation und Geschichte.* Zürich: Rhein-
            Verlag.
Goodenough, Ward H.
    1961   "Education and Identity." In *Anthropology and Education*, ed.
            Frederick C. Gruber. Martin G. Brumbaugh Lectures, fifth se-
            ries. Philadelphia: University of Pennsylvania Press.

1969   "Basic Economy and Community." *Behavior Science Notes, HRAF Quarterly Bulletin* 4(4):291–98. New Haven: Human Relations Area Files.

Grelier, Joseph
1954   *Aux sources de l'Orénoque.* Paris: La Tabla Ronda.
1956   *Zu den Quellen des Orinoko.* Leipzig: Brockhaus Verlag.

Grenson, Pedro J.
1950–51 "Nuestra primera música instrumental: Datos históricos." 2nd ed. *Revista de Estudios Musicales* 2 (5, 6). Mendoza: Universidad Nacional de Cuyo.

Gumilla, José
1963   *El Orinoco ilustrado y defendido.* Biblioteca Nacional de la Historia, vol. 68. Caracas.

Guss, David M.
1980   "The Atta." *New Wilderness Letter* (New York) 2(8):14–15.
1981   "Historical Incorporation among the Makiritare: From Legend to Myth." *Journal of Latin American Lore* 7(1):23–35.

Harris, C. J.
1968   *Otters.* London: Weidenfeld and Bicolson.

Heinen, H. Dieter, and Julio Lavandero
1973   "Computación del tiempo en dos subtribus Warao." *Antropológica* (Caracas) 35:3–24.

Heinen, H. Dieter, and Kenneth Ruddle
1974   "Ecology, Ritual, and Economic Organization in the Distribution of Palm Starch among the Warao of the Orinoco Delta." *Journal of Anthropological Research* 30(2):116–38.

Helitzer, Florence
1973   "The Princeton Galaxy." *Intellectual Digest* (New York) 3(10):25–32.

Henry, Jules, and Joan Whithorn Boggs
1952   "Child Rearing, Culture, and the Natural World." *Psychiatry* 15:261–71.

Herskovits, Melville J.
1970   *Man and His Works.* New York: Alfred A. Knopf.

Hilhouse, William
1832   "Notices of the Indians Settled in the Interior of British Guiana." *Journal of the Royal Geographical Society of London* 2:227–49.
1834   "Memoir on the Warow Land of British Guiana." *Journal of the Royal Geographical Society of London* 4:321–33.

Humbert, Jules
  1976   *Los orígenes Venezolanos (Ensayo sobre la colonización española en Venezuela)*. Biblioteca de la Academia Nacional de la Historia, vol. 127. Caracas.
Joseph, E. L.
  1970   *History of Trinidad*. London: Frank Cass. 1st ed. 1838.
Jung, Carl G.
  1959   *The Archetypes and the Collective Unconscious*. Bollingen Series, no. 20. Princeton: Princeton University Press.
  1967   *Symbols of Transformation*. Bollingen Series, no. 20. Princeton: Princeton University Press.
Koch-Grünberg, Theodor
  1923   *Vom Roroima zum Orinoco*. Vol. 3. Stuttgart: Strecker und Schröder Verlag.
La Belle, Thomas J.
  1975   "Liberation, Development, and Rural Nonformal Education." *Council on Anthropology and Education Quarterly* 6(4):20–26.
Lathrop, Donald W.
  1970   *The Upper Amazon*. London: Thames and Hudson.
Lavandero, Julio
  1982   "La nube de las cuatro jovenes." *Venezuela Misionera* 43 (508):56–58.
Lévi-Strauss, Claude
  1966   *From Honey to Ashes. Introduction to a Science of Mythology*. Vol. 2. New York: Harper and Row.
  1969   *The Raw and the Cooked. Introduction to a Science of Mythology*. Vol. 1. Trans. John and Doreen Weightman. New York and Evanston: Harper and Row.
  1973   *From Honey to Ashes. Introduction of a Science of Mythology*. Vol. 2. Trans. John and Doreen Weightman. New York, Evanston, San Francisco: Harper and Row.
Liddle, Ralph Alexander
  1928   *The Geology of Venezuela and Trinidad*. Fort Worth, Tex.: J. P. MacGowan.
Lizarralde, Roberto, J. Silverberg, and José Silva Michelena
  1956   "Etnografía." In *Los Guarao del Dalta Amacuro*, pp. 19–61. Caracas: Departamento de Sociología y Antropología Cultural, Universidad Central de Venezuela.
Lodares, Baltasar de
  1930   *Los Franciscanos Capuchinos en Venezuela*. Vol. 2. Caracas.

Lounsbury, Floyd G.
1959   "Similarity and Contiguity Relations in Language and Culture."
        In *Report of the Tenth Annual Round Table Meeting on Linguist-
        ics and Language Studies*, ed. Richard Harrell, pp. 123–38.
        Georgetown University Institute of Languages and Linguistics,
        Monograph no. 12. Washington, D.C.

Matthäi, Hildegard
1977   *Die Rolle der Greifvögel, insbesondere der Harpye und des
        Königsgeiers, bei ausserandinen Indianern Südamerikas.*
        Münchener Beiträge zur Amerikanistik, vol. 1. Munich: Klaus
        Renner Verlag.

Méndez-Arocha, Alberto
1963   *La Pesca en Margarita*. Fundación La Salle de Ciencias
        Naturales, Estación de Investigaciones Marinas de Margarita,
        Monografías, no. 7. Caracas.

Menezes, Mary Noel
1979   *The Amerindians in Guyana 1803–73: A Documentary History*.
        Totowa, N.J.: Frank Cass.

Métraux, Alfred
1948   "The Tupinamba." In Julian H. Steward, ed., *Handbook of South
        American Indians* 3:95–133. Bureau of American Ethnology
        Bulletin no. 143. Washington, D.C.: Smithsonian Institution.
1949   "Jesuit Missions in South America." In Julian H. Steward, ed.,
        Handbook of South American Indians 5:645–53. Bureau of
        American Ethnology Bulletin no. 143. Washington, D.C.:
        Smithsonian Institution.

Mondolfi, Edgardo
1974   "Taxonomy, Distribution and Status of the Manatee in Venezu-
        ela." *Memoria*. Sociedad de Ciencias Naturales La Salle
        (Caracas) 34(97):5–23.

Morey, Robert V.
1979   "A Joyful Harvest of Souls: Disease and Destruction of the Lla-
        nos Indians." *Antropológica* (Caracas) 52:77–108.

Müller, Jan
1956   "Report on a Botanical Reconnaisance in the Delta Amacuro."
        Unpublished.
1959   "Palynology of Recent Orinoco Delta and Shelf Sediments:
        Reports of the Orinoco Shelf Expedition." *Micropaleontology*
        5(1):1–32.

Oramas, Luis R.
1949   "Ceremonias fúnebres de los Caribes del Estado Anzoátegui."
        Memoria. Sociedad de Ciencias Naturales La Salle (Caracas)
        9(25):319–23.

Ortner, Sherry B.
  1973   "On Key Symbols." *American Anthropologist* 75:1338–46.
Osborn, Henry
  1969   "The Warao Self." *Bible Translator* 20:74–83.
Oswalt, Sabine G.
  1969   *Concise Encyclopedia of Greek and Roman Mythology.* Chicago.
Penard, F. P., and A. P. Penard
  1907–8 *De menschetende Aanbidders der Zonneslang.* 3 vols. Paramaribo: B. Heyde.
Raleigh, Sir Walter
  1596   *The Discovery of the Large, Rich and Beautiful Empire of Guiana.* London: Hakluyt Society. Reprint New York: Burt Franklin, Publisher, 1970.
Reichel-Dolmatoff, Gerardo
  1972   "The Feline Motif in Prehistoric San Augustín Sculpture." In Elizabeth P. Benson, ed., *The Cult of the Feline*, pp. 51–64. Washington, D.C.: Dumbarton Oaks Research Library and Collections.
  1978   "The Loom of Life: A Kogi Principle of Integration." *Journal of Latin American Lore* 4(1):5–27.
Rionegro, Froylán de
  1918   *Relaciones de las misiones de los PP. Capuchinos en las antiguas provincias españolas hoy República de Venezuela, 1650–1817.* 2 vols. Sevilla: Tipografía Zarzuela (vol. 1) and Tipografía La Exposición (vol. 2).
Rosenblat, Angel
  1964   "Los Otomacos y Taparitas. Estudio etnográfico y lingüístico." *Anuario del Instituto de Antropología e Historia* 1:227–377. Caracas: Universidad Central de Venezuela.
Roth, Walter E.
  1915   "An Inquiry into the Animism and Folklore of the Guiana Indians." In *Thirtieth Annual Report of the Bureau of American Ethnology, 1908–1909*, pp. 103–386. Washington, D.C.
  1924   "An Introductory Study of the Arts, Crafts, and Customs of the Guiana Indians." In *Thirty-Eighth Annual Report of the Bureau of American Ethnology, 1916–1917*, pp. 25–745. Washington, D.C.
Rouse, Irving, and José M. Cruxent
  1963   *Venezuelan Archaeology.* New Haven: Yale University Press.

Schomburgk, Richard
1922–23 *Travels in British Guiana, 1840–1844.* Trans. and ed. Walter
         E. Roth. 2 vols. "Daily Chronicle" Office, Georgetown, B.G.
         (First published: Leipzig: J. J. Weber, 1847–48)
1847–48 *Reisen in Britisch Guiana in den Jahren 1840–1844.* 3 vols.
         Leipzig: J. J. Weber.
Schomburgk, Robert H.
1840   *A Description of British Guiana.* London: Simpkin, Marshall,
         and Co.
Schuster, Meinhard
1976   *Dekuana: Beiträge zur Ethnologie der Makiritare.* Munich:
         Klaus Renner Verlag.
Schwarz, Herbert S.
1929   "Honey Wasps." *Natural History* 29(4):421–26.
Stevenson, Robert
1968   *Music in Aztec and Inca Territory.* Berkeley and Los Angeles:
         University of California Press.
Steward, Julian H., and Louis C. Faron
1959   *Native Peoples of South America.* New York: McGraw-Hill.
Suárez, María Matilde
1968   *Los Warao.* Caracas: Instituto Venezolano de Investigaciones
         Científicas.
Torquemada, Juan de
1759   *Veinte i un libros rituales i Monachis Indiana.* 3 vols. Madrid.
Tozzer, Alfred M.
1907   *A Comparative Study of the Mayas and Lacandones.* Archaeo-
         logical Institute of America. New York: Macmillan.
Turrado Moreno, Angel
1945   *Etnografía de los indios Guaraúnos.* Caracas: Comité Organi-
         zador, Tercera Conferencia Interamericana de Agricultura.
van Andel, Tj. H.
1956   "Note to Accompany a Provisional Sediment-Morphological
         Map of Delta Amacuro." Unpublished.
1967   "The Orinoco Delta." *Journal of Sedimentary Petrology*
         37(2):297–310.
van Andel, Tj. H., and H. Postma
1954   "Recent Sediments of the Gulf of Paria: Reports of the Orinoco
         Shelf Expedition" (vol. 1). *Verhandelingen der Koninklijke
         Nederlandse Akademie van Wetenschappen*, Afdeling Natur-
         kunde, vol. 20, no. 5. Amsterdam.

van Andel, Tj. H., and Pl. L. Sachs
    1964   "Sedimentation in the Gulf of Paria during the Holocene Trans-
             gression: A Subsurface Acoustic Reflection Study." *Sears Foun-
             dation: Journal of Marine Research* 22(1):30–50.
Vila, Pablo, et al.
    1960   "Geografía de Venezuela," vol. 1. In *El territorio nacional y
             su ambiente físico.* Caracas: Ministerio de Educación.
Voorde, P. K. J. van der
    1962   "Soil Conditions of the Isla Macareo, Orinoco Delta, Venezu-
             ela." In *Mededelingen van de Stichting voor Bodemkartering.
             Boor en Spade*, vol. 12, pp. 6–26. Wageningen: H. Veenman
             en Zonen.
Wasson, R. Gordon
    1968   *Soma, Divine Mushroom of Immortality.* Ethno-Mycological
             Studies, no. 1. New York: Harcourt, Brace & World. New ed.
             1971. New York: Harcourt, Brace Jovanovich.
Wilbert, Johannes
    1956a   "Los instrumentos musicales de los indios Warrau (Guarao,
             Guaraúno)." *Antropológica* (Caracas) 1:2–22.
    1956b   "Rasgos culturales circuncaribes entre los Warrau y sus infe-
             rencias." *Memoria.* Sociedad de Ciencias Naturales La Salle
             (Caracas) 16(45):237–57.
    1957   Prologue to Basilio María de Barral, *Diccionario Guarao-
             Español, Español-Guarao*, pp. 7–18. Sociedad de Ciencias
             Naturales La Salle, Monografías, no. 3. Caracas.
    1963   *Indios de la región Orinoco-Ventuari.* Fundación La Salle de
             Ciencias Naturales, Instituto Caribe de Antropología y Socio-
             logía, Monografías, no. 8. Caracas.
    1969   *Textos folklóricos de los indios Warao.* Latin American Stud-
             ies, no. 12. Los Angeles: Latin American Center, University
             of California.
    1970   *Folk Literature of the Warao Indians: Narrative Material and
             Motif Content.* Latin American Studies, no. 15. Los Angeles:
             Latin American Center, University of California.
    1972   *Survivors of Eldorado: Four Indian Cultures of South America.*
             New York: Praeger.
    1973   "Magico-Religious Use of Tobacco among South American
             Indians." In Vera Rubin, ed., *Cannabis and Culture*, pp. 439–
             61. The Hague: Mouton.
    1975   *Warao Basketry: Form and Function.* Los Angeles: Museum
             of Cultural History, University of California.

1977   "Navigators of the Winter Sun." In Elizabeth P. Benson, ed., *The Sea in the Pre-Columbian World*, pp. 16–46. Washington, D.C.: Dumbarton Oaks Research Library and Collections.

1979   "Gaukler-schamanen der Warao." In *Amerikanistische Studien*, Roswitha Hartmann and Udo Oberem, (2):294–99. Anthropos Institut, Collectanea Instituti Anthropos, vol. 21. Sankt Augustin.

1983   "Warao Ethnopathology." *Journal of Ethnopharmacology* 8:357–61.

1987   *Tobacco and Shamanism in South America*. New Haven: Yale University Press.

Williams, Thomas Rhys

1972   *Introduction to Socialization: Human Culture Transmitted*. St. Louis: C. V. Mosbey.

Index

Lord of Ritual and Dance, 217–18
Lord of the Dead, Soul-Hoebo, 92.
    See also Hoebo (Abode of Dark-
    ness, Land of Death); Scarlet Ma-
    caw
Lord of the Sacred Trumpet, 217
Lord of the Underworld, 93, 146. *See
    also* Scarlet Macaw
Lords of Rain, 221–22, 241, appear-
    ance and lifestyle of, 223, 234,
    240; chants to, 225–31; feared,
    242; origin of titles, 233–34; par-
    allels to, 234; ranks, titles, and lo-
    cations, 223–24 (Tables 8.1–2),
    225; regarded as foreigners, 233
Lords of Xibalba, 133–34
Lorenzano, Sr. Antonio, 146 n
lunar cult, ancient, 269
lunar symbolism, 63 n

Macareo *caño*, 4, 6, 17
Macaw God of the Underworld. *See*
    Scarlet Macaw
machete or bush knife, 35
Macuro mission, 260
maéma, a dance, 269
magic arrows, 123–25, 127, 154; sticks
    dropped by kites regarded as, 168
Maipure tribe, 259
maize, 16, 22, 34, 264
males: conditioned for navigation, 79;
    correct behavior of young men,
    63; life cycle of, 28
maluwana, decorated wooden disk of
    Wayana roundhouse, 198, 199
    (Fig. 7.10). *See also* roundhouse
Mamo River, 272
Mamo-araotuma, "People of the
    Mamo," 272. *See also* Carib Indi-
    ans
mamuse, ritual bonds, 156
manaca palm, *winamoru* (*Euterpe* sp.),
    14, 20, 29, 120; leafstalk used for
    cigar wrapping, 64, 71, 116, 138;
    used to build corduroy roads, 47;
    used to build houses, 217;
    winamoru tree shaman, 21–22

Manamo *caño*, 3, 4, 11 (Map 1.4), 17
manatee (*Trichechus manatus*), 17, 18
mangroves, 6, 29; red (*Rhizophora
    mangle*), 29
manioc, 16, 22, 254; bitter, 266
Manuel, *bahanarotu* of the Arawabisi
    subtribe, 147 n
mapuey, 264
maremare (dance), 257, 258, 261,
    266, 268, 272, 273; fiddler, 247;
    interpreted as dance of the moon
    and the jaguar, 269
Margarita Island, 26
marimataro, Calabash of Ruffled
    Feathers, 135. *See also* Calabash
    of Ruffled Feathers; rattle
Mariusa (subtribe of the Hoanarao),
    237 n, 247; swamp foragers and
    marine hunters, 17–18
marriage, 53. *See also* subtribes, en-
    dogamous
Masisikiri: spirit maiden in the *cachi-
    camo*, 67–72, 73 n, 77, 78, 82;
    spirit of the canoe, 62, 63. *See
    also* canoe; *cachicamo*
master builder. *See moyotu*
Master of Fire, 137, 138. *See also*
    priest-shaman
Master Spirit of Canoe Making,
    abode of, 75
Masters of Earth, the first, 151
mataruka aiwatu, "someone who
    pierces a calabash," 156
Mawari, 185, 197–98, 215; a Cariban
    deity, 148 n, 197; companions of,
    148–50; as Creator-Bird, 198;
    house of, 200–201, 208, 209;
    kanobo, 96; mountain of, 96; son
    of the God of Origin, 198; as
    sun bird, 208–9; the Supreme
    Bahana, 150–51; as swallow-
    tailed kite (*Elanoides forficatus*),
    148, 168, 198; in Yekuana lore,
    198. See also *bahana* shamanism;
    Cosmic Egg; light-shaman; swal-
    low-tailed kite

Quiche Maya of highland Guatemala, 133

rain, seen as polluting or as punishment, 239–42
Rainbow, and wife, 239
rainbow serpent, 77
rainbows, 239
rainmaker (weather shaman) 20, 219; apprenticeship and initiation, 220–22, 241; chants, 223, 225–29; communications with rain gods, 225–27; elderly, 231–32, 241; and food shortages, 244; stormy rains caused by, 240
rainstorms, 232–33. *See also* Orinoco Delta, climate and precipitation
Raleigh, Sir Walter, 25
rattle, 69, 133–35, 265; awakening and feeding of, 138, 140; as *axis mundi*, 140, 143; of *bahana* shaman, 157 (Fig. 6.2), 175; basketry, 267; Carib, 261; dancing or little (*habi sanuka*), 156, 157 (Fig. 6.2); fertilizing power of, 134–35; healing with, 139 (Fig. 5.2); infant, 40; as an instrument of fire, 135, 137–38; of Mawari, 148, 185; ritual (*hebu mataro*), 156; of ruffled feathers, 136 (Fig. 5.1); sacred, 20–21, 91, 121, 133–35; sanctuary of, 141 (Fig. 5.3); symbolism of, 156, 172–76 (Tables 6.2–3), 181; of Yaukware, 119. *See also* Calabash of Ruffled Feathers; Primordial Rattler
rebirth, of some children's souls, 105
red cedar (*Colophyllum lucidum* Benth.), 240
Red Faces, 16–17, 146, 272. *See also* Carib Indians
reduction policy, 260
refugee Warao, in Guyana, 19 n, 216
reptiles, 31
rheumatism, 244. *See also* illness and disease
rice, a cash crop, 34

Rio Grande, 3, 7, 11 (Map 1.4), 12 (Fig. 1.1), 13
Rionegro, Froylán de, 259
River Crab people, 151
Roaster (Haburi's father), 14–16
rocks, sacred, 21–22. *See also* quartz pebbles
rope bridge of tobacco smoke. *See* bridge, made of ropes of tobacco smoke
Roth, Walter E., 247 n
roundhouse, 202 (Fig. 7.11), 205–9 (Figs. 7.14 and 7.16); and annual path of the sun, 204 (Fig. 7.13), 205; of Aparai Indians, 198; center pole, 190, 194, 214 (Fig. 7.20); decorations on wall, 211, 212 (Fig. 7.19); diagrams of architecture, 188–91 (Figs. 7.3–6), 193 (Fig. 7.8); in photographs, 187 (Figs. 7.1–2); roof disk, 199 (Fig. 7.10); roof window, 192 (Fig. 7.7A–B), 201, 202 (Fig. 7.11), 203–6, 210–11, 214 (Fig. 7.20); sunbeam function and symbolism, 201–11 (figs. 7.11–7.18); symbolism of, 193–95; Wayana, 198, 199 (Fig. 7.10); and wind direction, 203 (Fig. 7.12); Yekuana, 186–93, 216–17
rum, 272, 273

sabke, white road, 127 n
sacred mountains. *See* world mountains
sacred rock cult, 10. *See also* quartz pebbles; sacred stones
sacred stones, 101, 103, 115, 138, 140; called "Grandfather," "Son of *Kanobo*," 117–18; temple of, 118. *See also* quartz pebbles
Sacupana *caño*, 4, 6, 16
sago, 11 (Map 1.4), 17, 145, 217, 263; festivals related to, 105, 264, 273; important traditional staple of the Warao, 30, 232–33, 242–43, 264; ritual uses of, 72, 74, 83, 238